Principles of information systems management

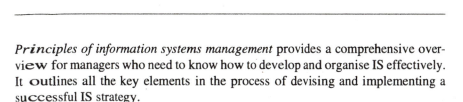

D0140001

Principles of information systems management provides a comprehensive overview for managers who need to know how to develop and organise IS effectively. It outlines all the key elements in the process of devising and implementing a successful IS strategy.

John Ward first looks at the background to developments in IS and IT. He then assesses the key issues in IS management for the manager wanting to develop a strategic approach. The book then covers the main processes of analysis for identifying information systems needs in the business and the application portfolio, including evaluating investments and setting priorities. It concludes with the development of IS and the management of resources as the IS function is aligned with the central activity of the organisation. Throughout, the management questions and problems are made clear, focusing on change management and strategic planning.

This will be ideal reading for all students and managers wanting to understand how IS can be managed successfully.

John Ward is Professor of Strategic Information Systems at Cranfield School of Management. He is the author of *Investment in IT* (CIMA) and co-author of *The essence of information systems* (Prentice-Hall) and *Strategic planning for information systems* (John Wiley)

Routledge series in the principles of management
Edited by Joseph G. Nellis

The Routledge series in the principles of management offers stimulating approaches to the core topics of management. The books relate the key areas to strategic issues in order to help managers solve problems and take control. By encouraging readers to apply their own experiences, the books are designed to develop the skills of the all-round manager.

Principles of service operations management
Colin Armistead and Graham Clark

Principles of applied statistics
M. Fleming and J. Nellis

Principles of operations management
R. L. Galloway

Principles of human resource management
David Goss

Principles of business environment
Nigel Healey and Peter Jackson

Principles of marketing
G. Randall

Principles of law for managers
A. Ruff

Principles of accounting and finance
P. Sneyd

Principles of information systems management
John Ward

Principles of financial management
Keith Ward and Keith Parker

Principles of information systems management

John Ward

London and New York

First published 1995
by Routledge
11 New Fetter Lane, London EC4P 4EE

Simultaneously published in the USA and Canada
by Routledge
29 West 35th Street, New York, NY 10001

Typeset in Times by LaserScript, Mitcham, Surrey
Printed and bound in Great Britain by
Mackays of Chatham PLC, Chatham, Kent

British Library Cataloguing in Publication Data
A catalogue record for this book is available from the British Library

Library of Congress Cataloguing in Publication Data
Ward, John 1947-
    Principles of information systems / John Ward.
        p.   cm. – (Routledge series in the principles of management)
    Includes bibliographical references and index.
    1. Information technology – Management. 2. Information resources management.
3. Management information systems. I. Title.
II. Series.
HD30.2.W36 1994
658.4′038 – dc20   94-46391
                                                                              CIP

ISBN 0–415–07267–0

Contents

Figures

Tables

List of boxes

Series editor's preface

In recent years there has been a dramatic increase in management development activity in most western countries, especially in Europe. This activity has extended across a wide spectrum of training initiatives, from continuing studies programmes of varying durations for practising managers to the provision of courses leading to the award of professional and academic qualifications. With regard to the latter the most prominent developments have been in terms of the Master of Business Administration (MBA) and Diploma in Management (DMS) programmes, particularly in the UK where virtually every university now offers some form of post-graduate and/or post-experience management qualification.

However, the explosion of formal management training programmes such as the MBA and DMS has tended to be in advance of suitably tailored management textbooks. Many of the core functional areas of these programmes have had to rely on some of the more specialized and thus more narrowly focused textbooks, which are more appropriate for undergraduate requirements. They have generally not provided a suitable balance between academic rigour and practical business-related relevance. The Routledge series covering the principles of management has been specifically developed to service the needs of an expanding management audience. The series deals with the full range of core subjects as well as many of the more popular elective courses that one would expect to find in most MBA and DMS programmes. Many of the books will also be attractive to those students taking professional exams, for example in accountancy, banking, etc., as well as managers attending a wide range of development courses. Each book in the series is written in a concise format covering the key principles of each topic in a pragmatic style which emphasises the balance between theory and application. Case studies, exercises and references for further reading are provided where appropriate.

It gives me pleasure to express my thanks to the staff of Routledge for the commitment and energy which they have devoted to the development of this series, and in particular to Francesca Weaver who has skilfully steered each book through the minefield of production from beginning to end. I would also like to express my gratitude to my secretary Christine Williams for maintaining her joviality throughout the development of the 'principles' series.

Joseph G. Nellis
Cranfield School of Management

Preface

As a management subject, information systems (IS) is relatively new. It has developed over the last thirty years, as organisations have employed information technology (IT) to improve the capture, processing and distribution of information.

During that thirty years IT and IT suppliers have evolved dramatically, business conditions have changed faster than ever before and organisations have become quite different in structure and how they work. With so much change affecting all the parameters that determine the role, nature and use of information, the management of information systems has been a challenging task! It has seemed so daunting in some organisations that general management has, in effect, delegated responsibility to its IT specialists or even its IT suppliers! Others have learned lessons from both success and failure and have established IS management as a key competence in their organisation. Others have succeeded at times and failed at times without ever really understanding why!

There are patterns that can be identified in the often frantic, seemingly random decision-making concerning IS issues. By understanding these patterns in relation to apparent success and failure in the use of IS, good, if not best, practice regarding most of the aspects of IS management can be described. Though much can be learned from the past thirty years, the environment within which IS will be managed over the next few years is uncertain and complex.

Much has been written about the use of information systems and technology as a competitive or strategic weapon through which business performance can be dramatically improved. At the same time many organisations are dissatisfied with their 'systems' and question whether all the investment has been worthwhile. Many senior executives are demanding better 'value for money' from IS/IT. Much has also been written about major failures of 'information technology', many of which reach the front pages of the national press. Recent surveys suggest that 70 per cent of all IS investments fail to deliver the expected benefits. Clearly given this range and diversity of experiences, organisations still have much to learn if their information systems are to deliver business improvements with certainty, repeatedly. This book aims to present an approach – a set of principles – which can help organisations, through better management knowledge and understanding, to increase their chances of success with information systems over time.

As such it is not a book about IT. It does however provide a comprehensive and coherent framework of concepts and methods to enable effective management of IT-based information systems in businesses and organisations. Whilst the technology itself is still changing rapidly in terms of price/performance and capability, the issues associated with managing its use are more stable and at times seemingly intractable. Knowledge of the technology itself can clearly help an organisation find opportunities to improve its operations or management. But too often technology-driven approaches to new or improved information systems have delivered disappointing results. When an organisation can define its needs for new/improved information systems, linking these clearly to the business goals and strategy, then the technology can be more appropriately employed to the benefit of the business.

Most people employed in modern organisations use and are affected by information that comes from technology-based systems. Many people are expected to contribute to the development and implementation of these systems and some have overall responsibility for their management. Given the apparent success rates there is obviously significant scope for improvement at all stages of the processes which produce the systems.

Chapter 1 of the book reviews the 30-year history of IS and IT in organisations and describes how and why their role has changed. Chapter 2 considers the issues that have arisen during that time, and the implications in terms of how they affect an organisation's ability to succeed in managing IS/IT. Chapter 3 describes how the planning for new and improved systems can be incorporated into the strategy of the business, to ensure that investments are driven by the need to satisfy business demands and issues. Chapter 4 describes a number of the most useful tools and techniques for determining how new systems investments can lead to significant improvements in business performance.

In Chapter 5 the balance changes from considering how to define what is required to determining how best to deliver the appropriate solutions. It considers alternative ways of managing different types of information systems, according to the contribution required in the business. Chapter 6 focuses directly on the processes of systems development, viewed from a business perspective, with particular attention being paid to delivering the required benefits and managing the risks involved. Chapters 7 and 8 consider the management of the key resources involved in the successful application of IS/IT in any organisation. Even though there are nowadays many more choices in terms of the supply of resources, the responsibility for their successful deployment still resides with the organisation's own management. The last chapter brings together the main messages from the rest of the book and considers how some of the issues will evolve over the coming few years.

Overall, the book attempts to enlighten and educate rather than instruct, but throughout the emphasis is on the practical application of sound management principles. In many cases those principles are well known in other fields of management. But perhaps due to the rapid evolution and relative mystique surrounding the subject of IS, good general management practice has not always been adopted in this increasingly important business activity.

Given the approach adopted, the book should provide valuable insight for those studying management subjects and practising managers looking for clear and comprehensive guidance on how to manage this complex and challenging aspect of business.

Acknowledgement

I am particularly grateful to Christine Afflick who prepared the typescript and diagrams with skill, diligence and, at times, considerable tolerance and patience.

Chapter 1

The evolution of information systems
A management perspective

INTRODUCTION

It is generally recognised that information is one of the assets that an organisation possesses. Like other assets and resources, such as people, finance, buildings, customers, products, etc., information must be well managed if the success of the organisation is to be ensured. Equally like the other resources, information, if badly managed, can lead to operational and managerial ineffectiveness and even to complete business failure. With the arrival of information technologies (IT) it has become possible to obtain new benefits from processing and using information more efficiently and comprehensively.

Information systems (IS) for gathering, storing, processing and disseminating information have been an integral part of every organisation's processes for ever. But the arrival of technologies which were capable of helping carry out those processes, changing them, eliminating the need for some of them and enabling new processes to be developed, has made the management of information systems a subject needing specific attention. Along with the new options have come new problems which have to be addressed, many of which are unfamiliar to the managers who have to deal with them. The suppliers of the technology have established an unrelenting pace of development and change such that the issues to be managed have been constantly evolving. In fact, what to do with IT and how to do it have become major sources of management concern and even organisational conflict.

The resolution of these concerns and conflicts must be sought in the overall context of the management of the business, not as an isolated set of problems 'caused by IT'. However, whilst the rate of change brought about by IT has been dramatic during the last thirty years, the pace of change in the environments within which organisations have to succeed has often been equally dramatic. This produces a major challenge for management – how to ensure the potential of IT is harnessed in an increasingly uncertain and complex environment. This was traditionally a challenge for managers in major corporations, but the ever-improving economics and capabilities of IT have meant that in every size of business the use of IT is now an item on the management agenda.

In parallel with the developing role of IT use in business, it has also evolved, albeit more slowly, in society at large. Most people are familiar with banks' cash machines, buy food at shops equipped with electronic point-of-sale systems, and many people have home computers. The new generation of employees expect to see IT on their desks. However, that does not mean that they are any more capable than their predecessors of managing the information resources and systems in an organisation. Just because someone can use a telephone does not mean they can communicate effectively!

IS as a management subject is barely thirty years old and the evolution of IS management in organisations over that thirty years has been both dramatic and erratic. Much has been learned both from success and failure. The cost of the failure to manage IS effectively in the past was often high, but rarely the cause of total business failure. The evidence from a number of industries today is that failure to manage IS appropriately in the future may well result in a business ceasing to exist! Equally effective IS management can become a major contributor to an organisation's success.

The rest of this chapter reviews the evolution of IS in organisations from a management perspective against the background discussed above. It is important to understand that general evolution in order to appreciate what has happened in a particular organisation and perhaps why. Much can also be learned from the past to help ensure that future management decisions about both IS and IT can be improved.

THE THREE-ERA VIEW OF INFORMATION SYSTEMS EVOLUTION

It is inevitably oversimplistic to describe the last thirty-plus years of IS evolution in terms of three eras. However, many researchers and observers have described it in such terms. They have used different words and emphasised different aspects of IS usage and/or IT developments, but in general they agree on the main changes that have occurred. Many of those views were built upon the early analyses of Nolan (1979), who based his six-stage model of how 'data processing' had evolved on observations of a number of large companies. Within the six stages (initiation, contagion, control, integration, data administration and maturity) he summarised two main eras: Computer Management (stages 1 to 3) and Information Management (stages 4 to 6) with a key transition at the end of the control stage. At that transition the objectives of deploying IT, the types of applications and the way it is managed all changed. Whilst the six-stage model can be criticised in its detail, at the higher level of the two eras it is still valuable.

Of course, a model developed by observing the 1970s is unlikely to cope with the changes that have occurred since. Wiseman (1985) extended the model into three eras where the objectives of IS use were suggested as:

Era 1   To improve business efficiency by automating basic information processes.
Era 2   To improve management effectiveness by satisfying information needs.

Era 3   To improve competitiveness by affecting the business strategy.

This effectively adds a third era to Nolan's original view. Galliers and Somogyi (1987) arrive at a similar three-era view based on a set of eight factors describing the technology, what it is used for and how it is managed. Both assessments recognise that in the latter part of the 1970s and early 1980s IT was being put to new uses, the effect of which was to change the way organisations conducted business or to develop new products or services or to manage the business differently, or all three. Both called these *strategic information systems* to describe the key aspect of the third era – strategic impact. Hirschheim *et al.* (1988) describe a similar three-stage evolution based mainly on the key issues involved in the development of information systems and the managerial and organisational implications. They describe how the focus of IS/IT management has changed from initial emphasis on *delivery* of specific systems, through *reorientation* of how information use needs to be supported through a variety of IS services, to *reorganisation* of responsibilities between users and IT specialists to ensure information is exploited to maximum benefit.

All of these are valuable views of IS evolution and are in many ways complementary. Each is a recommended article for further reading for those who wish to gain a deeper understanding of IS/IT history than can be provided here. Combining these and various other assessments the three eras can best be described by the following titles, each being determined by the main objective or purpose.

1 **Data processing**   To improve operational efficiency by automating information-based processes.
2 **Management information systems**   To increase management effectiveness by satisfying its information needs.
3 **Strategic information systems**   To improve competitiveness by changing the nature or conduct of business.

The word 'era' might be somewhat misleading since it suggests each has come to an end. As can be seen from Figure 1.1, the start of each era can be roughly identified, but each of the above are all continuing today. As the economics and facilities of IT improve, more activities are worth automating and more aspects of management can be aided by technology. As we move through the next decade further ways in which business can be changed through IT use will no doubt be discovered.

Each of the eras is now considered in more detail before drawing together an overall analysis of the various dimensions of the evolution.

THE DATA PROCESSING ERA

The concept of 'automating' basic information tasks, such as record-keeping and ledgers, predates the arrival of computers. Various electro-mechanical devices

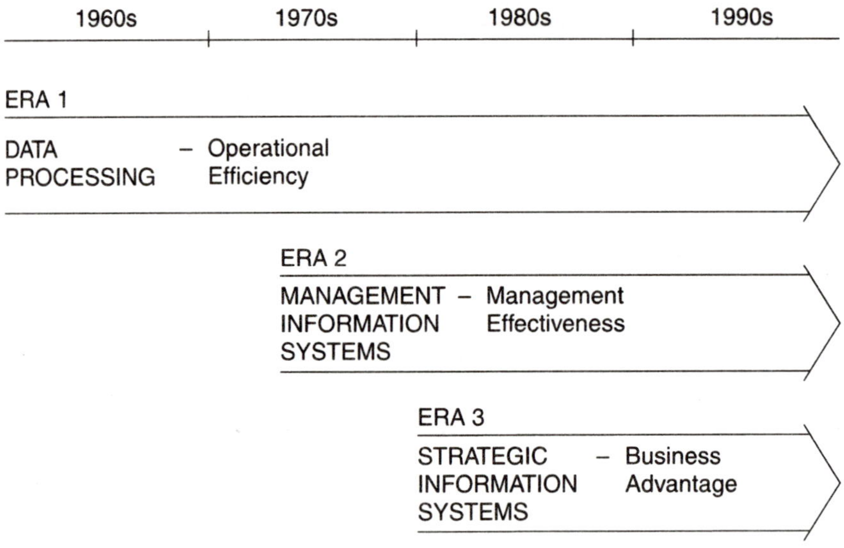

1960s	1970s	1980s	1990s

ERA 1

DATA   – Operational
PROCESSING   Efficiency

ERA 2

MANAGEMENT – Management
INFORMATION   Effectiveness
SYSTEMS

ERA 3

STRATEGIC   – Business
INFORMATION   Advantage
SYSTEMS

Figure 1.1 The evolution of IS/IT in organisations – the three-era model

could produce and use information via punched cards or paper tape to enable efficiencies of storing, extracting and analysing some items of data. Tabulators, sorters, accounting machines and the like were often used to improve the productivity of such tasks – and no doubt some are still in use! To utilise them effectively the skills required to develop paper-based business systems (commonly known as organisation and methods skills) had to be extended to incorporate the use of basic technology into the systems or methods.

When computers first arrived the main task appeared to be how to 'program the computer' to carry out routine processes more efficiently still. Like the electro-mechanical devices before them, they were seen as a way of automating a known task, in much the same way as a new machine could produce more widgets more cheaply. The capital cost of the equipment – computers and associated storage and input/output devices – was high, and a key issue for management was justifying the capital expense by measurable efficiency gains, producing a satisfactory return on investment or payback. Hence IS/IT investments, if they were evaluated at all, were justified in a similar way to other capital investments. This led to problems later as will be seen.

If the objective of using the technology is to improve efficiency, then the best approach is to clearly define the task or tasks to be automated and then to employ the technology to improve the efficiency of the specific processes involved. Activities such as running the payroll, producing invoices, maintaining ledgers and keeping stock records can be relatively easily defined and then the computer system can be designed to automate all or some of the clerical work involved. In theory, at least, the cost of carrying out these repetitive business transactions can be calculated before and after the change, to determine whether or not the investment has paid off.

The same rationale applies today, just as it did in the past. Investments in word- and text-processing technology can improve the productivity of secretarial and clerical tasks and those improvements can be measured. The same should be true of the use of spreadsheets for basic numerical manipulation by managers or the use of image-processing technology to store and retrieve documents, drawings and other 'pictures' which are by their nature not easily stored as structured 'data'.

This simple concept, however, was not easy to turn into reality, since the development of technology-based information systems was not merely a case of buying and commissioning pieces of equipment. 'Programming the computer' turned out to be the least of the problems in many ways, although the ongoing maintenance and changes to those computer programs proved more difficult and costly than expected.

It was soon realised that developing 'a system' which could combine the abilities of the technology with the way in which organisations and people work, was critical to the success of the investment in the longer term. Also, designing a system which could operate consistently and reliably, handling large volumes of transactions day in and day out, meant additional expenditure was often needed to ensure (a) the computer system was operational most of the time and (b) when it failed the situation could be easily recovered. This led to the need to develop standards, procedures and a whole set of disciplines which were previously unnecessary when people could intervene in the manual system to overcome problems. This combined with the limitations (in the early days) of the computer equipment and software, meant that the resulting computer systems often caused the people using the systems to work in new but far from ideal ways. The early batch-processing based systems may have optimised the use of the costly equipment but often meant one mundane clerical set of tasks was replaced by another. These tasks were determined more by the limitations of the technology than by the abilities of the people.

At the same time, due to the nature of the technology, a large number of specialists had to be employed. Systems analysis and programmers were needed to design, develop and maintain the computer systems. Data preparation staff were needed to 'punch' the batches of data, and computer operators and software specialists were needed to run the machines. As the workload grew a job or production control department was needed to schedule and organise the work going into and out of the computer room. The data processing (DP) department was born and it tended to grow rapidly in size, often to the dismay of the management!

In order to get the best from this increasingly expensive resource everyone was expected to use it in a way which was thought to be most effective. In practice this usually meant the way that the data processing department's management thought was most effective. Policies and procedures were established to ensure that data processing resources, both technologies and people, was used sensibly. This undoubtedly caused problems with other managers who felt that their ability to use IT to improve business performance was being unduly influenced, even dictated, by the data processing specialists. Resentment and conflict often developed and, though it originated ten or twenty years ago, those attitudes still cause problems today. As will be seen later these problems must be resolved if more strategic uses of IT can come about.

As has happened many times in the evolution of IT, technological advances offered new options in the 1970s. Smaller, cheaper machines (usually called 'minis') arrived to compete with the large mainframes. The programming languages became easier to use and data communications from terminals to machines (or machines to machines) became feasible. This resulted in two major steps:

(a) the systems could be designed to be more 'people friendly' and perform more functions, in a more natural, interactive way via screens attached to the existing systems;

(b) individual departments could afford to buy computers and use them on local tasks, for instance in warehouses, branch offices or on the production floor. Such machines had been in use in process control environments but they could now be employed for data processing.

This did not mean that the problem of developing data processing systems had been solved. In fact the problems increased, but it did give operational management an ability to get control, if they wished, of the systems in their departments. The result was often rapid progress, but in a fragmented way, producing systems which could not 'talk' to each other or share data. Further IT specialists were usually needed either at the centre or in the user areas to support the broader range of technologies. This often led to increased conflict as the DP department saw its role being reduced or even usurped.

This issue, who controls the technology and associated resources, often preoccupied the organisational management (and frequently still does). It deflected them from consideration of the main long-term issue: how the organisation could obtain maximum benefit from the deployment of IT. Over many years it has been realised in most organisations that to succeed in automating information-based tasks takes a co-operative approach between the users, who define the requirements and have to live with the resulting systems, and the IT specialists who design, develop and maintain the systems. This applies today, even when standard packages for such things as payrolls, accounting, stock control, etc., can be purchased. It is still a co-operative effort although the user has a more significant role to play, because the specialists no longer build the system. Such aspects are explored in more depth in later chapters.

Equally it has been realised that piecemeal automation, process by process, leads to incompatible systems, which in total may reduce overall business efficiency whilst apparently improving local productivity. A planned approach is required if overall benefits are to be maximised.

It must be remembered that many of today's large systems developments contain many components which are purely data processing. For example, electronic point-of-sale systems, based on barcode scanners, in supermarkets have essentially moved much of the data processing to the till – capturing, verifying, storing and processing the basic sales transactions. This data is then transmitted to other computers to be used for other purposes. Tasks which previously required manual intervention – keying in prices, checking shelf stocks and pricing the items have been automated or eliminated, resulting in reduced costs to offset the investment, and ongoing operating costs.

Key characteristics of the data processing era and associated applications are summarised in Table 1.1.

THE MANAGEMENT INFORMATION SYSTEMS (MIS) ERA

By the mid-1970s most large organisations had developed large numbers of computer-based systems addressing major areas of information processing in the various business functions. Data processing departments had also been established and most had become capable of carrying out projects to deliver and run the large transaction-based systems.

The second era dawned with the realisation that, with so much data now stored on the computers, it should be possible to provide managers and professionals with information from the computer, to aid decision-making in the control and planning of the business. This introduced a new purpose to the development of information systems – to increase management effectiveness by satisfying its information needs.

This new opportunity area was addressed with great enthusiasm by the IT specialists who saw their role increasing in importance in the organisation! Unfortunately the approaches which had been found to work in developing data processing systems were far from ideal in this new era. There is a significant difference between asking the invoicing manager 'how do we invoice our customers?' with a view to computerising the process, and asking a sales manager 'what information do you need to become more effective?'. The answer to the first is a description of a formal, repetitive process with rules and formulae using highly structured data. The type of answer to the second depends not only on the manager's perception of his or her role and ability to describe a variety of needs in a logical way, but also an understanding of how the manager's effectiveness depends on working with supporting staff and others in the organisation. It is a very difficult question to answer. Also, however good the answer, converting the needs to a definitive set of computer system processes and outputs is equally difficult.

Many aspects of management are impossible to define as formal, repetitive

Table 1.1 Characteristics of DP applications

Objectives of investment
- Improving efficiency and productivity of information-intensive tasks.

Focus of use
- High volume, repetitive, structured tasks mainly of a transaction-based type.
- Automation of known processes within existing business functions.
- Internal to business.

Justification
- Essentially cost savings, by reducing numbers of staff, waste and working capital needs.

Users
- Normally operators, clerical staff and first-line supervisors.

Key aspects of the development process
- Clear specification of user requirements and scope of system.
- Effective project management and methodology for designing, constructing and implementing the system.
- Sizing, procuring and commissioning appropriate technology.
- Using the capabilities of the technology and people in the most effective way to produce overall process efficiency.

Key issues for IT (DP) management
- Delivery of systems that work, on time, at an acceptable cost (quality and productivity).
- Organising resources to develop, operate and maintain the systems effectively on behalf of the users.

Examples of typical applications developed
Payroll, invoicing, sales and purchase ledgers, stock control, personnel records, shopfloor control, warehouse control, order processing, general ledgers, cost accounting, goods receiving, delivery documentation, etc.

processes. The information needed cannot always be anticipated and normally needs to be aggregated from a number of sources. Whilst some information is required regularly, much of it is required in an ad hoc fashion, at relatively short notice to help resolve an issue or assist in making a specific decision. Often the data from the computer systems has to be brought together with other data gathered through other formal organisational processes and informal sources – opinions and views of others, plus ancillary or unconfirmed items of knowledge. Equally the inevitable question of 'What if?' occurs – could the data be reworked, reanalysed on a different set of assumptions? – conditions which can only be introduced once a first analysis has been carried out. Clearly these needs cannot be defined in detail months or years in advance of the need. Generalised types of questions can be anticipated and hence allowed for as parameters which can be altered from time to time; for instance 'What would be the effect on total costs of an x or $y\%$ increase on operator basic pay rates?' or 'If stocks are reduced by $n\%$ how many stock-outs are likely to occur?' But these are only a small proportion of the types of analyses required.

An equally difficult issue is how to justify the investments in such systems of information provision. With automation, efficiency gains can be estimated and assessed in financial terms and measured afterwards. How can a major investment in, say, a sales forecasting system be justified? Clearly it might save time and effort in the preparation of forecasts, but the main benefits will arise from the accuracy of the forecasts and an ability to respond quickly and appropriately when demand changes. These benefits are difficult to quantify and express financially. Often, given the need to quantify the benefits to gain management approval for the investments, statements such as:

> more timely, pertinent and accurate information on sales could enable an $x\%$ increase in sales per annum which will pay for the system . . . [or] we should be able to reduce costs by $y\%$ by better control of stocks and work in progress . . .

were used to argue that better information leads to increased management effectiveness. Not only are they difficult to prove or disprove before the event, they are equally difficult to measure afterwards, especially since other business factors could easily cloud the picture even in the short term.

Hence, the issues in defining the requirements of and justifying MIS are quite different from the needs of DP systems. Equally the problems of delivering such systems are quite different. These problems were initially compounded by the need to derive data from the existing DP systems had been designed piecemeal with the objective of improving the efficiency of a specific process or set of processes – stock recording and control, general accounting, order processing, personnel records, etc. The data was structured in those systems to be used in those specific processes. Often the management information needs required access to data stored in a number of systems, and each had its own particular (even peculiar!) definitions and structure of data designed for that process. 'This month's sales' could mean quite different things in marketing ('orders placed'), Distribution ('goods shipped'), accounting ('invoiced items') and to some it could mean 'quantity' and to others 'value'. Yet it is quite likely that such a name existed in systems in each area. When a manager says, 'I need monthly sales data within one week of the end of the month . . .' it could mean a number of different things. Unless a coherent, explicit set of definitions of what data means is established, the MIS can produce more confusion in decision-making rather than less, and even lead to less effective management!

Most of these problems were discovered quite quickly and led to the concept of 'data-driven systems' rather than the 'process-driven systems' which had been the focus of the DP developments. By analysing the types of data in use in the organisation and the normal relationships ('customer buys goods', 'customer pays invoice', 'invoice describes goods purchased by customer'), data items could be defined and structured so that a number of systems could use the relevant parts whilst maintaining the coherence of the whole. This would avoid duplication of storage, inconsistencies leading to error and enable management to extract subsets of the data for analysis as needed, without having to extract them from many different sources each time. Hence the concept of data bases – coherent, structured sets of related items, accessible for multiple purposes whether they be transaction processing (e.g. invoicing) or management support (e.g. sales analysis).

From the mid-1970s many organisations invested heavily in data base developments, taking a long-term view of the potential benefits which were still unproved, rather than the short-term problem solving, payback-driven approach adopted to DP systems until then. But there were many problems:

- getting the users to agree definitions of data for multiple uses proved very time consuming and tedious, yet it was a precondition for the data base development;
- the software available to manage these large data bases was relatively inflexible, inefficient and required a new type of technical specialism to be developed;
- to use the new data bases required many existing systems to be rebuilt at great cost and for little obvious benefit;
- the software to enable managers to extract and analyse the data was poor and more often than not the DP department had to write a special 'one-off' program – meaning delays of weeks or even months before the information was available. Alternatively, user departments had to develop their own specialists in the retrieval languages and ended up with their own 'programmers'.

Overall, given the long time scale and uncertainty of the benefits and the seriously underestimated difficulties and costs of developing comprehensive management information systems, perseverance was more an act of faith than objectivity by the early 1980s. But once again potential solutions began to appear. The computer suppliers and software houses developed new types of data base management systems (DBMS) which provided more flexibility. They also developed new types of programming languages – fourth generation languages (4GLs) – which were simpler and easier to use.

More significantly new products arrived – micro-computers – which offered the vision of computer processing power on the desk under the control of the user. In the early days their capabilities were strictly limited but to many users they provided the opportunity to get things done, albeit not perfectly, that they had long wanted but had been unable to achieve via the DP department. Also the investment threshold had dropped an order of magnitude, to a few thousand pounds, a sum which could easily be found in the department budget. Initially the DP departments were generally dismissive – 'toys', 'not proper computing', 'a passing fad'! Had it not been for the early availability of excellent new software – spreadsheets – they might well have been proved right! Micro-computers took off dramatically, were cleverly renamed personal computers (PCs) and the rest, as they say, is history! Demand fuelled the rapid development of ever more powerful and capable hardware and software and increasing competition from major suppliers kept prices down. They proved a very effective way of satisfying some of the information needs that professionals and managers had been stockpiling since the mid-1970s and had been unable to get satisfied. The PCs also enabled them to do new things they had not envisaged, particularly due to the quality of the graphics. Whether or not this actually made the managers more effective (the original objective of MIS) is open to debate. Some no doubt were.

However, as in the early days of large computers, the technology was developing and changing very rapidly and within a few years large companies had acquired hundreds if not thousands of PCs of a variety of types with a variety of software. Management became concerned about the rapidly increasing costs and lack of control over the acquisition and use of PCs. At the same time the use of the wide variety of equipment and software to meet local needs had led to fragmentation of the information resource, duplicated effort and uncertainty about the quality and consistency of the information being provided. In response to these issues the DP department had developed new services to help users acquire and utilise the PCs. 'End-user computing support' groups and 'information centres' were put in place, partly to control the cost and potential proliferation of the PCs and partly to train and support the users. Many users realised that they needed data stored in the mainframe computers to be down-loaded onto the PCs to avoid rekeying vast amounts of data. Data held on different PCs needed to be shared and the DP department could provide the networks and controls to enable this. The users began to realise that there were benefits from having coherent data bases which were the repositories of the core business data. This renewed the drive to develop such data bases, but this time based on a perceived need by the users rather than an option provided by the technology. During the latter part of the 1980s, management information systems became a reality, but only via an expensive and extended learning curve, which eventually produced the appropriate balance of control between the user and the central DP department, now probably renamed the IS or IT department.

What had become clear was that managing IS was more than a trick of throwing one ball (DP) up into the air and catching it. At least two balls were involved (DP and MIS) and keeping both of these in the air simultaneously needed more carefully thought-out and consistently applied management techniques, or one or other would be dropped.

Table 1.2 summarises some of the key characteristics of MIS uses of IT. Many of these issues are far from satisfactorily resolved in many companies and it is also far from clear whether the objective of increasing management effectiveness has always been achieved. This will be discussed further below.

Table 1.2 Characteristics of MIS applications

Objectives of investment
- Improving the effectiveness of management decision-making by satisfying managers' information needs.

Focus of use
- Supplying managers and professionals with analysed information to meet regular and ad hoc needs.
- To support existing management processes.
- Mainly internal to the business.

Justification
- More timely, more accurate, more comprehensive information improves management decision-making and hence control and planning of the business.
- Using management and professional time more effectively.
- Speeding up the control and planning cycles of the business to enable more options to be evaluated.

Users
- Normally managers and professionals.

Key aspects of the development process
- Clear understanding of the information and purposes for which it will be used.
- Creating appropriate data bases and relationships to enable retrieval and analysis.
- Selecting and implementing suitable data management, retrieval, analysis and presentation software.
- Using the capabilities of the technology to enable people to be more efficient and effective.

Key issues for IT (MIS) management
- Establishing an effective data management process and services to enable the user to obtain and use the stored information.
- Organising resources to support variable, ad hoc requirements of users with ability to respond quickly.
- Educating users to obtain maximum benefit from the technology and systems.

Examples of typical applications developed
- Sales analysis, market research and analysis, capacity planning, budgetary control, management accounting, sales forecasting, inventory management, manpower planning, financial modelling, cash management, supplier analysis, etc.

THE STRATEGIC INFORMATION SYSTEMS (SIS) ERA

During the 1970s a number of organisations began to use IS/IT in ways which fundamentally changed the way their business was conducted. As a result they gained significant advantages over their competitors and had a major effect on the structure, relationships and economics of their industries. These *strategic* uses of IS/IT soon became well known, even achieving legendary status! The SABRE system installed in travel agents by American Airlines, American Hospital Supplies provision of on-line ordering for hospitals and Merrill Lynch's Cash Management Accounts were described time and again as examples of how IS/IT could create and deliver sustainable competitive advantage. Other such systems (e.g. Bank of America's Masternet accounting and ICI's Councillor systems) were less successful in the long term, but by the early 1980s the concept of competitive advantage from IS/IT was well established. That is not to say that excellent DP or MIS investments do not deliver advantage through lower costs and better management, but the impact on the business is less dramatic, more indirect. From the large number of documented examples of claimed competitive advantage from IS/IT four of the best known are briefly described in Box 1.1 case histories.

Box 1.1 Competitive advantage from IS/IT – some case histories

Thomson Holidays

On the night of 3 November 1985, Britain's bargain hunters camped in the streets to be the first in line for the cut-price holidays on offer in the tour operators' price war. The next morning, when the travel agents' doors opened, the computers of Thomson Holidays handled 3,291 bookings in the first frantic hours of business – almost a customer a second. Some of their competitors fared less well, as their systems ground to a halt under an avalanche of enquiries, leaving frustrated customers out in the cold.

Small wonder that Thomson Holidays' management will say that 'technology has become the basis of our business'. The firm's market leadership is actually founded on technological supremacy. It was the first tour operator to offer on-screen bookings to high street agents via TOP, its on-line viewdata system, which has earned a reputation as the most efficient in the business.

In the summer of 1986 Thomson carried a million extra passengers, one-in-four package holiday goers, and 85 per cent will have booked via TOP. It is this ability to handle mass bookings that has enabled Thomson to pursue its fiercely aggressive marketing strategy, and to stimulate huge demand.

In October 1986 Thomson announced it would only take bookings via the system in future.

McKesson

The company provided pharmacists and druggists with hand-held data entry terminals to record replacement stock details, and the information is down-loaded over telephone lines direct to McKesson's computers. McKesson fills the order overnight and delivers it the next day in boxes arranged to match the shelf divisions of the retailers' store. Druggists who signed up with the service, called Economost, typically doubled or tripled their order volumes. In many cases, they began to rely exclusively on McKesson. The total service helps retailers' stock, price-label rotate and display merchandise according to marketing reports generated.

In another area of its business McKesson provides a service via pharmacists to process the insurance claims for 23 million medical insurance customers' prescriptions. The system processes the claims via prescriptions completed and sends them to 150 healthcare insurers for reimbursing.

General Tire

General Tire arranged to have a telemarketing centre take over the service support functions that had been previously performed by the field sales force. Telemarketing specialists handle questions like: 'Have you got it?', 'Did it ship?' and 'There's something wrong with my bill.' This lowered General Tire's unit costs by freeing the field sales force to devote more of their time to selling. General Tire then decided to let the telemarketing centre take over the selling and account management role for some of the company's marginally profitable accounts – accounts that could not be profitably serviced by the sales team. In the first month of operation, General Tire's telemarketing people sold more to these accounts than the field sales force had sold to them over the entire previous year.

Pitney-Bowes

Pitney-Bowes has found a strategic application of information technology in the way it dispatches its service people. Currently, they dispatch over 3,500 customer engineers from each of their ninety-nine branch locations throughout the US. Drawing upon a central data base in Danbury, Connecticut, and twenty dispatch centres that feed into it, Pitney-Bowes puts it into a diagnostic system to see if it can be solved over the telephone – thereby saving the cost of dispatching a customer engineer. If not, he checks the data base to find not only the service engineer who is in nearest proximity to the customer but also the engineer who can handle it at the least possible cost. Before the new system was put in place, every customer engineer had to be trained to service every kind of machinery in his area: now the company can assign someone who has a skill that matches the problem, so that the high end of their product line does not suffer because of problems at the low end. The customer benefits from this arrangement.

These short extracts are based on examples as contained in articles by Large (1986) and Wyman (1985).

Based on this initial 'anecdotal' evidence for strategic information systems, researchers and observers analysed how IS/IT was being used differently from the past to gain such advantages – *what* were the characteristics of these new systems, *why* did they create advantage, and *how* were they brought to success. A number of writers were able to demonstrate how such uses of IS/IT had become a key component of the enterprise's business strategy, even if initially they had been isolated ideas, exploited with astute opportunism. Writers such as Benjamin *et al.* (1984), Notowidigdo (1984), Parsons (1983) and Wiseman (1985) not only analysed and classified the examples in a way that others could understand, but also suggested how various tools and techniques of analysis could be used to identify possible strategic IS/IT opportunities for any organisation. The most comprehensive of these articles by Ives and Learmonth (1984) is suggested as further reading. What the various tools and techniques of analysis are and how they can be used will be considered extensively later in the book. In this section the various characteristics of these information systems will be considered in more detail, based on the observations of others and the research work done at the Cranfield School of Management.

There appear to be four main types of strategic applications of IS/IT, each of which has different management implications.

1. *Those that produce more effective integration of the use of information in the key value-adding processes of the business*

By integrating the information resource and its use in the key activities of the business, companies cannot only carry out those activities in combination more efficiently but also use the resources in a more effective, co-ordinated way. In addition, integration of information provides management with better overall control of the business and an ability to respond more quickly in adapting its operations consistently when business conditions change. Integration can also enable the business to develop new more competitive ways of working, such as telemarketing in the General Tire example, or offer new levels of customer service as BMW and others have done with their integrated dealer, logistics and manufacturing systems.

However, to achieve such strategic integration requires the organisation to overcome some of the traditional barriers to successful IS/IT exploitation prevalent in the DP and MIS eras, i.e. sharing information, long-term planning of developments and reorganising to optimise the benefits from the systems. To overcome these barriers, senior management must become involved. They must understand the implications of this new information-based approach to managing the business, in terms of the roles of people and the organisation of business activities and functions. Reorganisation is likely to be necessary if significant benefits are to be obtained and the relative advantages sustained. Also the degree to which an organisation can obtain advantage from the second type of strategic IS/IT use below will depend to a large extent on its success in internal IS/IT integration.

2. *Those that link the organisation more efficiently or effectively with its main customers and suppliers*

A large proportion of the examples involve establishing electronic links to customers or suppliers. The objectives and implications vary. The simplest approach is the use of electronic data interchange (EDI) links for improving the efficiency of handling basic business transactions such as invoices and orders. Other companies are sharing information by allowing access by customers or suppliers to their computer-held data directly. This extends the information base of each company and allows both parties to make better combined decisions on requirements and resources, based on such things as stock data, forecasts and project progress. Further benefits are possible when the companies share out the work and responsibilities in new ways which use their combined resources more effectively, and avoid duplicated or error-prone activities. For instance, travel agents enter the data for Thomson Holidays, and British Steel manages North Sea steel stocks on behalf of BP. American Hospital Supplies and McKesson will take over the management of their customers' stocks.

These applications need a strong drive by the management of the key interfaces with the customers and suppliers, e.g. sales and distribution and/or purchasing, who must understand both the business implications of such links and have a clear understanding of the benefits they wish to achieve. Equally unlike all the systems investments described up to this point, these systems are not entirely within the power of the organisation to control. Customers, suppliers and competitors may take the initiative at any stage and the company may well have to adapt or change what it is trying to achieve and how, due to the actions or plans of the other parties.

3. *Those that enable the business to develop and deliver new or enhanced products or services to the market*

Many organisations are finding ways of using IS/IT to change the nature of the products or services they offer and even introduce new products or services enabled by IS/IT. Merrill Lynch's Cash Management Account – a consumer service which combines cheque, credit, savings and investment facilities – is probably the best-known example of the latter. In the UK, Nottingham Building Society and the Bank of Scotland offer similar 'products' – comprehensive financial services from the home or office. First Direct has introduced 'branch-less' banking, delivering the range of standard consumer banking products without the need for expensive real estate and staff, direct to the consumer. In areas like financial services the product is information and hence it can be delivered electronically. In other businesses the link is perhaps less obvious.

ICI's Counsellor system attempted to change the nature of the product, from a commodity chemical to 'consultancy'. The system enabled the farmer to diagnose the problem, identify which pesticide to use and evaluate alternative solutions (effectiveness, economics, etc.) based on general data and information specific to the farm. A scaffolding company developed a design system which prospective customers could use to develop and specify their requirements. In each case a competitive advantage was gained, at least for a time, by adding value to the basic product or service which tied the customer more closely to the company. In order to gain such advantages it is important to have a thorough understanding of the products of the industry and in particular how the customers obtain value from them. This enables the organisation to differentiate its products or services or find new ways of marketing and delivering the service more economically.

4. *Those that provide executive management with information to manage the business and its strategy more effectively*

The final type of strategic use of IS/IT is at present probably the least common, although the concept of executive information systems (EIS) is well established and heavily marketed by the software suppliers! The idea of providing executive management with pertinent information directly from IT-based systems is not new. It was one of the objectives of the MIS era, but an objective that was rarely achieved. There are three main reasons for this:

(a) defining what is pertinent to executive management is very difficult and subject to rapid change;
(b) the need for external information about the business environment to be included with internal information;
(c) the lack of sophistication of the MIS approach which does not allow easily for interpretations added to raw information – providing the context for strategic decisions and potential implications.

To develop an effective executive information system all these factors have to be considered. Techniques are needed to determine the items of information required to support strategic decisions. Often this is difficult if the business strategy is unclear. External sources of relevant data have to be identified, validated and incorporated in the data resource of the business. Flexible yet sophisticated analyses of the data have to be developed, as well as appropriate presentation of the results to executives with a limited time available to assimilate the details.

Various developments are facilitating progress towards making effective EIS a reality. A multitude of external data bases is now available – the problem is finding the 'right' ones! The presentation capabilities of IT have been dramatically improved. Knowledge-based or expert systems are now available to incorporate the knowledge managers have in the interpretation of the data. But all of these are not substitutes for knowing what information is required to make each type of strategic decision. Successful development of an EIS is more a question of understanding the management processes involved than delivering information to the executives. Much is still to be learned but some organisations have made significant steps towards building effective if not yet comprehensive systems to support executive decision-making.

The classifications above are intended to show the types of applications of IS/IT which are delivering strategic advantages to organisations today. These will be considered against the background of more traditional DP and MIS applications in the final part of the chapter. However, in analysing the many examples of strategic uses of IS/IT other lessons can also be learned. There are some factors which recur many times in the examples. These factors emphasise aspects of IS/IT development which are often different from the focus of attention in the DP and MIS areas. They imply that new approaches to identifying and then delivering strategic information systems are involved. These key factors are summarised in Table 1.3. The message for any organisation embarking on the development of a strategic information system is that to ignore all of these factors will almost certainly lead to failure and not to consider each one overtly will increase the risk of failure.

Table 1.3 Key factors for success in strategic information systems

1 **External rather than internal forms** Considering the information and systems needs in the context of the other firms in the industry and in particular the information that is exchanged with customers and suppliers.

2 **Adding value not cost reduction** Using technology to do things better rather than cheaper – improving the quality of the product or service and improving the way activities are performed. By focusing on quality, the lesson not just from IS/IT, is that costs are also reduced by getting it right first time, on time.

3 **Sharing the benefits** Ensuring that everyone, inside or outside the organisation, who uses the system obtains some benefit. Often, systems inside an organisation were developed by one function to gain leverage over others – rather than provide all parties with benefits. Unless all users benefit to some extent (particularly if they are external) there is no 'buy-in' to the system's long-term success and its effectiveness can deteriorate quickly.

4 **Understanding the customer** And what he does with the product or service the organisation provides, how he gains value from it, especially in terms of improving the exchange of information about the customer's needs and the service that can be provided. This also applies to 'internal' customers who depend on the services from the department.

5 **Business-driven innovation – adequate technology** Most success stories result from an innovative idea developed by business people and carried out using adequate, well-established IT. Very few successes come from leading-edge IT. It is really common sense, the advantage comes from the new idea carried out effectively. Using leading-edge technology is risky – it may not work – and since business innovation is risky enough there is no point in increasing the risk.

6 **Incremental development** Taking a gradual approach to achieve one set of benefits and then developing the system further. Few major successes were fully envisioned at the start but as some success was achieved new potential options became clear. Traditionally IS/IT developments became huge projects in order to offset the development cost against a greater range of benefits. These very large projects are very likely to fail and if many of the requirements and benefits are uncertain an incremental approach is logical. In many cases prototypes were first developed and often discarded to be replaced by the real system.

These are not the only factors but they can be seen to recur in many of the examples analysed.

A REVIEW OF THE THREE ERAS

The previous discussion attempts to describe, albeit briefly, the main changes that have occurred during the last thirty years of IS/IT use in organisations. Any such management overview is bound to oversimplify or even ignore some aspects of

IS/IT evolution. The intention at this stage is to highlight the general patterns and trends, because it is important that business managers understand the context within which they are required to make decisions about how their organisations use and manage IS/IT. Each organisation might think that its own IS/IT experience and history are unique. This is rarely the case. Its experiences will almost certainly relate to some stages of the evolutionary process described here.

Looking ahead, most organisations' future investments in IS/IT are not entirely within their own ability to determine and control. Hence an understanding of where they are now, in relation to others, and what will probably happen next is vital if IS/IT is to be managed successfully in the future. In order to depict the likely scope of that future, Figure 1.2 attempts to summarise the information systems environment within which organisations will have to plan and manage.

The two dimensions attempt to summarise (a) the purpose or objective of information systems developments and (b) the scope or focus of those investments. Whilst the discussion of the evolution of IS/IT identified three eras, the strategic era consists of extensions of IS/IT use in both of these dimensions: in part to achieve old objectives in a wider environment (boxes 4, 5 and 7 in Figure 1.2) and in part to achieve a new objective in both an existing and wider environment (boxes 3 and 6). This suggests a much more challenging management environment than the past. IS/IT was seen as a means of improving current business practices and activities within the organisation in the DP and MIS eras. To succeed in the SIS era, IS/IT must be seen as the means of changing how

PURPOSE / FOCUS	OPERATIONAL EFFICIENCY	MANAGEMENT EFFECTIVENESS	BUSINESS ADVANTAGE THROUGH CHANGE
INTERNAL	1. Data Processing	2. Management Information Systems	3. Internal Business Integration
		7. Executive Information Systems	
EXTERNAL	4. Electronic links between organisations to make data exchange more timely, accurate and efficient	5. Sharing information by direct access from one company to another	6. External Business Integration, changing the roles of the firms in the industry

Figure 1.2 The information systems environment

things are done, not just from an internal perspective, but also in the context of the industry. Understanding and managing those changes are not tasks for specialist IT managers to undertake, but tasks for organisational general management.

It might be worth reflecting at this stage on how successful organisations have been in exploiting IS/IT during the DP and MIS eras, i.e. how effective in general have management been in identifying and obtaining the benefits available? Strassman (1985) in his book *The Information Payoff* examines in depth the real contribution made by IS/IT when deployed to achieve the objectives of the first two eras - increasing efficiency and management effectiveness. Amongst his many assessments and conclusions based on extensive research, the following are clear:

(a) IS/IT use has generally been successful in improving operational efficiency – when applied to automate clearly defined, structured, repetitive tasks. However, the actual efficiency gains overall are lower than the claims made to justify the investment. Normally 5 to 10 per cent returns are achievable, not the 25 to 30 per cent usually claimed.

(b) It is very difficult to measure improvements in management effectiveness in relation to IS/IT investment. Strassman attempts to define effectiveness as the 'value added' of management over the cost of management. 'Value added' means the contribution to profits management makes by managing those aspects of the business it can control and influence. Whilst this is to an extent a subjective assessment the results from it are at least one view of management effectiveness. The first conclusion is that in general, until 1985 at least, IS/IT had made no noticeable difference to management effectiveness. However, by looking in more depth at specific companies and groups of managers it seems clear that satisfying the information requirements of good managers makes them better – but bad managers get worse! This is perhaps to be expected given the difficulty of defining the requirements. But also it appears that less competent managers adopt a piecemeal, cost-reduction approach (i.e. efficiency biased) to using IS/IT to address management tasks, rather than address the range of tasks in a comprehensive way with the intention of doing it better, not cheaper. Consequently there are few, if any, benefits and the net effect is to 'speed up the mess'.

These rather salutary reminders from the history of IS/IT (even allowing for the fact that things may have improved since 1985) show that even when the IS/IT environment was relatively simple, success was not easy. Today's more complex environment demands considerable management awareness, understanding and expertise to decide what to do with IS/IT and how to do it. To continue an earlier analogy, if juggling two balls takes a degree of co-ordination, juggling between three and seven requires considerable skill! That is the implication of the environment described in Figure 1.2.

KEY LEARNING POINTS

- The history of IS/IT in business and organisations has been somewhat chequered. Whilst many organisations have developed successful technology-based systems, few would claim total success. The technology and its capability have been changing rapidly, as has the business environment, but these changes do not wholly explain why managing information systems is problematic in many organisations.
- The evolution of IS/IT in business and organisations can be described in a relatively structured way in terms of what organisations were trying to achieve and how they were managing the process and resources. The 'three-era' perspective has been developed with the benefit of hindsight, but the many lessons that can be learned may help avoid future problems.
- The 'eras' are ongoing. Organisations are developing at different speeds from different starting points so that many should be able to learn from the experiences of the earlier 'pioneers'.
- In the discussion of IS/IT evolution a number of issues were identified almost in passing. Some vagueness may be left in the reader's mind about 'IS' and 'IT'. The terms may appear to have been used interchangeably, perhaps a more specific definition of terms is needed. It certainly would have helped in the past if everyone meant the same thing when bandying abbreviations about!
- It is necessary to define the terms more specifically in the context of understanding the management issues to be addressed with regard to information, systems and technology. Some of those issues are well known and are a product of the past, although they are not yet satisfactorily resolved.
- Other issues are newer and arise from the more strategic nature of IS/IT use. Organisations will have to resolve or at least cope with both types in the future, and it is likely that the environment will become more complex and the consequences of failure to address the issues more significant.

Chapter 2 will both develop a sensible set of terms and describe and structure the issues so that the rest of the book can address them in a coherent way.

Before moving to the next chapter the reader may wish to consider the questions below.

QUESTIONS FOR CONSIDERATION

1 For an organisation with which you are familiar, outline the way information systems have evolved in the terms used here. In particular identify:

   (a) two or three 'DP' systems that have clearly delivered efficiency benefits;

(b) any management information systems that have clearly made some managers more effective (describe specifically how this has happened);

(c) any strategic information systems – those that are gaining the organisation some form of business advantage.

Does the evolution show any variations from the models described? If so, can you identify the reasons for this?

2 For the same organisation, what issues have or are inhibiting progress towards coherent DP and MIS systems and the more strategic exploitation of IS/IT? Without attempting to structure the issues in detail, identify who in the organisation or outside it would appear to be responsible for the current situation and who can best resolve the issues. Use the following descriptions:

(a) The board of directors;
(b) Senior management;
(c) Functional/line managers;
(d) Staff;
(e) The IT department;
(f) Your IT suppliers;
(g) Customers or suppliers.

3 Discuss the pros and cons of the following proposition: *To exploit information systems effectively senior management must understand the technology.*

RECOMMENDED ADDITIONAL READING

Galliers, R.D. and Somogyi, E.K. (1987) 'From Data Processing to Strategic Information Systems', *Towards Strategic Information Systems*, Abacus Press, pp. 5–25.

Hirshheim, R., Earl, M.J., Feeny, D. and Lockett, M. (1988) 'An Exploration into the Management of the IS Function: Key issues and an evolving model', *Proceedings of the Joint International Symposium on IS* (March).

Ives, B. and Learmonth, G.P. (1984) 'The Information System as a Competitive Weapon', *Communications of the ACM*, 27, 12 (December).

Nolan, R.L. (1979) 'Managing the Crises in Data Processing', *Harvard Business Review* (March–April).

Strassman, P.A. (1985) *The Information Payoff*, Free Press.

Wiseman, C. (1985) *Strategy and Computers*, Dow Jones-Irwin, pp. 229–36.

OTHER REFERENCES

Benjamin, R.I., Rockart, J.F., Scott Morton, M.S. and Wyman, J. (1984) 'Information Technology: A strategic opportunity', *Sloan Management Review* (Spring).

Large, J. (1986) 'Information's Market Force', *Management Today* (August).

Notowidigdo, M.H. (1984) 'Information Systems: Weapons to gain the competitive edge', *Financial Executive* 52, 3, pp. 20–2.

Parsons, G.L. (1983) 'Information Technology – A new competitive weapon', *Sloan Management Review* (Fall).

Wyman, J. (1985) 'Technological Myopia', *Sloan Management Review* (Winter).

Chapter 2

Issues in information systems management

INTRODUCTION

In order to establish the appropriate principles and approaches for managing information systems in an organisation, it is essential to understand the issues which need to be resolved. The previous chapter outlined the typical stages organisations go through as the use of IS/IT evolves and develops. Many of today's IS/IT management problems and concerns result from that history. However, as organisations enter the 'strategic era', new issues have arisen and will continue to arise. In essence, most of the issues of the past revolved around the *supply* of technology-based information systems: how can IT-based systems be made to work effectively, economically and deliver the expected benefits? A much used phrase which expresses many senior managers' concerns is 'How can I get value for money from IT?' The words may express a genuine ignorance of the value or frustration because past investments have failed to deliver benefits or been excessively expensive. This anxiety to ensure benefits are gained at an appropriate cost will of course be a key aspect of the future, but the issues to be managed to deal with that concern will change.

As was discussed in the latter part of Chapter 1, organisations are not now able to control all aspects of their own IS/IT destiny. The actions of others may well affect what the firm has to do or can do. Future issues are likely to be more involved with deciding *demand*: what to do with IS/IT, why and understanding the business impact it will have. The supply-side issues – how to do it – will not disappear but they will need to be addressed in the context of the new demands. Whereas deciding the 'how' can, to an extent, be left to specialists in IT, deciding the 'what' is a business decision. Often in the past 'how' information systems were developed and managed effectively determined the 'what' – which systems were put in place; the capabilities of the technology intrinsically decided 'why' particular investments were made. The whole process was driven from the bottom up in a piecemeal fashion rather than directed and controlled in a planned way by management. No wonder management felt very uncertain that they were getting value for money.

Clearly the principles of how IS is managed in an organisation should be based on management processes which decide first what needs to be done and why, and which then decide how to do it. However, achieving such a logical approach in dynamic and complex business environments is not always easy – otherwise it would have been achieved in the past more comprehensively. The fact that supply-side options are continually changing does not help – but if you do not know what you want to do, it does not really matter how you do it!

Achieving a better balance between demand and supply management of IS/IT needs many preconceptions about the role of IS/IT to change. For instance the 'models' used to encapsulate and describe the last thirty years of history are precisely that – generalised descriptions of what has happened, to enable management to understand the past. Models for the future, on which to base the principles of IS/IT management will need to be different if greater success is to be achieved in a more challenging environment. This chapter will introduce some of those models. To provide a coherent set of approaches some definitions need to be established and used to achieve a better understanding of the management issues. The management issues and concerns need to be clarified, classified and understood in order to address them comprehensively. For an organisation to manage IS/IT successfully in the long term all the stakeholders involved need to establish a consensus on the principles which determine how it is managed. The first stage in gaining that consensus is to appreciate the issues perceived by the other stakeholders.

SOME KEY DEFINITIONS

The terminology of information systems and technology seems to be forever changing. In order to improve the communication in an organisation having an agreed set of terms which all understand and use is essential. Equally in this book terms will be used repeatedly and to aid understanding some definitions are needed. The way they are used here is (as far as is possible given the inconsistencies of use in the world at large!) the most common interpretation. Other specific terms will be defined later as necessary.

1 **Information and data**.   The *Oxford English Dictionary* essentially defines these as the same thing 'items of knowledge'. This does not clarify much! Probably the most useful way to define them is as follows. *Data* is the raw material which goes into a *process* to produce *information*. Information is what people require so that they can use their experience and skills to convert to knowledge. Equally a further computer-based process could be used to produce that knowledge – the concept of knowledge based or expert systems. Items of information can of course become the raw material, i.e. data for another process. *Data* implies not just numbers but also words and images which are input to some business process.

2 An **information system** links together data inputs, processes and information outputs in a coherent, structured way. In the context of this book the term

information systems implies *formal* systems, not *informal* systems of communication and discussion where the input data is uncontrolled, the processes are completely unstructured and not repeatable and the information output is not recorded in any way. Much of the information transfer and processing in an organisation is of the latter, informal type. It may be that some technology is now employed to facilitate informal information processes – word processors, electronic mail, computerised telephone exchanges and facsimile machines, etc. Here 'information systems' means the information processes needed to carry out the operations and management of an organisation in its business environment. None of these systems need rely on information technology.

However, all of the formal information systems of an organisation may (one day) be improved by technology. Any process by which data is collected, stored, retrieved, analysed, synthesised and formatted for a person or another process to use is a potential target for IT to be employed.

3 **Information technology.** This term is used here to mean the physical hardware involved in computers and communications networks, any software that runs or runs on the hardware. *IT resources* refer to any specialist resources or skills required to make the technology work in the organisation, i.e. if there were no IT, they would not be needed!

INFORMATION SYSTEMS ISSUES FROM THE EVOLUTION (DP AND MIS ERAS)

As has been said many of these issues concerned the delivery and supply of systems – in the terms used here, mainly 'IT' issues:

- how to develop and support the systems – methods which repeatedly delivered successful, working, maintainable systems;
- which technology to use, and hence which IT vendors, and how to control the proliferation of incompatible technologies, without limiting the potential uses to the detriment of the business;
- where in the organisation IT resources should be located, how they should work with the rest of the enterprise and how the use of IT should be decided;
- controlling the expenditure on IT and associated resources and ensuring accountability for their use.

In addition there are issues which were more specifically concerned with the information systems themselves:

- identification of potential benefits and the justification for using IT to improve the business performance;
- realising the benefits once the systems had been developed and implemented;
- the impact of the systems on people, job roles and on business practices.

Other issues became apparent as more and more IT-based systems were introduced, especially when the PC 'revolution' enabled IT to be dispersed throughout the organisation. These generally revolved around the data and information resources of the organisation:

- How should data be organised and stored to ensure coherence of the resource, avoiding unnecessary duplication, and the associated storage and processing costs?
- Who should be responsible for items of data to ensure their integrity and security. How should access to the data be controlled and how can it be protected from loss, misuse or even criminal use?

Finally, from the more detailed lessons from the DP and MIS eras it became understood that information systems needed to be integrated with each other and with other organisational processes. This raised two further issues:

- How to develop a long-term view that depicted how the systems should fit together within the business (an 'architecture') so that the systems could be developed in the optimum way.
- How to plan for the development and ongoing support of the systems, plus associated introduction of the supporting technologies and resources ('infrastructure'). This implies some setting of priorities and undertaking long-term investments which would only deliver benefits when later systems used the resources or facilities created.

Whilst these are not all the management concerns in every organisation, they do express many common issues which perplexed managers in the 1970s and 1980s, and still do! Many surveys were carried out during that period to understand those concerns and how they were changing over time. One of the most useful had its results published at three yearly intervals in *MIS Quarterly* (1987). By 1987 the strategic information sytems (SIS) era was well recognised and most of the technical issues that had caused concern in the 1960s and 1970s were considered by IT managers and general managers as being less important than those listed in Table 2.1.

Those items which are italicised can be related to the concerns which had developed during the DP and MIS eras, whereas the top four had become increasingly important during the 1980s in the emerging SIS era. Items which featured in earlier surveys but had dropped out of the 'top ten' by 1987 included: software development, integrating multiple vendor equipment, office automation, packaged software procurement and telecommunications management, i.e. more technical issues.

Whilst issues associated with these and other aspects of IS management cannot be neglected, the general view was that they could now be dealt with competently in most organisations – whereas the 'top ten' required senior management attention. One interesting feature of the list in Table 2.1 is that 'measuring IS/IT effectiveness' was more of a concern to the chief executive (ranked fourth) than the IT executive (ranked ninth). It is probably what one would expect!

Table 2.1 Top ten IS/IT management issues (in order of IT management opinion)

1	Strategic planning	(1)
2	Competitive advantage	(2)
3	Organisational learning	(3)
4	IT role and contribution	(5)
5	*Aligning IT resources in the organisation*	(7)
6	*Managing end-user computing*	(6)
7	*Data as a corporate resource*	(8)
8	*Information architecture*	(9)
9	*Measuring IS/IT effectiveness*	(4)
10	*Systems and technology integration*	(10)

Source: *MIS Quarterly* (1987).

The agreed need to improve the planning of IS/IT development and investment by making it more 'strategic' does not imply that planning had been totally absent in the past. During the 1960s, 1970s and early 1980s considerable effort had gone into some aspects of IS/IT planning within the business. Three types of planning predominated and the approaches to planning were decided mainly by the IT specialists within whatever administrative processes existed in the organisation. The three main types were:

(a) **Project planning** Detailed plans, networks of activities, bar charts and estimates of resource use and cost became a key IS management tool in the 1970s. Combined with structured methods for developing systems, project planning and control techniques greatly improved the predictability of individual project delivery and cost. They were less effective in ensuring benefits were obtained however.

(b) **Budgetary control** IT departments like all others would be expected to prepare budgets against which expenditure could be monitored. These would involve both capital and expense requirements and ensured that some forecast of resources, technology needs and costs, beyond the immediate project horizon, was developed. Not that these forecasts proved too reliable due to the uncertainty in the workplan – often 50 per cent or more of the work actually done was unplanned some twelve to eighteen months previously. Irrespective of that the 'budget' often became the controlling limit on what was done, regardless of the changed requirements.

(c) **Technology planning** Even given the uncertainty of the systems development plans, IT management had to forecast technology and resource requirements and convert them into long-term plans for the acquisition of hardware, software and services and recruit and train staff in the necessary skills. Given the high rate of turnover of IT staff in most organisations during the whole of the last thirty years (often greater than 20 per cent per annum) this planning was vital. Lack of appropriately skilled staff was often the main constraint to delivering the required project plan. The lead times for obtaining technology and staff often exceeded the budget horizon, so longer-term assessments and forecasts of needs was vital, even if the detailed plans were volatile.

Towards the end of the 1970s, often prompted by the major IT suppliers (such as IBM) and the management consultancies, senior management were invited to become involved in trying to develop longer-term, more stable IS/IT plans based on the plans for the business. This was the forerunner of 'strategic planning' as discussed later and normally involved management in a 'top-down' structured planning process driven by the business objectives.

Whilst it clearly helped set priorities from a business point of view the techniques used were really higher-level versions of systems development methods. Consequently the process probably helped plan better what was already intended to be done rather than uncovered new needs. The main benefit was that it produced far better understanding of the need for IS/IT planning throughout the organisation. Unfortunately neither the business nor the technology would stand still long enough for the resulting plans to be completed, and many of the plans were rapidly overwhelmed by short-term, event-driven priorities in the business.

The early 1980s also produced the 'PC revolution' which meant new types of technology becoming rapidly dispersed throughout organisations. The effect of this in many organisations was to reverse the process of business, top-down planning. Getting control of the expenditure, procurement of technology and the use of resources became the focus once more in order to deal with this new dimension of IT in the organisation. Management became more concerned with threats of technology proliferation and the associated cost explosion than with the cohesion of the IS/IT and business plans.

Another reason that the 'top-down' approach often delivered less than expected was due to the generally poor quality of the business plans on which it was based. They were either unclear, vague or not well understood or changed too frequently. Nor had they normally been developed with IS/IT in mind and, as already mentioned, IS/IT offers new ways of achieving business success. In the 1970s IS/IT was seen as a means of implementation, not as a source of change, to improve the business.

Whilst to combine all the issues of the past and future under the heading of 'planning' is somewhat simplistic, without a relevant, well understood and agreed plan many of the other issues become more critical. For ever changing requirements and priorities leads to low productivity in using resources, ineffectively used technology and only partial realisation of the benefits. Those problems are more obvious to management but the solutions cannot arrive without better planning for the future.

IMPLICATIONS OF THE STRATEGIC ERA

The strategic era implies that opportunities exist for businesses to gain advantages in their industry environment from appropriate IS/IT investments. On the other side of the coin potential disadvantages exist due to lack of investment and/or the effects of the investments of others in the industry. Sullivan (1985) suggested a simple grid to understand the issues facing management regarding how IS/IT impacted the business and the management implications. He described two axes against which the situation in any organisation could be assessed:

- **Infusion** is the degree to which an organisation becomes dependent on IS/IT to carry out its core operations and manage the business.
- **Diffusion** is the degree to which IT has become dispersed throughout the organisation and decisions concerning its use have been decentralised.

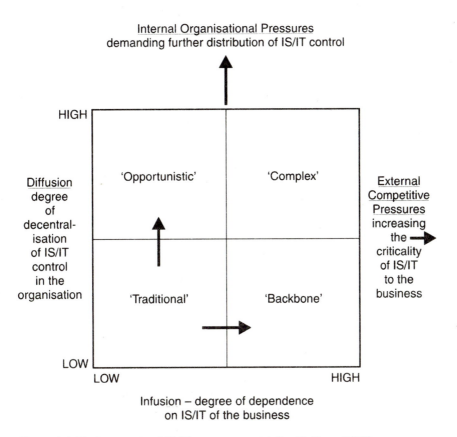

Figure 2.1 Environments of IS/IT management (after Sullivan 1985)

By plotting **high** and **low** degrees of infusion and diffusion, four, essentially different, environments are established as shown in Figure 2.1. Considering each one in turn:

(a) **Low diffusion, low infusion** i.e. highly centralised control of IT resources and IS is not critical to the business. Sullivan describes this as a 'traditional' environment typical of companies using IT solely to improve efficiency on a system-by-system basis (as described earlier as the DP era).

(b) **Low diffusion, high infusion** i.e. highly centralised control and IS is critical to business operations and control – the business could now be seriously disadvantaged if systems fail. Therefore high quality systems are needed, with normally a high degree of integration. The systems have become part of the 'backbone' of the organisation in Sullivan's terms.

(c) **High diffusion/low infusion** i.e. largely decentralised control giving business managers the ability to satisfy their local priorities but the resulting systems are not critical to the business generally. Any integration of systems occurs due to user–user co-operation, not by overall business or IT design. The management approach is essentially 'opportunistic' driven by short-term priorities which may create some business advantage in some areas.

(d) **High diffusion/high infusion** i.e. largely decentralised control but the business depends on the systems for success, both in avoiding disadvantage and achieving its overall business objectives. Sullivan describes this as a 'complex' environment which is difficult to manage. Too much central control to avoid poor investments will limit innovation and hence new strategic opportunities may be missed: too little control and the core systems may disintegrate.

As organisations evolved through the DP and MIS eras they tended to move from the *low–low* quadrant into one or other of the *high–low* quadrants. This often depended on the timing of their particular evolution and the availability of centralised (mainframe) or decentralised (distributed or PC) technology solutions to the DP and MIS needs. The arrival of the SIS era forces organisations to enter the *high–high* quadrant, and depending on the direction taken in the previous eras the changes to be made will be different. But in both cases senior business management will need to make some key decisions about IS/IT in concert, rather than allow local business managers total discretion or the IT department to control the types of investment.

The overall implications are that as the organisation becomes more dependent on IS/IT, essentially to avoid being disadvantaged, the more centralised and structured the approach to planning and control should become. But to facilitate the innovative uses of IS/IT to create future advantages, technology control needs to be close to the business user to enable appropriate connections between business need and technology solution to be made. In order to gain advantage and avoid disadvantage implies both high diffusion and high infusion and hence a complex, balanced set of management approaches (described by Sullivan as 'eclectic'). Most organisations are facing or will soon face this situation and both internal and external pressures will increase as indicated in Figure 2.1. Probably the best interpretation of the word 'eclectic' is to say that every organisation needs approaches to IS/IT planning and policy-setting tailored to its individual circumstances, as determined by the industry and business situation and organisation culture.

ISSUES IN IS/IT STRATEGIC PLANNING

By the end of the 1980s the need for organisations to have 'strategic plans' for their IS/IT investments was generally understood. In relation to that need a number of surveys have attempted to demonstrate how effective the IS/IT plans in organisations have become over the last ten years or so.

Lederer and Mendelow (1988) surveyed twenty US companies to determine the senior management problems preventing the development and implementation of IS/IT strategic plans. A previous survey had shown that obtaining top management commitment to the process was a prerequisite for success, but that it was often difficult to obtain. Their research identified the following reasons for this, in order of frequency of occurrence.

(a) Top management lack awareness of the impact IS/IT is having generally and did not understand how IS/IT offered strategic advantages. They tended to see 'computers' in purely an operational context (still a DP era view).
(b) They perceive a credibility gap between the 'hype' of the IT industry as to what IT can do and how easy it is to do it, and the difficulties their organisation has had in delivering the claimed benefits.
(c) Top managers do not view information as a business resource to be managed for long-term benefit. They only appreciate its criticality when they cannot get what they need.
(d) In spite of the difficulty in expressing all IS benefits in economic terms, top management demand to see a financial justification for investments.
(e) Finally and an increasingly apparent problem of the 1990s, is that top managers have become action-oriented with a short-term focus that mitigates against putting much effort into long-term planning, especially of IS/IT, given the other issues above.

In a similar UK survey, Wilson (1989) identified a number of barriers which prevented an effective strategic plan being developed and then implemented. These are listed in Table 2.2. The table lists the issues as stated in descending order of priority regarding (a) developing the strategy and (b) implementing it. In this survey top management attitudes seem less critical than the ability to measure benefits from the overall plan, deal with business uncertainties and provide appropriate user and IT skills. Again the consensus perhaps reflects views based on the past evolution of IS/IT as much as its future implications. The survey also highlights one or two of the 'softer' or cultural issues involved – politics and middle management's insecurity in the face of change.

Table 2.2 Barriers to success in IS/IT strategic planning

Barrier	*Importance ranking*	
	(a) Development	*(b)* Implementation
Measuring benefits of the plan	1	3
Nature of the business – rate of change	2	2
Difficulty in recruiting IT staff	3	1
Political conflicts in the organisation	4	6
Existing IT investments – constraining effect	5	5
Lack of resources to educate users	6	4
Doubts about application benefits	7	10
Telecommunications problems	8	9
Middle management attitudes to change	9	7
Senior management attitudes	10	8

Source: Adapted from *International Journal of Information Management.*

In spite of these difficulties in developing and the implementing strategic IS/IT plans, many organisations have spent considerable time and effort attempting to do so. Research by Galliers (1987) showed that 55 per cent of major UK companies claimed to have developed strategic IS/IT plans, although the same research questioned the efficacy of the planning, given the limited objective in many cases of merely prioritising an existing 'wish list' of projects. What the objectives should be and how they can be best achieved will be considered in detail in the next chapter. In the meantime it might be simply worth stressing that, to most organisations, having some form of IS/IT Strategy which attempts to link IS/IT plans to the business objectives and priorities is preferable to not having one! The consequences of a total lack of strategy, (i.e. merely adding up lists of projects, summing resources and buying whatever technology seems to fit each system best and calling it a plan) are by now well understood. Table 2.3 lists a number of the typical problems faced by organisations due to the lack of IS strategic planning. The list was developed by discussion with IT and business managers of organisations in both private and public industry sectors and most items on the list seem applicable to many companies today.

A report by the Kobler Unit (1990) based on a survey of thirty-four UK companies indicates that the consequent business problems caused by IS/IT in organisations which do not have IS/IT strategies are in total even more severe than the individual issues in Table 2.3. The following are typical:

(a) a loss of control of IS/IT investments leading to individuals or departments often striving to achieve incompatible objectives through IS/IT;

Table 2.3 Common business problems due to the lack of an information systems strategy

- Systems investments do not support business objectives.
- Systems are not integrated – causing duplication of effort, inaccuracy and delay and fragmented information resources.
- No means of setting priorities for projects and resources. A constantly changing plan reduces productivity and wastes scarce resources.
- No way of deciding optimum resource levels or when/how to use outside resources.
- Poor management information – not available, inconsistent, inaccurate and slow. Does not support key decision processes.
- Misunderstanding between users and IT – conflict and dissatisfaction result.
- Technology strategy is incoherent, incompatible and constrains business options.
- No infrastructure investments are made.

(b) problems caused by IS/IT investments can become a source of conflict between parts of the organisation;

(c) localised justification of investments can produce benefits which are actually counter-productive in the overall business context;

(d) systems on average have a shorter than expected business life and require overall considerably greater IS/IT spend to redevelop more frequently than should be necessary.

A STAKEHOLDER VIEW OF THE ISSUES

If the approaches adopted to managing IS and IT in an organisation are to be successful, then the views of all the parties, who both contribute to and determine that success, have to be considered. By understanding their perception of the issues their viewpoints can be included appropriately in establishing both what is done and how it is done.

These parties are the *stakeholders* who benefit or otherwise from the way IS is managed and whose views need to be reconciled in establishing IS management principles in the organisation.

Figure 2.2 describes the main stakeholders. Their particular interests in the success of IS management in the organisation could be summarised as follows:

(a) **Business partners** These are becoming more directly involved in the information systems of the organisation as the new strategic systems span organisational boundaries. Although traditionally their view might have been limited to the 'output' of the systems (i.e. will I get my order on time,

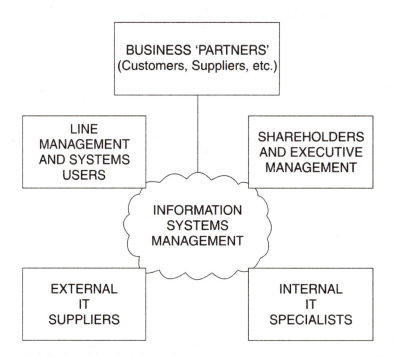

Figure 2.2 Stakeholders in information systems management success and/or failure

or will I be paid?), now they may require a direct involvement in deciding how systems are designed and implemented and demand a share in the mutual benefits delivered. A factor which may well influence a company's choice of trading partners may be the quality of the systems or their compatibility to ensure trading with each other is done in the most effective way.

(b) **Shareholders and executive management**   They clearly want to be sure that IS/IT investments overall are delivering benefits to the organisation and enable business targets to be achieved. That implies that the available benefits are being identified *and* the systems are being optimally managed – hence achieving value for money! Top management also have a direct input to make in defining the needs for executive information which enables the business to be controlled effectively at all times – so that management know what is going on in and around the organisation and can make appropriate decisions.

(c) **Line management and systems users**   They must not only ensure that the systems do what they are supposed to and that the intended business benefits are realised, but also understand their functions and relationships in the business to identify where potential benefits from IS lie. As we have seen, most future benefits will arise through change of functions or relationships, not just automating what exists. Identifying and managing those changes are business responsibilities. But they will only be achieved if the systems which enable them are designed and implemented in partnership with the IT specialists.

(d) **Internal IT specialists** They normally have two sets of objectives: (i) satisfying the needs of the organisation and (ii) furthering their IT careers. These can cause a conflict of loyalties if not effectively reconciled. Furtherance of an IT career requires gaining appropriate experience in how systems are developed, implemented and used *and* having experience and knowledge of technologies which are employed widely in the world at large. These skills increase the value of the individual, but may not coincide with the organisation's needs. This potential conflict must be recognised and dealt with if the high quality IT resources are to be obtained and retained in the organisation. Overall IT management's main concern is ensuring that they have the resources and technology to deliver the systems to the business, i.e. their primary focus is on managing supply successfully.

(e) **External IT suppliers** It may appear on first sight that they are merely there to sell things (hardware, software and services) to the organisation! Whilst all IT suppliers clearly want the organisation to buy their products in preference to others, most take a view that balances short-term cash flow with long-term partnership and growth in income. They want their products to be used effectively so that the business becomes more successful and buys more! They also have a lot of knowledge which can be used as a resource to help the organisation make appropriate uses of IS and deliver the systems more effectively. No IT supplier wants to be associated with a major systems failure, which will reduce the probability of repeat business and may jeopardise its ability to sell to others. In other words, if IT suppliers are managed well they can contribute to the strategy and they clearly will see the potential benefits to them of doing so.

These points are meant to illustrate that there are a number of stakeholders each with a major, if different, interest in how IS/IT is managed and equally each has an ability to affect how well it is managed. Therefore ignoring the views of any of the stakeholders is to risk the future success of IS in the business and to create an imbalance which is likely to cause many of the problems discussed.

KEY LEARNING POINTS

- **There are a number of common concerns which most organisations share regarding the management of information systems. Most research over the last ten years shows how the business (or demand-side) concerns have gradually increased in importance relative to those about the technology (supply-side).**
- **To achieve success with information systems, organisations must manage**

both demand and supply in a balanced, coherent way. This cannot normally be achieved by a purely reactive approach, responding to the most recent business problem or latest development in technology.

- A longer-term *strategy* is needed which enables demand for information systems to be established from a clear understanding of the business, its environment and what it is trying to achieve. Only then can an appropriate set of supply processes be put in place to satisfy those requirements over time.
- A key objective of the strategy is to obtain business and IT consensus on the target benefits to be achieved, the priorities for investment and the appropriate way of managing those investments. The key word is consensus, since if everyone is pulling in different directions, due to ignorance or vested interests, the sum total of benefits delivered may be very small, even negative.
- But a strategy is merely a means to an end – the end is having an appropriate set of information systems in place, delivering the range of available benefits at an acceptable cost, for the foreseeable future of the organisation.

The next chapter considers how an information systems strategy can be developed.

QUESTIONS FOR CONSIDERATION

1 Based on the brief case histories described in Boxes 2.1 and 2.2 outline the issues that exist regarding IS management in each of the companies, and the reasons for them. What would you recommend the CEO in each case should do next to improve the situation?

2 For a company with which you are familiar, attempt to relate the current state of IS/IT management in the organisation with the issues, concerns and problems covered by this chapter. For those that exist, describe any consequent business or organisational problems that clearly result. What, if anything, is being done to address them and by whom?

Box 2.1 Information systems management issues – case history 1

The company manufactures high-tech equipment for use in the oil, chemical and other process industries. Turnover exceeds £300 million but profits are very variable depending on cycles in its customers' industries. It is continually trying to diversify in terms of customers to achieve more stability of income and earnings. It produces high quality products and invests heavily in R&D to provide ongoing product innovation. Much of its component manufacture is subcontracted and its main manufacturing process consists of assembly, testing and commissioning. It provides on-site maintenance to its customers.

The CEO is an engineer and most of the management and key staff have technical backgrounds. The IT department which runs a number of mini-computers has reported to the administration manager for several years. She is also responsible for finance and purchasing. The minicomputers run the accounting, production control and purchasing systems and users have access via terminals or PCs. The computers are essentially full, further capacity is needed, and the systems are unreliable. Much of the IT department's time is spent on day-to-day fixes and maintenance, often associated with data problems. There is a long list of enhancements and new systems requests which never seem to get done due to short-term priorities. Management is reluctant to invest in more capacity, which they do not believe is the real source of the problems, merely an IT view of how to buy their way out of them.

Due to user frustration business departments have bought a considerable number of PCs of various types and have developed a variety of small systems from marketing to product development, mostly using packages, but some areas have written their own programs. Many of these systems duplicate aspects of the central systems and due to capacity constraints cannot all be linked to the central data bases. None of the users' systems communicate directly with one another. There is now considerable friction between many of the users and the IT department.

The latter are seen as both obstructive when users wish to obtain equipment and software and then unhelpful when users need training and technical support. Most department managers no longer attend the IS planning meeting each quarter. Staff turnover in the IT department has been rising steadily and the systems development manager recently resigned when a request to buy more capacity and recruit more staff was refused at the company finance committee, in spite of his boss's support.

The CEO and other department heads realise that to support future growth plans better systems would be needed and the current ad hoc developments, whilst locally very useful, were a fragile base on which to build. However, their overall concerns could be summed up by the production director's comment at the finance meeting – 'to give more money to the IT department is to pour it down the drain'. His suggestion to the meeting was that the central IT department be disbanded and distributed to each department. Many of the others nodded but no decision was made.

Box 2.2 Information systems management issues – case history 2

The company is a wholesaler/retailer which buys household goods (including electrical, furniture and furnishings) from manufacturers and sells them through a number of different retail chains which it owns. The turnover is over £1 billion. Traditionally the business was split into a wholesale division which procured, stored and distributed the goods and several retailing chains varying in size and type but with a wide geographical coverage in the UK. The business was organised as profit centres and the wholesale decision 'sold' the goods to the retail chains.

The information systems were mostly centralised at head office and covered most head office functions and the needs of the wholesaling business. In the past the retail companies had had limited systems but some had invested in point-of-sale technology and two of the larger ones now had IT departments. However, the links between the new retail systems and the centre were only of a batch type. Interfaces with ordering systems etc. were being developed. Other retail groups could not easily justify such investments given the tight profit margins and the need to justify such capital investment to head office, who were keen to use available capital to fund new outlets or takeovers.

The performance of the business had been declining for some years, despite revenue growth and a new business strategy had been developed. This involved reorganisation into new business units based on the retail chains who would become responsible for purchasing goods from suppliers through to sales to consumers. The wholesale division would become a warehousing and distribution company serving the retail chains, who would have the choice of using the service company or external services. Equally the distribution company could sell its services to other external companies, provided internal demands were met first.

In future, each retail company and the distribution company would be responsible for its own information systems. The main IT centre at head office would remain and would provide technical support and facilities for use by the businesses as well as continue to provide the systems needed by head office. The new business strategy was seen as giving more freedom to the retail managers to develop appropriate strategies for their markets, but also increasing accountability for success or failure. Most greeted the change with enthusiasm.

The head office IT Manager was less enthusiastic. He had informed senior management that to implement the change would require widespread changes to existing systems, the redevelopment of a large number and many new systems just to make the new structure operational. The cost would be in tens of millions of pounds, and require resources they did not currently have. This did not allow for any further developments required by the new businesses after the change. These would probably not be able to *start* for some years. Some of the business unit managers shared his concern but on balance felt the benefits of the new strategy far outweighed any potential problems with IS/IT. They would 'get by', although before the change many of them had been the harshest critics of the IT department. As a result few of the IT staff had any intention of transferring to the new companies.

RECOMMENDED ADDITIONAL READING

Brancheau, J.C. and Wetherbe, J.C. (1987) 'Key Issues in Information Systems Management', *MIS Quarterly* 11, 1, (March).
Sullivan, C.H. (1985) 'Systems Planning in the Information Age', *Sloan Management Review* (Winter).

OTHER REFERENCES

Galliers, R.D. (1987) 'Information Systems and Technology Planning within a Competitive Strategy Framework', published in Pergamon Infotech State of the Art Report (Ed. P. Griffiths) *The Role of Information Management in Competitive Success*.
Kobler Unit (1990), 'Regaining Control of IT Investments – A handbook for senior UK management' (ISBN 0-9516016-0-1).
Lederer, A.L. and Mendelow, A.L. (1988) 'Convincing Top Management of the Strategic Potential of Information Systems', *MIS Quarterly* (December.)
Wilson, T.D. (1989) 'The Implementation of Information System Strategies in UK Companies: Aims and Barriers to Success', *International Journal of Information Management* 9, pp. 245–58.

Chapter 3

Developing a strategic approach to information systems management

INTRODUCTION

The previous chapter explained why a lack of strategy for information systems can seriously reduce an organisation's ability to take advantage of information technology. Worse still, a lack of an agreed IS strategy can cause business and organisational problems beyond the immediate issues associated with IS/IT management. Obviously, to be fully effective, the IS strategy and plans should support the aims and direction of the business and if possible enable more ambitious goals to be achieved or better ways of doing business to be developed. Before considering this in more detail it is worth first clarifying what is meant by a strategy. It can perhaps best be defined as

an integrated set of actions aimed at increasing the long-term wellbeing and strength of the enterprise.

This definition applies equally well to the business strategy itself or the set of IS investments or the range of technology options selected. The key words in the definition are:

(a) **integrated** a coherent, related, compatible
(b) **set of actions** which will be carried out in order to improve the
(c) **long-term** future (not just react to current or even past problems or satisfy short-term financial objectives) wellbeing and strength of the
(d) **enterprise** overall, not just improve the performance of some of the activities.

For the purpose of the first part of this chapter the enterprise will be considered to be what in business strategy terms is known as a *strategic business unit*. This can be defined as a part of the organisation that

'Sells or provides a distinct set of products or services to an identifiable group of customers, and is a source of income to the organisation'.

This broad definition can include commercial businesses, public sector and non-profit-making organisations. In the commercial arena words such as 'profit' and 'competition' can be included in the definition. In fact all organisations cannot afford an extended loss (deficit of income over expenditure) and most face direct or indirect competition as will be explained later.

Most organisations are in practice composed of more than one business unit and how IS and IT strategies can be developed in multi-business unit organisations is dealt with at the end of the chapter.

The scope of this chapter is to explain how an organisation can establish appropriate management approaches which ensure IS/IT investments link effectively to the business strategy. The next chapter then considers a number of tools and techniques which enable specific investment options to be determined.

THE SCOPE AND CONTEXT OF IS AND IT STRATEGIES

In the last chapter the terms IS and IT were defined and in the first chapter the way IS/IT can become an enabler of business strategic change was discussed. Figure 3.1 brings these together to describe the relationship between IS/IT opportunities, business and IS and IT strategies.

The process of fully integrating the relationships is obviously an iterative one over time but following the rationale through from the start the main aspects of what is involved can be summarised as follows based on Figure 3.1.

1 **The business strategy.**   The development of the business strategy in many ways is a prerequisite for determining IS requirements. However, it may be that there is potential for change in the business environment enabled by IT, which implies that the business may wish to or have to change what it does and/or how it does it. Like many other parameters IS/IT is an input to the discussion of where the business should be going, just like economic and market factors, product development, etc. which are considered when defining the strategy. It might be considered under a general heading of technology development, except that the focus should be on what it is being used for within the industry and by others, not on which technologies should be used. How this can be done will be considered later.

2 **An information systems (IS) strategy**   defining the information and systems needs for the business and its component functions. The strategy should define what the business needs for the foreseeable future, based on an analysis of the business, its environment and strategy. The objective is to establish the demand for IS applications, aligned closely to the business plans and issues. These needs will clearly change over time and the demand must be continually updated, reviewed and prioritised based on business imperatives. It may not be feasible to satisfy all these requirements, economically or technically, in the short term but over time more applications become feasible.

3 **An information technology (IT) strategy**   which defines how the needs will be met based on the priorities in the IS strategy. This involves determining how applications will be delivered and how technology and specialist resources

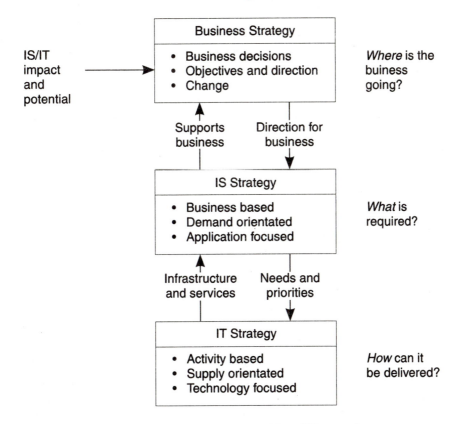

Figure 3.1 The relationship between business, IS and IT strategies

will be used and managed in support of achieving the business needs. It will describe the activities which need to be performed, how they are to be organised and the means to be employed in developing and operating systems and in acquiring and controlling technology – i.e. how the supply can be achieved.

A corporate or general management responsibility is to balance the demand-and-supply issues to ensure the business plans are achievable. This will require continuing reconciliation based on business priorities and supply constraints. In order to do this the organisation must establish a process for integrating business and IS/IT planning.

Considering the interaction of these three together it is worth summarising the scope of the potential benefits available if all three strategies can be successfully integrated. The Massachusetts Institute of Technology (MIT) study entitled

'Management in the 1990s' (see Scott Morton 1991) identified five levels of potential business benefit from IS/IT investments. The conclusions are very similar to those described in Chapter 1 (see Figure 1.2) but are expressed in a slightly different way (see Figure 3.2). The terminology used can be explained as follows.

1 **Localised exploitation** involves the use of IS/IT to automate selected business processes and satisfy particular management information needs based mainly on a functional approach to IS/IT investments. The benefits are limited but little change to the business or organisation is needed to get the benefits, i.e. relatively low risk.

2 **Internal integration** involves some internal reorganisation and the creation of new job roles and relationships both to facilitate the development of and obtain the benefits of systems which integrate major business activities. Whilst change is needed, it is entirely within the organisation's ability to define the changes and implement them.

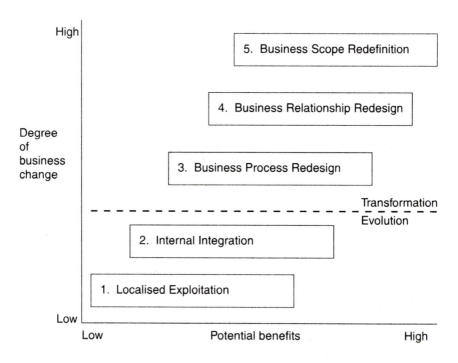

Figure 3.2 The relationship between the benefits of IS investments and the degree of business change needed to realise them

Source: N. Venkatraman (1991) 'IT Induced Business Reconfiguration', *The Corporation of the 1990s*, pp. 122–58.

Both these stages can be described as evolutionary, building logically from one stage to another at a pace the business and organisation can accommodate. The further stages require degrees of transformation in terms of what the business does and its external relationships, which in turn will affect its internal processes and structure.

3 **Business process redesign** involves the realignment of business activities to improve relationships with customers and suppliers and hence the overall performance of the businesses. This may well create direct systems links and require internal processes to be redefined to fit better the overall set of processes in the industry, i.e. it will require change in the way the business is conducted.

   An often quoted example of this was the redesign of the Ford Accounts Payable process and system which dramatically reduced the costs of internal processing of invoices, etc., and automated payments to suppliers.

4 **Business relationship redesign** involves the reconsideration of how information is shared and used by the organisation and its business partners. This is more than merely linking the processes together and may require the development of new relationships based on mutually designed information systems, and probably further organisational changes. Some activities may be done by different parties, to avoid duplicated effort or to enable subcontracting of non-core activities. This will normally require new management control systems to monitor the performance of these new business relationships.

   Examples of major changes in the way business is conducted in relation to consumers can be seen in First Direct, the bank with no branches and Direct Line Insurance, both of whom have caused major rethinks by competitors of how to market and deliver those types of products.

5 **Business scope redefinition** involves the realisation that, based on 1-4 above, the organisation may be able to extend its market or rationalise its activities to grow or become more profitable as part of a restructuring of the industry. This will obviously depend not only on the extent and quality of its information systems but also on the vision of the management to see how new opportunities can be derived from its information resources. In this case the organisation may change what it does as well as how it does it and this may well require more external industry information being available to the executive team to decide on future directions.

   The two previous examples quoted (First Direct and Direct Line) are causing major financial service companies to consider whether or not they can compete in traditional ways in those and other similar markets, and whether by innovative uses of IT they can open up new market opportunities.

Whilst this may seem rather theoretical, many companies are moving through these various stages of evolution and transformation, often at a pace that is controlled by others in the industry. The choice is either to react to change as and when it arises — effectively deal with threats to the business — or attempt to understand the implications and identify the potential opportunities for the business. The key message of the MIT study is that benefits from IS/IT investments are inextricably linked over the long term with business and organisational change. In which case the process of defining the IS and IT strategies must consider how information systems can produce beneficial change and also anticipate the effects of changes initiated by others in the industry. This requires a management framework that views IS/IT from an external perspective as well as an internal one, and tools and techniques of analysis which enable specific options to be identified and assessed.

IS/IT STRATEGIC PLANNING – A BASIC FRAMEWORK

In order to develop appropriate strategies for IS and IT it is vital that the relevant inputs are considered. Those key inputs to the planning process are described below. In the next chapter tools and techniques that can be used to bring together and analyse the inputs are reviewed and later in the book the various outputs from the planning process are considered in more depth to show how plans can be turned into successful implementation. The overall framework is described in Figure 3.3.

Inputs

In summary the inputs are:

1 The **external business environment** – the economic, commercial, social and competitive climate in which the organisation operates.
2 The **internal business environment** – the objectives, strategy, resources, activities and culture of the business.
3 The **external IS/IT environment** – technology trends and the use of IS/IT by others in the industry or by similar organisations.
4 The **internal IS/IT environment** – the current situation of IS/IT in the organisation both in terms of what it is used for and how it is managed – the contribution it makes in what areas of the business and the quality of the resources and technology in place.

  A particular aspect of this is the *applications portfolio* – the systems in place and being developed. These need to be analysed in terms of how effectively they contribute to the business and they should be managed according to that contribution like any other business asset. A way of enabling management to classify and understand that contribution is discussed in some detail later in the chapter.

Each of these inputs needs to be considered in more detail.

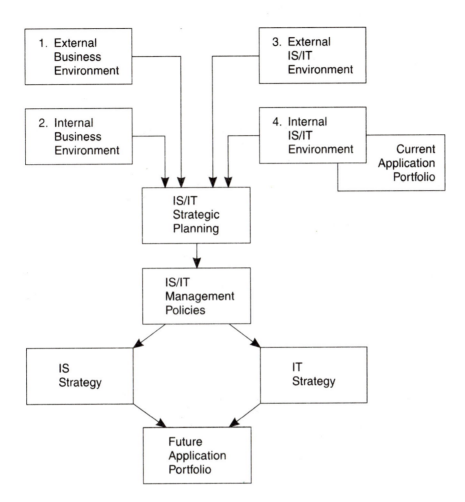

Figure 3.3 A basic framework for IS/IT strategic planning

The external business environment

This is an assessment of the forces which are affecting the industry in which the business operates, the economics of the industry, its structure and competitive basis and within that the particular issues and pressures facing the business. This should normally be part of any business strategic analysis, rather than a part of a specific IS/IT strategic planning process. Based on such an assessment, the role that IS/IT is playing or could play in changing any aspect of the industry, can be examined to identify potential opportunities or threats. For example, the increasing power of retailers over manufacturing companies has been enhanced by retail point-of-sale systems and the information this provides the retailer. Manufacturers need to consider how their IS/IT might be developed to either counter that pressure or perhaps better understand the potential of retail systems to gain some mutual benefit. Business environments are changing ever more rapidly, in some cases faster than the lead time for developing new systems! In such a case that speed of change needs to be reflected in reduced systems development lead times, which in turn will determine many aspects of the IT strategy – just as increasingly competitive environments impose constraints on product development lead times, and hence the methods of product design and manufacture.

The internal business environment

This consists of an analysis of what the business does, how it does it, and how it is organised and managed – in order to identify the information and systems needs. Such an analysis must obviously be related to the external business environment and this, again, should be done as part of the business strategic planning process. In particular the following need to be considered.

(a) The mission and objectives of the business must be clearly expressed along with the strategies being pursued in order to achieve those objectives. These will need to be accurately interpreted to define information and systems' needs and also to set investment priorities. Often objectives and strategies are rather vaguely expressed and not well understood by all the management. Unless these are clearly defined and agreed the resulting IS/IT strategy will be equally vaguely focused and become subject to 'flavour of the month' changes which will continually disrupt the planning and implementation of key systems.

(b) The business activities must be analysed and the relationships and interdependencies understood. This analysis must be as independent as possible of the current organisation structure, describing the main processes of the business which enable it to provide customers with products and services, plus what has to be done to control and develop the business. This will lead to the definition of a business information architecture, which should be robust enough to accommodate any changes in how the business is conducted and organised. The same analysis may well reveal weaknesses in the current organisational allocation of activities which either better systems can address or which cannot be addressed without organisational change. Once this activity 'model' is established it is important to describe the economic implications of the various activities in order to identify areas of high potential benefit.

(c) The strengths and weaknesses of the business and the reasons for these need to be assessed and agreed. This will include an analysis of the resources of the business – financial, people, products, technology, etc. – to identify where IS/IT can focus on exploiting the strengths and redressing weaknesses.

(d) Whilst the 'ideal' information and systems model should be derived from a logical view of the business activities in the industry context, the eventual systems will have to be appropriate to the structure and style of the organisation. Hence it is important to understand how the organisation functions, how decisions are made in both the formal structure and the informal network of interpersonal relationships. This will determine the types of information needed, who will need it and how it is presented and used.

Many structured management information systems fail to produce any benefits where the basic decision-making processes are relatively informal, based on interpersonal trust rather than formal exchange of information. The rate of change of both organisation structure and senior personnel will also determine the type of system and information required. Whilst no system will ever be flexible enough to cope with all the complexity and variety of organisational relationships, the structure, culture and style of the management will determine how information systems are developed to support the management processes.

The external IS/IT environment

This essentially consists of two parts:

(a) The organisation needs to appreciate and interpret the developments in information technology and the trends in both the economics of its use and the practicalities of applying new technologies to its business needs. An understanding of potential supply options, and different vendors and their product offerings, will enable more appropriate solutions to business needs to be considered and new application opportunities to be identified.

Technology trends and developments need to be evaluated both to select short-term options with a view to the long-term implications and also to plan when it looks most appropriate to intercept a new technology. When, for instance, would it be most appropriate to consider introducing electronic mail or image processing? No expressed need may exist but the cost of other forms of communication and document management must be compared over time with the ever-improving economics of the newer technologies.

All new technologies imply some risk and a learning curve for the business. Early understanding, interpretation and selective use of developing technologies may enable a future advantage to be identified and obtained. How many organisations did not consider the long-term implications of personal computers? The result has often been excessive direct expense plus enormous, often hidden, organisational costs.

If the need for more rapid development of new systems is not identified in time, the learning curve for adopting new systems development tools may be too long to improve the business situation.

Often short-term expediency forces continued use of known technologies and tools and continually overrides the long-term need to migrate to more appropriate technologies.

(b) More specifically the organisation needs to know how information technology is being employed by others in the industry, to what purpose and how successfully. In fact, knowledge of the use of IS/IT in *other* industries can provide a source of good ideas that can be transferred. Most critically what competitors, customers and suppliers are doing must be interpreted in terms of the business implications. Using the example above, manufacturers of retail goods took a long time to appreciate the business implications of the use of point-of-sales systems plus electronic data interchange and barcoding of products by retailers, and have had to react quickly and often at great cost to pressures from their customers.

A very successful flower auction suffered a short-term set-back when one of its competitors offered buyers the ability to buy flowers remotely through viewdata terminals. The competitor increased its potential market and in the short term attracted buyers away from the auction until it responded with a similar system. This shows not only the need to consider the available technology but how it can be applied in the industry. In practice most companies who have gained strategic advantage from IS/IT have not used the 'latest' technology – it is too risky. They have innovated in a business sense, but used proved, often well-established, 'adequate' technology.

THE INTERNAL IS/IT ENVIRONMENT

This again consists of two main components.

(a) The business systems and information resources that are in place and currently being developed must be assessed according to their contribution to the business. These need to be analysed in terms of how effective they will be in the future, not based on historical needs. The strengths and weaknesses in business terms of existing systems (*current application portfolio* in Figure 3.3) must be fully understood before further developments are undertaken – otherwise they may fail due to the inadequate foundations on which they must be built.

(b) The IS/IT assets and resources need to be catalogued and examined to identify whether the current capability and technology of the organisation are adequate for future needs. This is not just an 'audit' of current technology (hardware, software, etc.) but also a review of the people, their skills, how they are managed and the methods used to develop and support the systems and underlying technologies. One of the main reasons that IS/IT strategic planning often fails to deliver the changes required is that the organisation is not capable of implementing the plans, due to lack of resources, skills or management process. One key aspect is understanding the culture and style of the IS/IT department and how it relates to the business culture. This reconciliation of the IS/IT approach and attitudes with the business environment is often a critical aspect of the strategy development.

The current application portfolio

Before embarking on the development of new systems it is important that management understand the contribution that existing applications of IT are making to the business. When looking to the future, different IS/IT investments will be expected to deliver different types of benefits to the organisation and varying degrees of business change will be needed to realise those benefits. That implies that the investments will need to be managed in different ways and hence some form of classification of those investments is required in order to determine the appropriate management approach. Obviously this *portfolio* of existing and planned systems evolves over time, so it would be most beneficial if the same method of classification is used to manage *applications* over the whole of their business lives. That classification should be based on the business contribution expected from the application, in the same way that products or services of the business should be managed in different ways according to the contribution they make to the business.

A number of approaches to categorising systems for management purposes have been proposed over the last thirty years. The rationale for using the 'model' described here has been explained by the author in detail in previous publications (Ward 1988 and Ward *et al.* 1990). In the context of this chapter it is a way of assessing the contribution being made by the existing information systems. The same model will be explored in more depth at various stages throughout the book as a basis for understanding how to manage the whole portfolio of existing, planned and potential investments. The basic model is described in Figure 3.4.

The axes suggested for the matrix are based on work by McFarlan (1984) which described the overall role of IS/IT in a business and enabled the role of IS/IT in different organisations to be compared. However it is clear that every organisation will have a mix of IS/IT applications which contribute in different ways to the business. The matrix is far more useful when analysing this mix in order to manage each application according to its intended contribution. The matrix considers applications to be of four types.

(a) **Support applications** where IS/IT is used to improve the performance of business activities, achieving productivity or efficiency improvements which deliver mainly economic benefits. They are obviously valuable and over time good support systems reduce business costs and enable people to be used more appropriately. But they are not vital to the business achieving its current or future objectives. Examples would be such things as general accounting, personnel record keeping, expense reporting systems, etc. Many of the uses of spreadsheets and other PC-based packages would fall into this category, as well as some major organisation-wide systems. Often 'package'

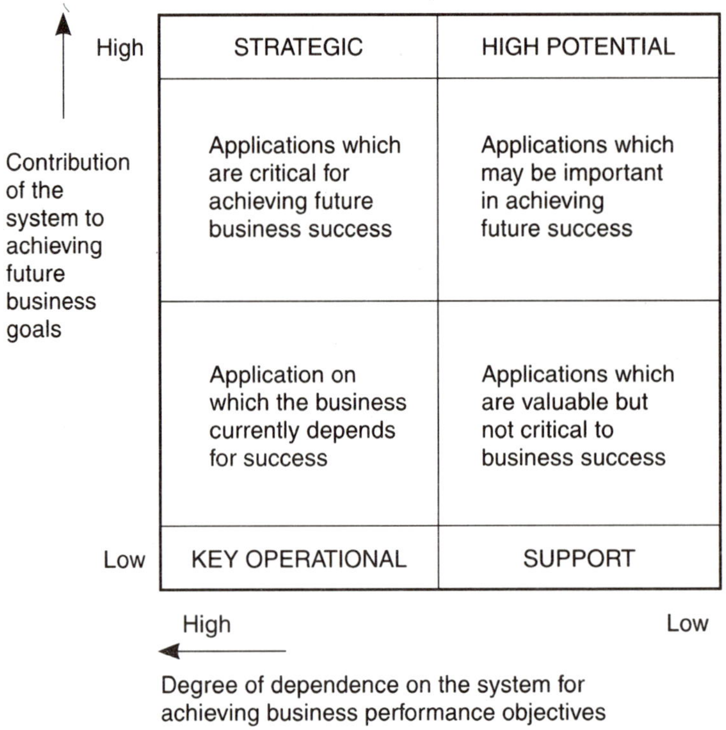

Figure 3.4 An application portfolio – based on business contribution

solutions are available for such systems because the needs are very similar in many companies.

(b) **Key operational** (sometimes called **factory**) applications where IS/IT is embedded in the core activities of the business such that if the system fails the business has immediate and significant problems – orders are lost, customers are lost, income is lost, etc., leading to real loss of profitability and control in the short term. Essentially problems and weaknesses in these systems lead to business disadvantages, since there is no realistic alternative way of running the business from day to day. Examples might be order management, inventory control, accounts receivable or production scheduling in a manufacturing company. The quality of the data and the degree of integration between these systems are critical to their success, if disadvantages due to errors, inconsistencies and delays are to be avoided.

(c) **Strategic** applications are those which are giving the organisation the ability to achieve its future objectives and in a competitive environment should deliver some advantage to the business. That is either because others do not have such systems (as was the case with Thomson Holidays) or because the system is significantly better than those of competitors. Examples might be a sales forecasting system which reacts more quickly to market changes or a PC-based system used by sales people to capture business from new customers or links to suppliers to achieve just-in-time (JIT) delivery of components and hence reduce inventory costs to virtually zero. The nature of strategic applications will depend on the stage of development of IS/IT in the industry and how well the organisation can link IS/IT investments to specific business objectives.

(d) **High potential** applications are not really systems at all, in that they are areas of research and development which may eventually lead to new systems developments. This part of the portfolio is where new ideas for systems or new technologies are evaluated to determine what the potential benefits are and whether further developments are worthwhile. Many will prove to be worthless but a few may well provide the basis for strategic investments. Examples might be the evaluation of image processing technology for document management or the feasibility of using expert systems to model the behaviour of competitors.

The evaluation may be by means of a prototype, or by assessing market acceptance of an idea or by a purely 'paper' evaluation of the economics and capabilities of new technology.

The matrix can be used by management to understand the value of its existing investments in IS/IT as a basis for determining future areas of required investment and actions to improve the contribution, get better value for money, from investments already made. In the latter case a simple SWOT (strengths, weaknesses, opportunities, threats) analysis of each system (as shown in Table 3.1) can be made to decide what, if any, action needs to be taken.

APPROACHES TO INFORMATION SYSTEMS PLANNING

The whole purpose of IS planning is effectively to populate the future applications portfolio with the appropriate suite of information systems that meets the business requirements at any particular time. Given the lead time associated with acquiring those systems, which can vary from a few weeks to several years, it is essential to identify future needs and opportunities as far as possible. That is not easy, given the rate of change of the business environment, but it means that the organisation must establish processes which enable the IS strategy to be derived from analysis of the various inputs (as in Figure 3.3) and also enable it to be updated as and when anything changes.

Once the applications required are known in overview, then the portfolio approach helps define how they can be successfully managed in order to deliver the expected benefits, i.e. to determine the *supply-side* strategy that is most appropriate. Therefore the IS planning process has to determine *what* is needed. The next chapter describes a range of models, tools and techniques that enable

Table 3.1 SWOT analysis of existing applications (Strengths, Weaknesses, Opportunities, Threats)

For example, when assessed, an application might be described in one of the following ways as an indication of actions required:

- High future potential, currently under-exploited, known benefits still to be realised.
- Can be easily extended or enhanced to be of more value.
- Could be of greater value if used more extensively.
- Benefits would increase if system were more integrated with others.
- System is critical but data quality is poor and causes problems.
- System needs significant redevelopment to meet future needs due to inadequate functionality or obsolescent technology.
- System still required but needs to be reimplemented to reduce complexity or cost less, and/or use less IT or user resources.
- Will be less important in the future; functionality should be rationalised or replaced by a package solution.
- System is no longer of value – should be discontinued.
- System operates satisfactorily – no changes needed at present.

etc.

that to be done, but it is important to understand the management approaches to IS planning that can be and are used, when and where they are appropriate and what they produce.

In essence *key operational* and *support* applications in the matrix enable the organisation to avoid suffering disadvantages in its business environment when compared to its competitors, or in its dealings with customers and suppliers. It does not take much creativity to identify what applications are required – they can be discovered by observing other companies in the same or similar industries. However, since *strategic* and *high potential* applications are aimed at achieving a competitive advantage, by definition there must be something new or unique in what the systems do or how they do it, otherwise no advantage can accrue. These will therefore require considerably more creativity in defining them. Competitors will not have them – otherwise the business is already at a disadvantage and catching up – but it may be possible to translate an idea from another industry to advantage. For example the 'yield management' systems employed by the largest US airlines to maximise the revenue from their flights, could be adopted by a cold store and refrigerated transport company to maximise its revenue during the summer when the demand increases dramatically – especially in a long hot summer – but when capacity is essentially fixed. (However, care is needed – when the French railways attempted to adopt a system derived from airline reservation systems it did not work and caused chaos!)

In summary, the planning process must be both analytical and creative, and must include formal and informal components in order to use organisational skills and talent effectively. The organisation needs to develop an approach that combines these attributes in a process that is tailored to the organisation and its overall planning and management processes. That is what is meant by the term 'eclectic' in the discussion of planning in complex environments described in the last chapter (see Figure 2.1).

Returning to that model which considered the impact of IS/IT on a business (infusion) in relation to the ability to devolve IS/IT decisions (diffusion), an organisation in the complex quadrant will have almost by definition a comprehensive application portfolio. Diffusion equates to 'informality' in that each part of the business can decide what it wishes to do, but some formality is needed if applications which span different parts of the business are to be identified and the benefits delivered – and most strategic systems cross organisational or functional boundaries and/or require business processes or organisational relationships to change. Organisations who are not in this complex quadrant will probably have an incomplete applications portfolio. Figure 3.5 attempts to show this.

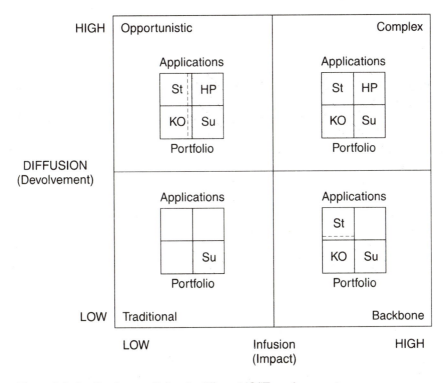

Figure 3.5 Application portfolios in different IS/IT environments

Figure 3.5 suggests a number of cause-and-effect relationships which are generally borne out by observation in many organisations.

(i)   Organisations that have a traditional, low-impact view of the role of IS/IT with highly centralised IT will tend to have a predominance of *support* applications.
(ii) Those that have decentralised IT control, because it is not seen as particularly critical to overall business success, will also produce a profusion of *support* systems, solving local problems. A number of *high potential* ideas will probably be developed but it will be difficult to bring them to strategic fruition because of the localised view of their value and the limited IT skills available in each area. Decision-making has been localised, and so, although some *key operational* systems will be implemented, integration across the business will be poor because system inter-relationships have not been considered in satisfying the local needs.
(iii) Where the impact of IS/IT has increased, probably due to external pressures, but IT is kept highly centralised, both *key operational* and *support* systems will be developed and continually improved, but more innovative uses of IS/IT will not be instigated because of the lack of perception in the business of what can be achieved.
(iv) Achieving the right balance of control, to enable business creativity without fragmentation of the resulting systems and hence develop truly *strategic* applications is far from easy, unless these cause-and-effect relationships are understood throughout the organisation.

There are reasons for these cause-and-effect relationships, based on the way IS evolves in organisations and the way in which IS planning becomes more sophisticated and better balanced over time. This also implies that a number of different planning methods need to be in place at any one time to develop a relevant, complete portfolio of applications.

Earl (1989) describes five different approaches to IS planning which imply increasing organisational maturity as the impact of IS/IT on the business is understood. The key aspects of the five stages are described in Table 3.2.

Earl's analysis considers the main task which is carried out, the main objectives, who drives the planning forward and the approaches adopted. By looking at each of these aspects the effectiveness of the linkage between IS planning and business strategy can be determined, and consequently how likely is the organisation to be gaining strategic advantage from IS. The stages can also be mapped onto the application portfolio model. This implies that although the organisation needs to develop more 'mature' planning approaches in order to achieve a full and relevant portfolio, some earlier stage planning approaches need to be maintained in order to manage the total matrix of applications. Not every application needs all the complexity implied in stage 5.

An organisation can identify from the types of planning approaches in place:

Table 3.2 Increasing organisational maturity with respect to IS planning

	Stage 1	*Stage 2*	*Stage 3*	*Stage 4*	*Stage 5*
MAIN TASK	IS/IT application mapping	Defining business needs	Detailed IS planning	Strategic/ competitive advantage	Linkage to business strategy
KEY OBJECTIVE	Management understanding	Agreeing priorities	Balancing the portfolio	Pursuing opportunities	Integrating IS and business strategies
DIRECTION FROM	IT led	Senior management initiative	User and IT together	Executives/senior management and users	Coalition of users/ management and IT
MAIN APPROACH	Bottom-up development	Top-down analysis	Balanced top-down and bottom-up	Entrepreneurial (user innovation)	Multiple method at same time
SUMMARY DESCRIPTION	'TECHNOLOGY LED'	'METHOD DRIVEN'	'ADMINISTRATIVE'	'BUSINESS LED'	'ORGANISATION LED'

After Earl (1989)

(a) where it is in relation to the eventual need for integration of IS and business planning; and

(b) which approaches it needs to adopt in the short term to move it towards that eventual goal.

The names given by Earl to the dominant rationale at each stage (see 'summary description' in Table 3.2), imply the following:

1 **Technology led**: carried out mainly by IT specialists to establish technology foundations, architectures and resources which should satisfy expected application needs of users.

2 **Method driven**: the use of techniques (often a consultant's methodology) to identify IS needs by analysing business processes – an 'engineering' philosophy based on top-down analysis of information needs and relationships.

3 **Administrative**: the main objective is to establish IT capital and expense budgets and resource plans to achieve approved IS applications – usually based on a prioritised wish list from users.

4 **Business led**: business plans, usually at a functional level, are analysed to identify where IS/IT is most critical in meeting short- to medium-term needs.

5 **Organisational**: the development of key themes for IS/IT investment derived from a business consensus view of how IS/IT can help meet overall business objectives – agreed by the senior management team.

Figure 3.6 shows how the evolving approaches to planning map onto the portfolio model. This is a very commonly observed pattern of evolution in organisations, although there is always some overlap across the stages. It can be explained as follows.

Stage 1   Technology led

Typical early IT-led planning – the IT department need to plan the interfaces between applications, each of which is developed to meet a particular need at a particular time in a particular area in order to make them work efficiently and effectively, and to plan for resources and technology to meet potential needs. Obtaining management understanding of the increasing dependence of the business on its systems is the key objective – to enable a more coherent business-related approach to be adopted. Essentially **support** applications are being built and management perceives IS/IT in that limited role – but the dependence is steadily increasing.

Stage 2   Method driven

Management, now aware, usually because of some crisis or key system failure, initiate a top-down review of IS/IT applications in the light of business dependence – priorities are to be agreed based on the relative importance of business

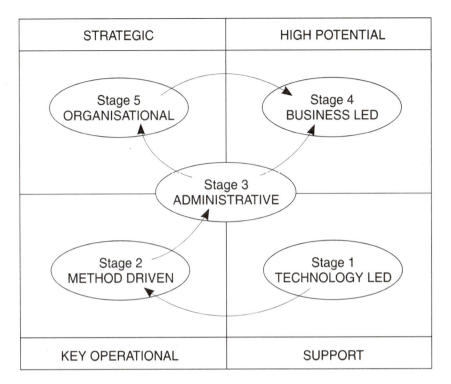

Figure 3.6 Mapping the stages of IS planning onto the application portfolio

needs. Should the order processing development take precedence over the new sales analysis system etc.? The approaches used are very methodological, normally based on derivatives of IBM's 'Business Systems Planning' and involve gaining a management consensus of criticalities and priorities. An extended, prioritised list of **key operational** applications is the usual result – to ensure the business is not being disadvantaged.

Stage 3   Administrative

The next task is detailed IS and IT planning – to determine the best way of implementing **key operational** and **support** applications or, in some cases, re-implementing existing systems in more appropriate, less costly ways. The portfolio needs to be better balanced – greater attention is paid to the critical **key operational** systems and less resource is dedicated to **support** applications – each having been 'prioritised' in stage 2. The 'information centre' concept may be implemented for support-type systems, and application packages will probably be introduced. Stage 3 can take considerable time to plan and implement effectively and whilst this is going on, nothing else can really happen since all resources are budgeted against a known detailed two–three-year plan.

So far, the process has essentially made IS planning a structured rather than unstructured process – aiming to stop IT-based systems causing at best no disadvantage – but the objective has not yet been overt use of IT competitive advantage.

Stage 4   Business led

The users take the reins, with the tacit agreement of their senior management often at a department level. Users see new opportunities, using IS/IT in new ways to provide business leverage/competitive advantage. This may start during stage 3 as frustration builds up in the 'jam tomorrow' stage of detailed planning and implementation. It is important that users, unfettered in any way by IT procedure or control, exercise this freedom to innovate, even if 90 per cent of the ideas are of little strategic potential. It is the source of **high potential** ideas, which with later IT support can be turned to advantage. The only problem is that too much development at this stage produces large numbers of local support systems – ideas of less potential – that have to be maintained, often at great cost.

Stage 5   Organisation led

This is the difficult stage to achieve, particularly if stage 3 is delayed and stage 4 is more user-rebellion than business-stimulated innovation. The innovative ideas of stage 4 need to be evaluated, in the business strategic context along with the opportunities now made available from the key operational and support infrastructure – i.e. the knowledge of what to do and the ability to deliver it effectively. Linking IS/IT potential to the business strategy is the main task. This requires the simultaneous attention of senior executives, line management and IT specialists – the first time in this process they have all acted together as a coalition. There is no 'methodology' available – multiple methods implies business planning methods plus IS/IT top-down and bottom-up approaches. Strategic applications can now be identified in the context of the business strategy and agreed to by all concerned.

In a further study based on these planning concepts, Earl (1990) assessed how organisations at different stages, using different approaches or mix of approaches, were satisfying the top management that maximum benefits were being obtained from IS/IT. The strengths and weaknesses of each approach were assessed using a number of factors. Not surprisingly perhaps the approaches were ranked as follows:

1 Organisation-led   ***   (very satisfactory)
2 Business-led   **   (satisfactory)
3 Administrative   *   (less than satisfactory)
4 Method-driven   *   (less than satisfactory)
5 Technology-led   *   (less than satisfactory)

One might argue that perception is all – the more involved you are in deciding what happens the happier you are! – and it is more likely that top management will accept a business view that IS is successfully deployed than accept the same story from the IT management! The reality may be different?

INFORMATION SYSTEMS PLANNING IN A LARGE (MULTI-BUSINESS UNIT) ORGANISATION

There is a considerable amount of evidence, described in detail in Ward *et al.* (1990), that developing IS strategies and plans at a Strategic Business Unit level is most effective in focusing the use of IT on the key business needs. Lower level, functional or departmental plans for systems lead to fragmentation of information resources and miss opportunities for improvements through integration.

Equally, in organisations that consist of many businesses, a top-down or 'corporate IS/IT' strategy usually fails to meet the specific needs of each business. The applications that result from such planning tend to focus on only those things the businesses have in common and these are generally those in the *support* quadrant of the applications portfolio. Hence, many strategic opportunities are missed. Such an approach also causes resentment in the units who have to devote significant efforts and resources to implementing systems they see to be of marginal importance, i.e. not critical to the business. Resources are often not available, therefore, to deliver systems the unit deems more important. That is not to say that major benefits cannot be obtained by looking across the corporation as a whole, rather than just at each business's needs. These benefits can accrue in a variety of ways; e.g. from sharing information about customers and markets, from using similar systems and saving money on IT resources. Therefore an organisation needs to develop IS plans to obtain benefits at all levels. Figure 3.7 expands the basic structure seen earlier in the chapter to demonstrate the overall relationships.

In essence, the diagram shows that an organisation should develop IS strategic plans for each business unit *and* for the corporate body – treating the latter as a business unit that manages a number of businesses, and consequently will have its own information needs. Depending on the amount of potential commonality in the business units and/or their degree of interdependence for success, further benefits will be available from combining the business units' IS plans. Ways of assessing these additional potential opportunities and benefits are considered in the next chapter. The degree of similarity of IS strategies will be determined both by the real similarities of business processes, products and environments and by the view corporate management take as to whether they run a 'conglomerate' of unrelated businesses or a 'corporation' of potentially synergistic businesses.

Based on IS plans, derived and expressed in similar ways, IT strategies can be devised to satisfy the range of needs in the most effective way. At one extreme, each business unit may have its own IT strategy for resources and technology. At the other extreme one overall IT strategy may be applicable across all businesses,

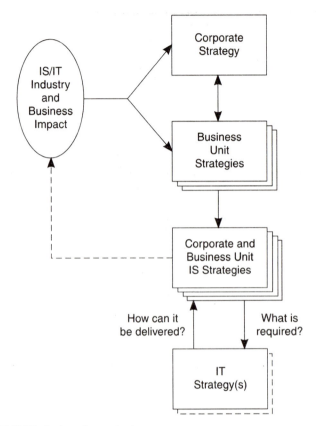

Figure 3.7 IS/IT strategy in context

although (as will be seen later) a mixture of supply strategies will probably be most appropriate. Unfortunately in many large companies, supply-side options are often considered first and hence the IT strategy often determines the IS potential of the various businesses. This may give top management a comfortable feeling that IT is under control but may mean the businesses are failing to achieve all the benefits available and may even be suffering disadvantages as a consequence.

Whilst all the key ideas and techniques which follow apply specifically to *a* business unit, they can also be used, as will be shown, to manage all aspects of IS and IT in a large organisation consisting of many businesses.

KEY LEARNING POINTS

- **Developing a strategic approach to information systems management, ensuring the right things are done in the right way for the overall benefit of the business, is a complex task, to be achieved in a complex environment.**

It implies bringing together the right inputs, considering all the relevant factors that affect decision-making. The old computer programming adage 'garbage in, garbage out (GIGO)' applies to the IS strategy as well as the detailed programming.

- There must also be an understanding of the potential scope for business change and development enabled by some of the applications of IT. Some information systems can create significantly better ways of carrying out the business, when related changes in business processes and organisation are made to exploit the technology.
- This implies an understanding of the different contributions made by different applications, all of which are valuable, but in a variety of ways. The *applications portfolio* view is a valuable way of creating this understanding across the business.
- Given the different nature of the applications, different approaches to planning for information systems are needed, if the full range of applications is to be discovered, agreed and delivered.
- There are models which can be used to understand why an organisation is or is not gaining the potential benefits of IS/IT. From that diagnosis, and an appreciation of the options available a process of change can be instigated to improve the overall effectiveness of IS management in the organisation.
- To achieve a fully effective approach a range of tools and techniques are needed to determine what the organisation should be doing – to ensure that the appropriate portfolio will be in place in the future that matches the business situation and strategy.

The next chapter describes the main tools and techniques available to do this.

QUESTIONS FOR CONSIDERATION

1   Figure 3.8 shows an example of an applications portfolio for a manufacturing company. Attempt to describe the systems with which you are familiar in your company in a similar way. For each system described identify its main strengths and weaknesses (Table 3.1 is a useful guide). What conclusions can be drawn about the contribution and quality of the systems you describe?

2a   Again using an organisation with which you are familiar describe how IS planning is carried out using the types of planning approaches described in the chapter – which of the five approaches is used and hence at what stage of evolution is the organisation? (See Table 3.2.)

2b   Based on the answer to (a), what needs to change if the organisation is to become more mature/capable of linking its investments in IS to the business strategy? Which of the aspects of IS planning described in the chapter are satisfactory and which need improvement and what should be done, and by whom, to bring about those improvements.

STRATEGIC	HIGH POTENTIAL
ORDER MANAGEMENT	EDI WITH WHOLESALERS
LINKS TO SUPPLIERS (JIT)	MANPOWER PLANNING
MRP II (MULTI-SITE)	DECISION SUPPORT (CAPACITY PLANS)
SALES FORECASTS AND MARKET ANALYSIS	EXPERT FAULT DIAGNOSIS
PRODUCT PROFITABILITY ANALYSIS	DOCUMENT PROCESSING
BILL OF MATERIALS DB	TIME RECORDING
INVENTORY MANAGEMENT	BUDGETARY CONTROL
SHOP FLOOR CONTROL	GENERAL ACCOUNTING
PRODUCT COSTING	MAINTENANCE COSTING
MAINTENANCE SCHEDULING	COST ACCOUNTING
EMPLOYEE DB	CAD FOR LAYOUT DESIGN
RECEIVABLES/PAYABLES	PAYROLL
CAD (PRODUCT DESIGN)	
CUSTOMER DB	
etc.	etc.
KEY OPERATIONAL	SUPPORT

Figure 3.8 Example portfolio for a manufacturing copmpany

3   Identify five reasons why organisations fail to develop a comprehensive application portfolio that enables them to realise the maximum business contribution for IS/IT, and discuss the implications of each.

RECOMMENDED ADDITIONAL READING

Earl, M.J. (1990) 'Approaches to Strategic IS Planning: Experience in 21 UK companies', *Proceedings of the International Conference on IS*, Copenhagen.
Scott Morton, M.S. (Ed.) (1991) *The Corporation of the 1990s*, Oxford University Press. Chapters 5 and 6.

OTHER REFERENCES

Earl, M.J. (1989) *Management Strategies for Information Technology*, Prentice-Hall.
McFarlan F.W. (1984) 'Information Technology Changes the Way You Compete', *Harvard Business Review* (May–June).
Ward, J.M. (1988) 'Information Systems and Technology: Application Portfolio Management – An assessment of matrix based analyses', *Journal of Information Technology*, 3, 3 (December).
Ward, J.M. Griffiths, P.M. and Whitmore, P., (1990) *Strategic Planning for Information Systems*, John Wiley, Chapter 1.

Chapter 4

Identifying the information systems needs for a business

INTRODUCTION

Chapter 3 considered how to develop an overall approach to the strategic management of information systems in a business, based on an understanding of the differing contributions that IS investments make to business success. In order to determine the specific IS investments that a business should make, tools and techniques are needed to analyse the business and its situation within the context of the overall planning processes described in Chapter 3.

The purpose of the 'tools' is to enable business and IT managers to assess the business from a variety of viewpoints and agree where and how IS investments would be most beneficial. At the same time the use of the various analysis techniques enables the value and usefulness of the existing information systems to be reviewed and improvements determined. To establish the appropriate suite of future applications requires the business situation and strategy to be analysed in a number of different ways, using a number of different tools, each of which will help uncover some of the opportunities. These tools and their application are described in the first part of the chapter in the context of *a* business. In the latter part of the chapter the various techniques will be reviewed to show how they relate to one another and hence can be brought together with a framework for deciding on the future requirements in total. Also how the techniques can be extended to deal with a multi-unit organisation will be discussed.

The various techniques discussed below can be considered in two main categories:

(a) those which enable the business strategy to be interpreted in terms of information and systems needs; and
(b) those which enable the information relationships associated with external and internal business processes to be analysed and improved.

In both categories the analysis may well highlight areas where changes to business processes, relationships and organisation structures may be required to take full advantage of IS options available. It is usually this combination of IS investment and business change that results in strategic developments, as described in earlier chapters.

Before each of the various techniques can be used, the business situation – the environment within which the organisation has to succeed – needs to be fully understood by the business management. This understanding is a key part of developing the business strategy itself, and should lead to establishing appropriate objectives for the business. However, some aspects of that situation appraisal have direct implications for the IS strategy, so the next section deals with how to consider IS investments at a high level in the context of the business situation. As will be seen, the result may be a need to revisit and reconsider the business strategy at a high level before proceeding further.

SITUATION APPRAISAL AND THE IMPLICATIONS FOR IS INVESTMENTS

As part of establishing a business strategy a number of high-level models can be used to assess the situation faced by the organisation. Two of these in particular have implications for the options for IS investment in any business. First, the stage of maturity of the industry and the resulting competitive forces will determine the priority areas for not only a particular firm, but also its competitors. Second, the product portfolio and the contribution that the mix of existing and new products make to the overall performance of the company should determine the allocation of all types of resources, including IT resources.

Figure 4.1 summarises a standard model of industry development in terms of the relationship of supply and demand, and shows how the focus on information requirements varies according to the stage of maturity of the industry. Clearly in a declining industry (such as ship-building) there is a heavy focus on using information to reduce costs in order to retain profitability against fierce competition. But in a growth industry (such as electronics) much of the focus of the information is matching the needs of the market to product development and establishing effective distribution channels to the customers, to capture a significant share of the available demand. Whilst oscillations in the overall economic cycle will moderate the rates of growth in any industry and hence set short-term priorities, the IS strategy should be appropriate to the general state of the industry in which the business competes. That implies a more defensive strategy and a more focused, careful use of IS/IT in mature/declining industries and a more aggressive strategy with more varied and perhaps riskier use of IS/IT in emerging/growth industries. In mature industries situations are better understood by management and also are generally more stable, and hence IS/IT investments can be derived from a rational structured business analysis. In emerging/growth industries less is known, more is uncertain and more opportunities exist to be creative in the use of IS/IT to develop the business. Also the IS strategy is likely to evolve more quickly as the business understanding increases.

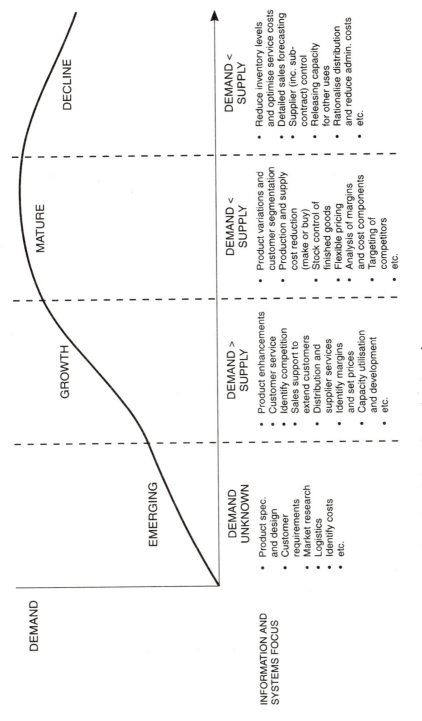

Figure 4.1 Industry/product life cycles – information and systems focus

PRODUCT PORTFOLIO ANALYSIS

Businesses which have a mix of products – a product portfolio – which compete in different industries, at different stages of maturity, may have to devise different IS strategies to support products for each industry and each stage of maturity. The best-known model for classifying the product portfolio is the Boston matrix which assesses the market growth/market share relationship of a company's products to determine product investment and resource allocation strategies. There are many similar models which relate the industry life cycle and product strategies, and each can be considered in a similar way to that discussed here in the context of the Boston matrix. The basic matrix is shown in Figure 4.2.

The four quadrants relate to the different stages of maturity in the life cycle in terms of the stage of evolution of the product in the market place. Bringing the two models together suggests the different emphases that will be given to the IS strategy to support groups of products in the different quadrants. These differences are summarised in Box 4.1. An example may serve to explain how important it is to understand the key differences between parts of the business in order to develop appropriate systems.

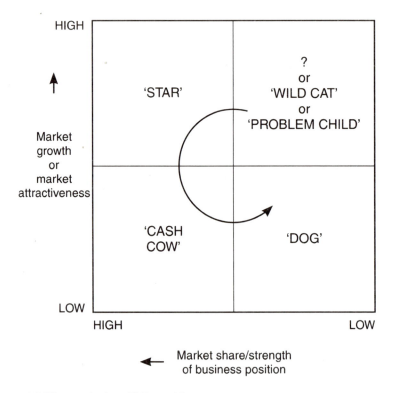

Figure 4.2 The product portfolio matrix

Box 4.1 IS/IT investment and the product portfolio

1 **'Wild cat' or '?' or 'problem child'** (low market share–high growth market)
To succeed with such a product an organisation would generally need to innovate with the product or how it is delivered to the market place to capture a high share, or to focus on a particular niche in the market.
IS/IT should therefore focus on product or business process development (e.g. logistics) and on the identification of potential customers, their needs and enable them to be segmented to advantage. The key then is getting information about the product or service to the relevant customers effectively. These IS uses are likely to be quite innovative in the industry to attract the attention of potential buyers.

2 **'Star'** (good market share in high growth market)
The route to long-term success – sustaining the position – requires continuous innovation in product and/or services, to keep ahead of competing products and meet the developing customer needs. Systems will tend to address the business needs from the customer end enabling demand to be satisfied and customer preferences and changes to be detected and matched. The systems should enable growth of activity and be able to handle increased volumes and complexity of business without incurring equal increases in business costs. Whilst some systems effort will be directed at understanding and controlling costs, the majority of effort will be to support business development and innovation, with the aim of differentiating the product in the market place. The investment focus will be to understand the market, add value and cope with growth.

3 **'Cash cow'** (strong market position in mature, lower growth market)
The business strategy is to 'milk' the 'cash cows', ensuring that available profits are gained and a significant net cash inflow achieved. This involves defending the market position, keeping customers, lowering costs and satisfying demand in the most efficient way. Therefore systems will focus on the detailed matching of demand and supply, optimising the overall business logistics and the use of capacity and resources to achieve lower total costs. Productivity and control of the business are the main aims to prevent competitors gaining advantages, rather than creativity and innovation.

4 **'Dog'** (weak market position in a low growth or declining market)
Dog products are unlikely to attract much investment, unless it an be clearly directed at improving profitability and/or gaining a greater market share. Alternatively a valuable niche in the market place may be available by focusing on a subset of customers. In both cases the use of IS/IT will be selectively targeted at detailed aspects of the business to reduce costs and increase profitability. The eventual aim may be divestment and hence some of the functions of the business may be subcontracted to minimise overheads and IS/IT may be subcontracted, at least in part, with those activities.

A leading door manufacturer had three factories, each making a range of products, which could be segmented into two distinct product groups:

(a) **Standard doors** of some 200 designs sold through a catalogue to house builders and by merchants and shops. Several million such doors were sold each year and the company had a large market share (cash cow – mature market).

(b) **Special doors** (e.g. safety, security, fire doors and high quality and odd shape/side doors). These were made to meet particular customer specifications in small batches. This segment of the market was growing rapidly and the company had a good share of the market, in which there were many more competitors including imports from Holland and Germany, (star-growth market).

The information systems in the business had been designed to meet the needs of the standard door business. They were very effective in ensuring that costs were kept low through automation, and satisfying the customer demands in terms of efficient service. However the business was trying to use the same systems to manage the special doors business. But the basic needs are different for special doors: e.g. to deal with a wider range of types of customer, to enable quotations and designs to be produced quickly to win orders, and to track specific orders from obtaining the raw materials through manufacture, testing and delivery to the customer. Each special door should yield considerably more profit. But due to the large administrative overhead per order, caused by having to use systems designed for large-volume standard items, significantly reduced actual profits were being achieved. Worse still, some orders could get 'lost' in the system for long periods – causing customer dissatisfaction, which probably meant lost future business.

Given the market growth and strategy of the business to expand in this latter area, serious problems resulted from this use of unsuitable 'second-hand' systems in a growth business. Once the problem was understood it proved relatively easy to implement a suite of systems to manage the special doors business effectively. Those systems were focused on winning and satisfying the customer order, rather than optimising the efficiency of production and stock handling.

COMPETITIVE FORCES ANALYSIS

Once the business situation is clarified in this way, and the overall implications of IS to the business or segments of the business are understood at a high level, another analytical technique used in business strategy can help focus more specifically on the key areas for IS investment. Again this is a form of industry analysis, implying that the conclusions drawn for a particular company could be similar for competitors. Michael Porter (1980, 1984) describes it in terms of 'competitive forces' analysis. He describes five forces which affect an organisation's ability to succeed in its industry. These are: *the threat of new entrants*, *the threat* of *substitute products or services, the bargaining power of buyers* and *of suppliers* as well as the more obvious *rivalry of existing competitors*. These forces are considered in more detail below, from the point of view of asking: 'Can IS investments help deal with these forces?' The intention is to ensure that investments are aimed at addressing external pressures on the business as well as improving the performance of internal activities. As part of the business strategy development it is valuable to assess the impact of each force (high, medium, low, for instance) and then describe the nature of the impact where it is high, in order to identify ways of counteracting that force.

Table 4.1 summarises some of the key implications when each of the five forces is impacting success and also gives examples of the ways in which IS/IT investments can influence the situation. A few of these (see column 3 of Table 4.1) are described in more detail below to exemplify the potential relevance of IS investments.

(a) By analysing the nature and buying patterns of customers, apparently homogeneous markets can be segmented in order to tailor product offerings more

Table 4.1 Impact of competitive forces and potential IS/IT opportunities

Key force impacting the industry	Business implications	Potential IS/IT effects
Threat of new entrants	Additional capacity Reduced prices New basis for competition	Provide entry barriers/reduce access by: • exploiting existing economies of scale • differentiate products/services • control distribution channels • segment markets
Buyer power high	Forces prices down Demand higher quality Require service flexibility Encourage competition	Differentiate products/services and improve price/performance Increase switching costs of buyers Facilitate buyer product selection
Supplier power high	Raises prices/costs Reduced quality of supply Reduced availability	Supplier sourcing systems Extended quality control into suppliers Forward planning with supplier
Substitute products threatened	Limits potential market and profit Price ceilings	Improve price/performance Redefine products and services to increase value Redefine market segments
Intense competition from rivals	Price competition Product development Distribution and service critical Customer loyalty required	Improved price/performance Differentiate products and services in distribution channel and to consumer Get closer to the end consumer – understand the requirements

Adapted from James I. Cash (1988) 'Inter-organisational Systems: An information society opportunity or threat?' *The Information Society* 3, 3.

appropriately or provide ways of buying that suit different groups of customers. At the same time this can ensure that marketing and selling resources are better utilised. For instance, small customers may be served by a frequent telemarketing service to help them keep low stocks, and reduce the costs of handling small 'random' orders. At the same time large customers may be offered on-line ordering facilities to make buying easier. Both these enable experienced sales staff to be released to gain new business or 'protect' vulnerable customers. Both require good information systems to support the new processes. A number of organisations have adopted similar mixtures of customer account management.

A similar, but slightly different example, is the use of portable computers by insurance salesmen, pioneered by Allied Dunbar, which both enabled the new demands caused by the Financial Services Act to be met efficiently and also a broader service, 'Financial Planning', to be offered to the more valued clients at little extra cost. Such systems clearly differentiated the early users in the high-value segments of the market.

(b) Many organisations have used IS/IT to speed up the development and introduction of new products, through the integration of design and manufacturing systems (CAD/CAM) which can reduce lead times by factors of 50–80 per cent. Often this was done by reusing existing product data. A locomotive manufacturer reduced lead times from eighteen to six months, when it was understood that 80–90 per cent of components were reused from one design to another. Previously each design team had interpreted the customer requirements in terms of a 'unique' product rather than compare requirements against previous designs to enable designs and components to be reused. This example is for a product which is designed to order but in other types of product development IS can play a key role.

For instance a pharmaceutical manufacturer has identified two critical forces that are related, and will significantly impact future success. First the 'time to market' of new drugs must be reduced, both to increase profits in the long term and ensure that others do not dominate certain key market segments. Second, the organisation must have more flexibility where drugs are made throughout the world, in order to optimise manufacturing resources and distribution costs across a large range of products. Both of these require a more integrated approach to systems and information management throughout the whole business. Improving each function's use of information systems may reduce lead times by 10 per cent overall, but by looking at the whole R&D process, and optimising the gathering and production of information the lead time could be reduced by the 40–50 per cent which may well be needed to compete successfully in the next ten years. If that succeeds and more drugs are brought to the market more quickly, then manufacturing optimisation will be critical to avoid huge capital costs and risks. Therefore international planning and control systems for product manufacture (which is subject to rigorous registration processes) need to be undertaken now. The intention is to reduce both product lead times and eventual manufacturing costs in the face of fierce competition.

Many more examples can be quoted showing how IS investments can directly affect the competitive forces in an industry. Clearly where, as discussed earlier, companies have gained advantages through IS, they have in some way changed the balance of forces in their favour. Often IS investments affect more than one of the forces, as shown in the examples above.

The main benefits of the types of analyses described to date are:

(a) to ensure that IS/IT, along with other resources, is focused on dealing with aspects of the business which have a significant effect on success and failure;
(b) by focusing on specific business pressures, people can be more creative in thinking about IS in terms of how it could be used to advantage by changing some of the ways business is carried out – an external rather than internal focus;
(c) to get agreement at a high level between business and IT managers on the importance or otherwise of IS investments to the future success of the business. This is in part because these techniques help management learn from how IS/IT has affected other industries, by translating the ideas and implications in a structured way to the forces affecting not only one firm's position but also the major stakeholders in the industry. A lack of such a high-level view may mean that major opportunities or major threats are ignored.

However, in order to understand the potential benefits to an organisation, more detailed assessment of how IS might affect success is needed.

INTERPRETING THE BUSINESS STRATEGY IN TERMS OF IS REQUIREMENTS AND PRIORITIES

Michael Porter (1980) argues that organisations achieve long-term success in competitive environments by pursuing one of two 'generic' business strategies: *Low cost* or *differentiation*. Low cost means that the organisation is more efficient and more effective in using resources than its competitors and hence overall has lower real costs of doing business, but produces a product or service of comparable quality. Low cost does not imply low price! Hence if the firm can obtain similar prices to its competitors, it will have higher margins. But if a 'price war' occurs the low-cost firm will be able to reduce its prices furthest in the battle for market share and still remain profitable. Obviously in such organisations IS investments will tend to be aimed at, and justified by, reducing costs and improving control of business activities. This may limit the type of IS investments and will tend to focus on the automation or elimination of activities. For instance, to achieve low cost a standardised order entry and processing system will minimise order handling costs. 'Standardised' is the key word here, since by automation, simplification and standardisation of process and hence systems, lowest cost of operation *and* tightness of control can be achieved. Hence in any organisation, whatever its specific objectives, that is following a 'low-cost' strategy, highest priority is likely to be given to IS investments which enable costs to be steadily reduced over time. This may lead to problems with IT if a too short-term focus is used. The emphasis on cost may mean that in evaluating IS investments the least-cost IT solution may be chosen. This often produces poorly integrated, problem-driven solutions, that may actually increase overall business costs – 'low cost' is a long-term, total view of business costs. More innovative uses of IT may enable overall business costs to be reduced in the long term, but this may be difficult to prove in advance.

In a similar way the IS investments for a firm which has chosen to succeed through differentiation, will follow a philosophy intended to make the company unique in the eyes of its customers in some way and hence be able to gain a premium price for its products and services. 'Differentiation' does not deny the importance of controlling costs but balances that with the need to provide the customer with aspects of the product or service which customers value so much that they will pay a premium. Hence the organisation's profitability will be greater than its competitors provided its costs are no worse. IS can clearly be used to differentiate an organisation as has been seen in earlier examples. In comparison to the 'low-cost' company's standardised order processing system to reduce costs, a differentiating company may offer a variety of ways to place orders, making it easier for each major type of customer. Its internal costs may increase but the customers may value the way the system fits their way of working. The overall role of IS/IT in such companies is likely to be more varied than in 'low-cost' companies, given that it will be used to both reduce and control costs *and* enable the higher quality of service or product the customer demands to be delivered. If customers are paying a higher price they often expect much better information about what they are getting and when, so good information systems can often be at the heart of a differentiation strategy.

Porter argues that companies who succeed have clearly achieved differentiation or low cost, or in some cases both (if only for a limited period). Those who achieve neither, by definition will be less successful and may fail totally in the long term as their margins disappear. A lot of organisations are in this middle category where the 'generic' strategy is confused or oscillates between the two as economic conditions or management changes. This can often be seen in the rather arbitrary approach companies adopt to making IS/IT investments and setting priorities amongst them. Where the overall strategy is clear, IS/IT investments can be seen to be part of a pattern – driven by 'themes' as mentioned in the previous chapter. Seeing the long-term implications of IS in the organisation is critical if full benefits are to be achieved. At this stage we are talking about identifying appropriate opportunities, but the systems have to be designed and implemented effectively and the benefits realised to succeed. This is much easier if the generic strategy is clearly understood and sustained over time.

Returning briefly to the door manufacturer described earlier, the standard doors business was essentially low cost, whereas the special doors business relied on differentiation, and hence the nature and specific functions of the systems needed to support each were significantly different. It was only when this was recognised that all the benefits available from IS could be achieved.

Within that overall long-term 'generic strategy', organisations need to set short- to medium-term objectives that can be achieved. The *mission or vision statement* of the company will normally encapsulate its long-term aims and describe the culture and ethics or values that the management believe should be adopted in pursuit of those aims. However, the mission statement will provide only the vaguest of business targets and more specific *objectives* need to be set to direct the efforts of the organisation for the next year or two. However a further step is needed to ensure that throughout the organisation actions that are taken at all levels, at all times are consistent with achieving those objectives. The objectives must be interpreted and translated into relevant actions. This is true for all aspects of the business and the process described below could apply to any set of business activities. Here the emphasis is on ensuring the right IS investments are made and that IT resources are deployed to achieve the objectives of the business, not something that has always happened in the past.

A number of techniques are available to carry out this interpretation and translation, the best known and probably most used is *critical success factor* (CSF) analysis. Critical success factors are: *those things which we must get right in order to achieve the objective*. For instance if the objective is '*to* increase market share by 2 per cent' a critical success factor might be '*by* increasing the number of customer calls by sales staff'. This might lead to a number of actions concerning how the sales staff spend their time and are supported by other parts of the organisation. It should also lead to some measurement. After a few months it should be possible to measure whether or not the number of calls has increased and hence whether progress towards the objective is being made. The basic relationship between the components of the approach is shown in Figure 4.3 and an example of the linkages between objectives, CSFs and IS actions is shown in Box 4.2.

Looking more closely at how this helps define IS needs, it should be reiterated that the determination of CSFs for each business objective should be a part of business management, not something which is done solely to decide on IS needs. IS actions are merely one of the products of the process, albeit an important one. The process should be carried out in a number of clear stages.

(i) Establishing and agreeing the mission or vision statement of the business. This is clearly a task for the board or chief executive of the organisation and will be done infrequently – every few years – and it will have a time horizon of several years.

(ii) Setting or updating the objectives for the business. Again this is a task for senior line management and the final objectives must be agreed by the board or executive body of the business. All objectives should have certain basic

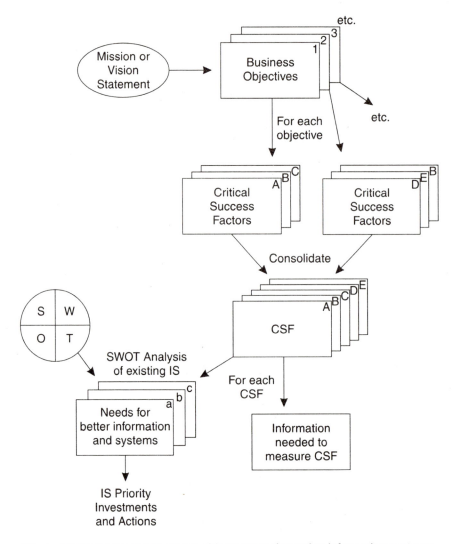

Figure 4.3 Analysing the business objectives to determine information systems needs

attributes – relevant, achievable, unambiguous, measurable! They are also likely to have a time horizon of one to two years, although this will depend on the nature of the business and the stability of the business environment. Some organisations, such as utilities, can and do set objectives to be achieved over several years. Others, where either economic conditions or market forces have more effect, will have to make some assumptions about the

Box 4.2   Example of critical success factor analysis (for a fictitious petroleum retailing company)

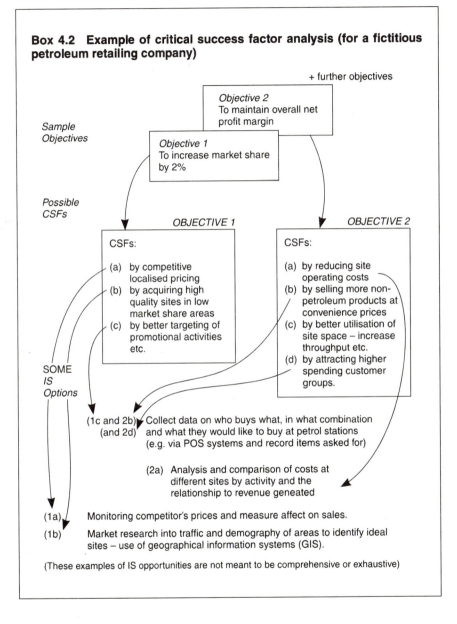

Sample Objectives

+ further objectives

Objective 2
To maintain overall net profit margin

Objective 1
To increase market share by 2%

Possible CSFs

OBJECTIVE 1

CSFs:

(a) by competitive localised pricing
(b) by acquiring high quality sites in low market share areas
(c) by better targeting of promotional activities etc.

OBJECTIVE 2

CSFs:

(a) by reducing site operating costs
(b) by selling more non-petroleum products at convenience prices
(c) by better utilisation of site space – increase throughput etc.
(d) by attracting higher spending customer groups.

SOME IS Options

(1c and 2b) Collect data on who buys what, in what combination
(and 2d) and what they would like to buy at petrol stations (e.g. via POS systems and record items asked for)

(2a) Analysis and comparison of costs at different sites by activity and the relationship to revenue geneated

(1a) Monitoring competitor's prices and measure affect on sales.

(1b) Market research into traffic and demography of areas to identify ideal sites – use of geographical information systems (GIS).

(These examples of IS opportunities are not meant to be comprehensive or exhaustive)

future, but will probably set precise objectives for six to eighteen months ahead. It is vital that the objectives are specific and agreed and understood by the senior management before the next stage in the process. Vagueness, misunderstanding or discord at this stage will lead to confusion and conflict later.

(iii) The best way of agreeing the critical success factors (CSFs) is through a workshop process that involves the 'owners' of the objective and the line managers of functions or departments who are key to achieving the objective. Different people will have different views of what is 'critical' and very few people will understand the whole picture. Therefore it is important to elicit, reconcile and agree the critical factors amongst the group of managers that will have to act on them. This may take some time or more than one iteration. In the process it may be necessary to clarify, revise or refine the objective.

It is likely that CSFs will recur against different objectives and so, before looking at how IS can help, the CSFs should be consolidated. If one CSF affects several objectives then the necessary actions for that CSF have a higher ranking than when only one objective is affected. This part of the process may require some reconciliation of the language used to express the CSFs by the different groups who may have generated them. The consolidated list of CSFs, cross-referenced against the objectives, becomes the input to the next stage.

(iv) Whilst the above steps are structured and very analytical, deciding on actions, in this case IS-based actions, to deal with the CSFs takes a degree of creative thinking. Also to this point involving IT specialists has been on a 'for information only' basis. Now a group of business and IT people need to convene to determine how, if at all, new IS investments or improvements to existing systems could satisfy the success factor. To help the process, the use of SWOT analysis (Strengths, Weaknesses, Opportunities and Threats) can help review how well or otherwise the existing information systems contribute to the CSF.

The product of the combined analytical and creative process is to identify IS options for further evaluation – ideas which can be tested or subject to more searching feasibility analysis. Often, for instance, relevant data exists but is not ideally structured to use in the required way or relatively simple changes or extensions to existing systems may meet the need. It is important at this stage merely to get some understanding of the likely size of the task. Where only small amounts of work are required, rapid action can be taken and an early 'winner' achieved. Major developments or revisions will obviously need to be planned within the context of resources available.

One of the products should always be the provision of information to measure progress or achievement of the success factor. Since management have defined the factor as critical, they would clearly need information to monitor performance of the business against it. By definition therefore, such measures should become part of the management (or executive) information system. IT may or may not be the best means of delivering such feedback, but where IT is the best way, existing information systems will need revision or new ones will need to be developed.

(v) As the potential ways of meeting the CSFs through IS are devised the IS/IT plan will have to be revised and new priorities established. However, it should not be assumed that IS/IT is always a relevant solution and many CSFs may produce no consequent IS/IT action. Where they do, however, the IS/IT implications become 'Strategic' in terms of the applications portfolio – since if they are not completed successfully in the relatively near future the implication is that the business objective will not be achieved. These particular IS investments should therefore be endorsed, given priority for resources in the business and IT function and monitored closely by senior management.

Whilst the above uses a specific terminology – critical success factors, the approach is a general one for interpreting business objectives in terms of how information systems can directly support the achievement of the objectives. Some such structured set of techniques is essential both to define some required IS investments and also to enable priorities to be set amongst the variety of possible investments.

UNDERSTANDING THE ROLE OF INFORMATION IN THE INDUSTRY AND THE BUSINESS

Over the last twenty years IT specialists have devised techniques to enable business processes and activities to be described in information terms in order to define the details required to develop a computer-based system. These analysis and modelling techniques, such as data flow and data entity analysis, have been successfully integrated into systems development methodologies and more recently have been 'automated' by inclusion into software designed for systems developers (CASE tools and 'workbenches'). Once an information system can be described in outline, then precise techniques can be used to define what it consists of and how the processes and flows of information relate to one another. These 'systems' tools will be summarised from a management view later in this chapter and then dealt with in more detail in a later chapter. However, before those tools can be used in detail, the areas of potential business opportunity, improvement and change have to be determined. As has been shown earlier it may be necessary to reconsider the nature of the information exchanges with other organisations and perhaps redefine or redesign the business processes themselves before considering how best to apply technology to them. A higher level, business overview is needed to determine areas of opportunity for IS before studying the detailed needs. This is considered below under the heading 'value chain analysis' which is a business-based set of concepts used in formulating business strategic options and can be adapted to consider the information-based options in that strategy.

VALUE CHAIN ANALYSIS

The concept of 'value chain analysis' is described at length by Michael Porter (1984) who says:

Every firm is a collection of activities that are performed to design, produce, market, deliver and support its products or services. All these activities can be represented using a value chain.

Equally the value chain of the firm is only one part of a larger set of value-adding activities in an industry – the value system. The value chain of any firm therefore needs to be understood as part of the larger 'system' of related value chains – those of its suppliers, customers and competitors, before it can be optimised. The actions of those other parties will have a significant impact on what the firm does and how it does it. This is especially true in the area of information systems. For example, the considerable investment made by food retailers in point-of-sale systems has changed the way information is passed to food manufacturers and has dramatically changed the delivery service required from those manufacturers. This has implications for the information systems within the manufacturing companies and in turn the systems which relate to their suppliers. For an organisation to identify the overall implications of IS for its business in terms of opportunities and threats, the information flowing through the industry – the **external value chain** – needs to be analysed before the use of information can be optimised inside the business – by considering the **internal value chain**.

The external value chain

Figure 4.4 gives a schematic view of an industry value system. In particular it shows the key role information plays throughout the chain. The overall performance of the industry in terms of its ability to maximise value added and minimise its costs is primarily dependent on how well demand-and-supply information is matched at all stages of the industry. To achieve the highest possible income and profit from the consumption of goods or services produced by the industry, the resources of the industry need to be focused on producing those goods and services as efficiently as possible to the satisfaction of the consumers. If poor information means that those resources are wasted or used inefficiently, costs rise without increases in revenue, and profitability falls overall. In such situations all that firms can do to improve profit is compete with their suppliers and customers to share out the limited available net profit. This almost inevitably leads to some firms going 'bust', the equilibrium is destroyed and the industry has to be re-organised in some way. It is not always the least efficient that suffer, it is often those with the poorest information about what is happening in the industry who go to the wall.

Whilst the above discussion is primarily about 'profit', the value chain approach can be used in any industry, since every industry uses funds, incurs cost and uses resources to deliver services of some sort to consumers. In 'non-profit' industries, such as government, health care and charities there is always a matching of supply and demand to achieve a break-even, if not a profit.

Obviously if an organisation can match the demand for its products and

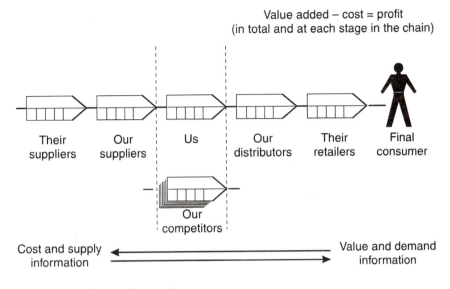

Figure 4.4 Industry value system

services very closely to the supply of resources, at all times, performance can be optimised and efficiencies maximised. Equally obviously if the firm, as depicted in Figure 4.4 ('Us'), is operating at some distance from the ultimate consumer and primary suppliers it is difficult to obtain precise demand-and-supply data. Interestingly, one would expect organisations that have component businesses in different parts of the same industry value chain to be able to exploit their combined information to outperform others who cover less of the chain. In fact that is often not the case, especially when the businesses operate as profit centres – the 'competition' that produces often means that they actually co-operate less well than independent firms in sharing information!

Box 4.3 is an analysis of a particular value chain for part of the timber industry in the UK. The notes describe how the chain was used to identify threats and opportunities in terms of information systems from the viewpoint of a major importer/wholesaler.

When starting to understand how industry information flows affect the firm itself, the firm should be treated as a 'black box', i.e. how things are done inside the firm should be ignored – that will be considered later when looking at the internal value chain. The consideration should start at the end consumers in terms of what information is available about the consumers' needs, who they are, etc., and how they can be influenced. Then the needs for information exchange with more immediate customers can be examined in terms of how effective it is for both parties. Eventually all the flows of information to and from the firm down-

Box 4.3 Value chain for timber importer/wholesaler (softwood)

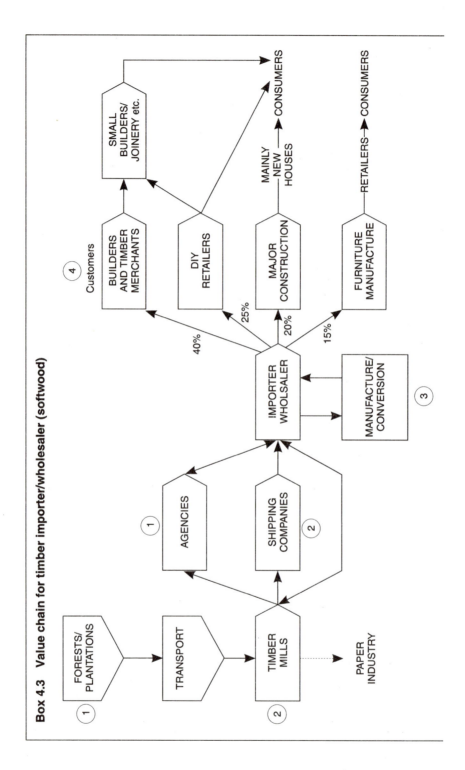

(Box 4.3 cont.)

TIMBER IMPORTER/WHOLESALER

Issues/threats and opportunity areas in the value chain

1 The main sources of softwood imports to the UK are Scandinavia, Canada and Russia. The disruption in Russia has thrown a key area of supply into disarray. Previously the importer dealt with a single government agency to agree contracts and then arranged shipping etc. through the Baltic ports. No agency now exists and to obtain supplies the importer needs to deal with a number of parties who 'own' the timber, provide logistics and run the mills. The whole supply chain has broken down and new arrangements need to be established – who to contract with, for what, can they deliver, etc., are problems, and how far up the chain does the importer need to go – new IS?

It is worth noting that the Scandinavian Mills may be better placed to procure the raw timber for their far more efficient mills.

2 The way timber is shipped is changing from bulk carriers to container loads. Previously the importer bought the whole load and stored it in warehouses at the ports. Now containers can be prepared for specific customers and transported direct from the docks to customers. This implies that major buyers, e.g. DIY and timber merchants, can order some or all of their timber direct from the mills – reducing the need for wholesalers/importers. In the US domestic timber market retailers buy direct from the mills – it could happen in Europe.

However, these smaller orders significantly increase the costs at the mill for essentially commodity materials. In response the mills are producing higher value products, e.g. tongue and groove floorboards, rather than ship basic timber – this can also reduce shipping costs.

Clearly the threat of the mills moving further down the value chain needs to be dealt with – by both addressing the supplier relationships and securing better customer relationships – adding value that cannot be obtained by dealing direct.

3 Manufacture/conversion involves adding value to basic timber, by recutting to customer required sizes, planing, etc., and making wooden products, e.g. roof trusses, architraves, skirting boards, etc. Given (2) above clearly these operations have to be efficient and responsive to customer needs. Given that a major importer may 'manufacture' on every one of its, say, ten to twelve sites, economies of scale can be achieved by product/site specialisation, providing customers can be served everywhere in the country – this requires centralising control of operations – not a traditional approach in the industry.

4 Customers: specifics of each of the four types:

(a) Furniture manufacturers – loyal customers who want a combination of product quality, responsive service and price, which cannot easily be met without a close, knowledgeable working relationship.

(b) Major construction – building: price and delivery are key issues to large buyers. Can add value by providing total wood supply by taking off from designs and supplying 'whole pack' of materials to sites to meet building plans. Also increasing numbers of houses are timber framed increasing the demand: could add value by erecting the frames on site?

Both furniture manufacturing and construction are cyclical businesses and predicting changing demand is critical to profitability of sectors.

(c) Builders and timber merchants: traditionally were small companies but have become large chains (e.g. Jewson, Graham) with more buying power. They take bulk deliveries, cut and deliver to small builders, etc., and some consumers. Often builders merchants are part of a group which includes timber merchants, (e.g. Wickes recently took over Hunters, Meyer International owns Jewson and International Timber). Risks that (i) parts of market not available due to mergers; (ii) others go direct to mills for some/all products.

(Box 4.3 cont.)

Importers/wholesalers have little knowledge of merchants' customers which number in the tens of thousands. They are small operators who hold no stock and rely on frequent/small deliveries from merchants who hold the stock. Wholesalers only deal in bulk deliveries. Why cannot wholesaler establish logistics with a third party to deliver direct, from nation-wide wholesale branches and reduce role of merchants?

(d) DIY retailers (e.g. B&Q, Texas, Homebase). These sell only a partial range of 'packaged' timber products, purchased centrally often through EDI-based systems. Price is critical, as is conformance to product standards and delivery patterns – very demanding. Each prefers to deal with a limited number of suppliers and each is attempting to attack the small builder market as well as the consumer. Timber is essentially an unbranded product, but could consumers be educated to expect a branded range of timber products, as with paint etc? The big DIY retailers are seen as a major threat, given their growth/share and buying power, and are more likely to bypass the importer to reduce costs for a limited range of products in large quantities.

Based on this analysis of the value chain one particular timber importer drew the following conclusions about the focus of its business/IS strategy (this is not a full list).

(a) Establish closer links through joint ventures, planning and stock/logistics management with a few key suppliers – perhaps sharing manufacturing capability to provide a mix of higher value-added products more efficiently. This should prevent supplier bypass.

(b) Gather information about the Russian supply chain to establish reliable combinations of raw material/logistics/mills and hence be able to procure Russian timber as needed. New information systems would be necessary to support this and monitor the situation.

(c) Rationalise its own manufacture/conversion activity to become more efficient and establish systems/logistics to supply all depots from few sites to meet customer orders and forecasts. This would require new internal systems.

(d) To manage the overall UK stock, rather than each depot separately to reduce overall stock holding, supply from multiple sites, satisfy move orders in total and perhaps extend stock management back into suppliers and forward into major customers.

(e) Extend embryonic facility to derive timber needs from builders' drawings to a service available to all builders.

(f) Become pro-active in establishing electronic trading links with a variety of large customers to improve service and reduce costs, rather than merely react to the demands of the major DIY chains.

(g) Establish customer data base of the small builders/joiners etc. and identify those who could be supplied direct or in combination with another party. Get to know their customers' customers in order to add more value where possible.

In essence the importer/wholesaler faces a number of threats which are clearly demonstrated by the value chain. To deal with those threats they must:

(a) be seen to add value by suppliers and customers;

(b) be more efficient in moving goods through the chain in relation to customer demand;

(c) develop a better understanding of the end customer requirements etc. to provide appropriate services/products – 'one-stop shopping';

i.e. all parts of the value chain can yield opportunities. In the particular case the importer was part of a group that included a major builders' merchant chain and opportunities exist to link the two operations together, rather than allow them to trade 'at arm's length' as separate profit centres.

stream in relation to the consumers and intermediaries can be documented, in terms of critical information the firm needs and the current and potential sources of that information. The same process can be repeated in terms of immediate suppliers and their suppliers of key resources, raw materials and services.

Then each of the key flows can be examined to see how it could possibly be improved in terms' of accuracy, speed, cost or timeliness and how that might benefit the business. It might be, beneficial, for instance, if a distributor could provide raw sales data directly, rather than consolidate their sales in order to place larger orders. This may enable the firm to give that distributor a more reactive service, allowing the distributor to hold lower stocks, yet satisfy more of its customers. At the other end of the chain it may be possible to do similar things with suppliers, and whilst these are simple examples they form the basis of 're-engineering' the way the industry operates to everyone's benefit.

It may be, of course, that many of the information exchanges cannot easily be improved, or cannot be improved without the willing co-operation of trading partners. Co-operation may only be forthcoming if there is some mutual benefit in changing that particular information flow or by changing another flow to provide the partner with a balancing benefit. It could be that to produce the improvement, existing trading partners have to be bypassed and information exchanged with other parties further upstream or downstream in the chain. This may eventually lead to significant realignment of business relationships. Many options will usually present themselves from the analysis, only some of which will prove feasible and beneficial to implement, at least in the short term. However, an understanding of the whole picture may lead to further options in the longer term. It will certainly enable the organisation to understand the implications of potential actions by others and then determine a more strategic response. This, for instance, became immediately obvious in the example given in Box 4.3.

The value chain analysis should only consider those items of information that affect the organisation's ability to develop, produce, distribute, market and service its products and services. Non-critical items should be ignored at this level of analysis.

The role of EDI in the value chain

Obviously, electronic data interchange (EDI) may be used to improve the gathering and dissemination of information. EDI-based information systems' links can be developed to various levels of sophistication and mutual dependence. Figure 4.5 shows four 'levels' of relationship. At the basic level, replacing the postal systems by EDI for invoices, orders, etc., could be used by a company with **all** its customers and **all** its suppliers who have computers, simply by connection to a public network. This has indeed happened in some industries, especially those dominated by large retailers, where the majority of basic business transactions are now electronic. This basic use of EDI is spreading through different industries at different rates. The same is true of stages 2, 3 and 4 in Figure 4.5. At each stage an organisation will develop closer systems links with fewer and fewer customers/suppliers owing to the degree of mutual dependence and the certainty of their long-term trading relationship. For instance, stage 1 may be appropriate for all of a company's 5000 customers, yet it will only develop interactive links as in stage 3 with, say, the largest fifty where a slow response or a mismatch of information could cost both parties dear.

As has been said, a firm will not be able to determine its own destiny with regard to its use of EDI. It is not just a matter of company size, but clearly the larger players have more to gain from EDI and hence tend to force the smaller companies to comply with their strategies. As most industries develop standards for EDI, the potential risks for the small company diminish since it will not have the cost of satisfying a variety of requirements for different suppliers or customers.

Any organisation needs to understand how EDI use is developing in its industry, identify the business implications and then define its position with regard to its use of EDI. Much has been written on the implications of EDI-based systems in different industry situations (e.g. Cash and Konsynski 1985) and about

Essentially can occur at four levels:

1.   Transaction passing systems

2.   Enquiry into other companies' data or information exchange

3.   Transaction-driven interactive systems, responding to one another

4.   Interactive processing systems

Figure 4.5 Inter-company 'trading' systems – levels of EDI

the strategic options available for firms in relation to the competitive position (e.g. Robinson and Stanton 1987). Others have questioned whether the effects are really that significant. Clearly there is still much to understand about the full implications of EDI – perhaps the situation is similar to our understanding of where computers were taking us circa 1972?

When EDI is used to enable better information exchanges through the industry value chain, significant benefits can be obtained from the improved links. These benefits should enable a firm to spend more of its business energy in outperforming its real competitors rather than competing with its trading partners for the available profit. The essence of the argument is:

(a) At any one time an industry generates a certain amount of net profit (total sales – total costs). That profit is shared amongst the organisations contributing to the value chain for the industry.

(b) If, in the version of the value chain that includes our firm, the overall net profit can be increased, we can take a share of that increased profit and hence outperform our direct competitors, who are not part of that version of the chain.

(c) If we initiate the changes but also share the benefit with our customers and suppliers (i.e. they too become more profitable), they will prefer to trade in our more efficient version of the industry. It is very likely that rival firms will be competing for those suppliers and/or customers – but they should give us preference because they are more profitable when they do. This brings about long-term advantages and in due course affects the whole industry structure.

To achieve (b) only, three things can be done:

(i)   create more demand;
(ii) satisfy more of the available demand (gain market share);
(iii) reduce the cost of satisfying the demand.

By better information exchange through the value chain, all or any combination of the three can be done at the same time. For example, by sharing consumer market research information carried out by retailers, a manufacturer may be able to enhance a product to open up a new market segment. Or earlier feedback on changing tastes may enable the production plan to be rescheduled to meet the new consumer preference. This is particularly important in fashion goods and in very seasonal products such as toys. Benetton, the clothing company, has developed highly integrated systems which link the franchised shops right through to the subcontractors who make the clothes. This enables them to respond faster than their competitors to changes in fashion and they are far more profitable than the average clothing company.

There are many ways in which better information exchange can reduce costs which occur at the boundaries between companies. Table 4.2 provides a number of examples, all of which can be seen in a number of industries, with the effect of reducing inter-organisational costs very significantly.

Table 4.2 Reduction of inter-company costs due to better information exchange along the value chain

Cost	Potential IS impact
1 Administration	Electronic transmission of orders and invoices direct from one firm's computer to another.
2 Inventory	Sharing information on stocks to avoid both companies carrying unnecessary stock.
3 Transport/storage	Optimising delivery to ensure transport or storage space is utilised effectively and emergency loads/space are not needed.
4 Quality control	Checking the quality where it is most appropriate and allowing others access to quality data to avoid later rework.
5 Design	Sharing product design data to enable faster development of a better product.
6 Financing	Ensuring payments are made to avoid the need for additional bank loans (and hence loss of profit) to fund the business operation.
7 Capacity	Matching the use of resources across firms to avoid idle resources in one part of the chain and/or overload in another.
etc.	

One final example may serve to illustrate the long-term effects of excellent information flow through a value chain. In 1982 Thomson Holidays introduced the TOP system which enabled travel agents to book holidays via a viewdata system directly on the Thomson computer. This immediately reduced some of the double handling costs of bookings (in the agency and at Thomson) and speeded up the process of booking, hence saving agency time and cost. As a result agents 'directed' consumers towards the Thomson brochure, since they earned more commission per man-hour spent booking the holiday. Later, Thomson developed similar links to their suppliers (airlines, hotels and other service providers). In effect this enabled Thomson to respond better to changing demand than others, which for a number of years gave them an advantage, but other tour operators were still profitable since demand for holidays was increasing. The 'system', however, gave Thomson a major advantage when demand dropped suddenly as it did in 1987 (USA bombed Libya) and 1991 (Gulf War). In 1987 Horizon Holidays (no. 3 in the industry) failed and in 1991 International Leisure Group (no. 2 in the industry) went bust. Neither of them were able to respond to the rapid changes in demand as effectively as Thomson, and both had lower margins due to higher cost structures. Thomson were able to adapt more quickly and were more efficient in the context of the overall industry value chain.

It is often the case that the investments which enable demand and supply to be matched effectively through the chain, deliver the real strategic advantage not in the good times, when demand is high, but when demand falls. The investments pay off in recession. This implies that an organisation needs to understand how information flows affect industry performance and what the critical success factors are for the industry in changing economic conditions.

In summary, an understanding of the industry value chain, and the key information flows in the industry, can enable an organisation to intercept and influence those information flows to its advantage, to the benefit of its trading partners and at the expense of its competitors. Whilst this ability is not a substitute for good products and services or good marketing, it can complement those strategies and ensure the organisation maximises the profits from them, over the long term.

The internal value chain

Much of what has been said about the external value chain above applies to the firm's internal value chain – the relationship between its value-adding activities. Before trying to improve the organisation's internal use of information, its wider role in the industry needs to be understood, since those external interfaces should be a major influence on the way information is gathered, organised and used in the organisation. In many cases the actions of trading partners and competitors will have a direct impact or constrain what the company would ideally like to do.

The purpose of internal value chain analysis, like many other techniques for assessing and improving how a company operates, is to divorce **what** the company does from **how** it does it, i.e. to look at the activities it performs to contribute to the value-adding processes of the industry rather than its organisation structure. Historically the information systems a company has will have usually resulted from the organisational needs at functional and departmental level. Only subsequently will these systems and information resources have been aligned to the processes that the firm carries out to satisfy its customers and govern the business. This means that the systems fit the hierarchical organisation structure well but are less effective in ensuring an appropriate flow of key information through the business to optimise its overall performance.

The value chain approach first distinguishes between two types of business activities:

(a) **Primary activities** Those which enable it to fulfil its role in the industry value chain and hence satisfy its customers, who see the direct effects of how well those activities are carried out.
(b) **Support activities** Those which are necessary to control and develop the

business over time and thereby add value indirectly – the value being realised through the success of the primary activities.

In a multi-unit business, each operating unit will have a set of primary activities it must perform successfully to satisfy its set of customers. The support activities, or some of them, may be shared by the operating units because it is more cost-effective to do so, or because there are synergistic benefits by providing a central service to each of the units – e.g. human resource management or IT. The degree to which shared 'head office' support activities are provided or support activities are distributed to the operating units will be determined by the diversity and geography of the operating units and the corporate strategy for managing those units. Even in a financial conglomerate of very diverse businesses some activities, such as financial control, are likely to be retained at the centre to control and direct the business unit's activities.

Michael Porter (1980) classifies the primary activities into five groupings which can be considered in sequence starting with suppliers and ending with customers.

1 **Inbound logistics** Obtaining, receiving, storing and provisioning the key inputs and resources of the right quality and quantity to the business. This may include recruiting staff as well as buying materials, components and services and dealing with subcontractors and acquiring equipment.
2 **Operations** Transforming the inputs into the products or services required by the customers. This involves bringing the resources and materials together to make the 'product' e.g a car; or provide the service, e.g a banking current account.
3 **Outbound logistics** Distributing the products to the customers either direct to the consumer or to the appropriate channel of distribution, so that the customer can obtain the product or service and pay for it appropriately, e.g. a car would go via a dealer to the customer although it would be possible for the customer to collect the car from the factory; or the delivery of cash to a bank customer via an automatic telling machine (ATM) installed in a grocery retailer.
4 **Sales and marketing** Providing ways in which the customers and consumers are aware of the product or service and how they can obtain it, including how to induce them to buy or use the product or service. This would apply to a new car model, or a bank account, but also to cancer screening in the National Health Service for instance.
5 **Services** Which add further value by ensuring the customer gets full benefit or value from the product once purchased (e.g. car warranty, or information on how to use a bank account to avoid unnecessary charges).

Porter's structuring of the activities fits most easily to a manufacturing company but using the same logic of obtaining resources, transforming them, delivery, getting the customer to 'buy' and then get maximum value from the product or service, value chains can be drawn for any business even if they are somewhat different from that shown in Figure 4.6 for a manufacturing company.

Figure 4.6 shows sets of activities grouped in the structure described above and also some of the associated support activities one would expect to find in a manufacturing company. The nature of the primary activities a firm performs will to an extent be predetermined by the industry, its products, customers and suppliers – its success is determined by how well it performs the range of primary activities in concert. That will decide how much value is derived and how much the activities cost and hence the primary profit margin.

With regard to the support activities, however, the business has more discretion as to what they are, how they are organised and how they relate to the primary activities. There is no natural or imposed logic for them, unlike the primary activities, but support activities have three main contributions to make:

(i)   to enable the primary activities to be carried out at optimum levels of performance, i.e. support activities provide services to the primary activities;

(ii) to enable the business to be controlled, governed and developed over time by coordination of the acquisition and deployment of resources and processes in the business;

(iii) to satisfy the statutory obligations that the organisation has, e.g. financial, legal, health and safety.

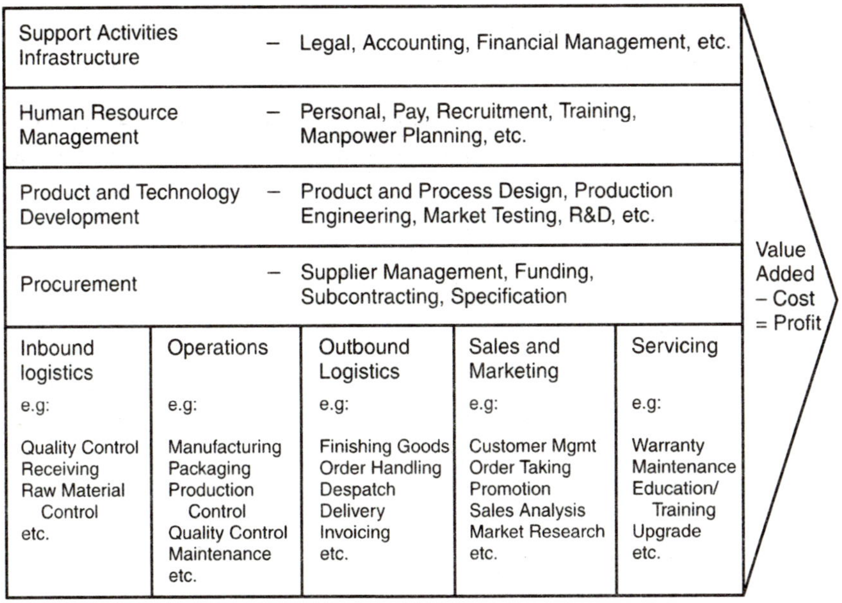

Support Activities Infrastructure		– Legal, Accounting, Financial Management, etc.			
Human Resource Management		– Personal, Pay, Recruitment, Training, Manpower Planning, etc.			
Product and Technology Development		– Product and Process Design, Production Engineering, Market Testing, R&D, etc.			
Procurement		– Supplier Management, Funding, Subcontracting, Specification			
Inbound logistics	Operations	Outbound Logistics	Sales and Marketing	Servicing	
e.g:	e.g:	e.g:	e.g:	e.g:	
Quality Control Receiving Raw Material Control etc.	Manufacturing Packaging Production Control Quality Control Maintenance etc.	Finishing Goods Order Handling Despatch Delivery Invoicing etc.	Customer Mgmt Order Taking Promotion Sales Analysis Market Research etc.	Warranty Maintenance Education/ Training Upgrade etc.	

Value Added – Cost = Profit

Primary Activities.

Many activities cross the boundaries – especially information-based activities such as: Sales Forecasting, Capacity Planning, Resource Scheduling, Pricing, etc.

Figure 4.6 A typical manufacturing firm's value chain

These support activities will often be very significant users and generators of information and it is important that the needs of those activities are balanced with the needs of the primary activities when developing information systems that both primary and support activities use. Unfortunately in many organisations the needs of the support activities (e.g. accounting) have imposed a considerable burden on or even constrained the options available to the primary activities resulting in inappropriate or very complex systems in the primary activities. In concept at least the information flows through the primary activities should operate like a 'pipeline', as represented in Figure 4.7a.

Information about what customers want and how that demand can be satisfied should flow freely through the organisation enabling the management of each activity (A, B, C, D, E) to determine how best to deploy its resources to maximise customer satisfaction in the most effective way. Any action taken would be immediately visible to other activities in the chain who can then take further action accordingly or inform the other activities of problems in meeting the requirement. The chain can be continuously rebalanced across all the activities. In addition to the flow through the organisation, each activity (e.g. warehousing, sales-force management) will need information systems to carry out and manage its part of the business. These in themselves may be very extensive but should link in to the flow as required. For instance, the warehouse management system must know where every item is in the warehouse, but the rest of the business only needs to know what is in it, and whilst the manufacturing department needs to schedule each machine in detail, the rest of the business only needs to know that product will be ready to meet orders from customers.

Often, however, the reality is more like Figure 4.7b – it is meant to look like a maze! – and attempts to illustrate a number of typical problems, caused by the way systems are developed to satisfy organisational rather than the overall business needs.

(a) The organisation structure does not coincide with the logical relationships of activities in the value chain and hence information processing occurs in a different structure from the business flow.

(b) Organisational boundaries act as 'valves' in the 'pipeline' restricting the speed of flow while one department massages the information to meet its own needs while delaying others from access. Valves in a pipeline cause turbulence and heat! The heat in this case will come out in the meetings held to resolve problems across departments caused by delayed, incomplete or inconsistent information!

(c) Supply-and-demand information take different routes through the organisation, some faster, some slower, with more or less accuracy making it very difficult to make decisions with the confidence that the best decision is being made and that the decision will not cause major problems elsewhere.

(d) Support activities become part of the primary chain, in that information has to go through them between stages in the primary chain causing delays in the

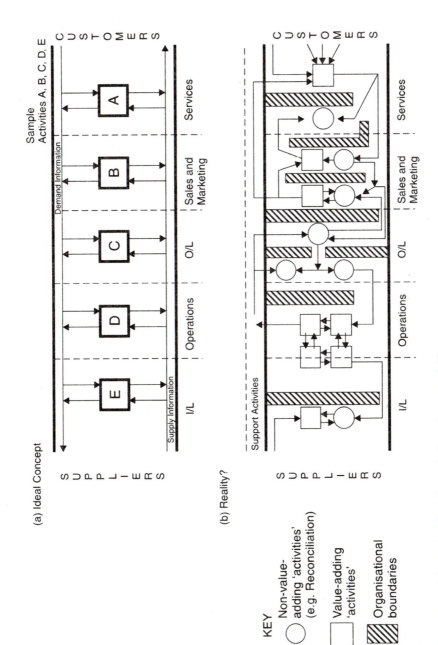

(a) Ideal Concept

Sample Activities A, B, C, D, E

(b) Reality?

KEY

○ Non-value-adding 'activities' (e.g. Reconciliation)

☐ Value-adding 'activities'

▨ Organisational boundaries

Figure 4.7 **Information flow through the primary activities**

information being used for its main purpose. As one computer salesman said, 'I know what you mean – our sales prevention system, designed by the accountants to ensure salesmen aren't selling the company down the river. Problem is it stops the customer getting what they want, when they want it!'

(e) Very complex systems that are designed to meet the needs of a particular activity, **and** be integrated with other systems in that function **and** with systems in other functions and not doing any of the three things very well.

These are just examples of the problems that occur and they can become much more severe when all the support activity systems are taken into account. One engineering company producing electrical switching systems studied how information flowed through the primary activities involved and were able to simplify the flows from the customer enquiry through to the component suppliers, and back again, to reduce delivery lead times from twenty-seven to five days. The result was a 37 per cent increase in sales – sales they were losing because their delivery times were too slow and unreliable. That was for only one product, but when the same logic is applied across the whole product range and associated processes, dramatic performance improvements can be made, often at very little cost and with the result that the systems become much simpler.

In practice, the situation depicted in Figure 4.7b is untenable and in order to operate effectively managers bypass the formal systems to gather information and decide how to use resources – making the systems merely a historical record of what happened (and often not a very accurate one!) – rather than use the systems to ensure business activities are harmonised effectively. The 'informal' systems replace the 'formal' systems as a means of managing. If that is the case, the formal systems should be replaced by systems that support a more appropriate way of working. It is not the ideal solution, but it is better than them becoming an inaccurate record of what has happened. When the value chain for a major exporter of products was examined in detail a senior executive was heard to comment, 'That explains why every order we take becomes an adventure – an adventure for the customer and an adventure for us!' People had to intervene everywhere in the supply chain to overcome the limitations of the systems, but people intervened in different ways at different times with no certainty of repeating success in meeting the customers' needs. A combination of systems and organisational changes was needed to ensure more certainty of satisfying the customer at least 95 per cent of the time.

Summary of the use of value chain analysis

The purpose of using value chain analysis is to understand the opportunities (and potential threats) that IS/IT offers the business. As has been said earlier, many of those opportunities involve the external exchanges in information and others require greater integration of the internal use of information. Value chain analysis forces business managers to ask questions about both the information and systems they need and have, and about the way the business processes themselves work, in relation to the way the firm creates value for its customers. As a technique, value chain analysis is independent of the organisation structure and focuses on **what** the organisation does, not **how** it is organised to do it. This enables questions about 'why can't we do it better, differently or at a lower cost?' to be asked more pointedly. Existing ways of doing things can be challenged, leading to redesign of processes where this is of benefit and better information systems which improve the **business** performance, not just the performance of some functions or activities.

To get the most benefit from value chain analysis it should be tackled in a logical way with clear objectives for each stage, i.e.:

(a) To improve relationships with customers and suppliers in all aspects of their involvement with the organisation. Table 4.3 shows how IS opportunities exist over the whole life cycle of customers using the resource acquired from an organisation.

(b) To improve the critical information flows through the primary activities, removing bottlenecks and delays and ensuring the accuracy and consistency of information in use. The key to success is getting information of the right quality, to the right place at the right time, so that further value can be obtained from it or added to it.

Table 4.3 Customer resource life cycle

Requirements

Establish requirements	To determine how much of a resource is required.
Specify	To determine a resource's attributes.

Acquisition

Select source	To determine where customers will buy a resource.
Order	To order a quantity of a resource from the supplier.
Authorise and pay for	To transfer funds or extend credit.
Acquire	To take possession of a resource.
Test and accept	To ensure that a resource meets specifications.

Stewardship

Integrate	To add to an existing inventory.
Monitor	To control access and use of a resource.
Upgrade	To upgrade a resource if conditions change.
Maintain	To repair a resource

Retirement

Transfer or dispose	To move, return or dispose of resource as necessary.
Account for	To monitor where and how much is spent on a resource.

(c) To improve the systems within each primary activity to obtain functional performance improvements and greater efficiency.
(d) To improve the way in which support activity information systems assist the management of primary activities and enable activities and resources to be controlled and co-ordinated across the business.
(e) To improve efficiency within the support activities.

This may seem logical and is certainly the way in which IS can be focused on where and how it can contribute most to the business. However, in reality, it is almost the reverse of the way IS has been developed in most organisations over the last thirty years! Reversing that 'logic' is not an easy task. The value chain approach can result not only in much better systems, but also simpler systems at less cost than the complex, ill-fitting systems of the past.

Once the role of information and systems in the value chain is understood, a number of further steps can be taken, based on the value chain model.

1 The critical success factors, as defined earlier in the chapter, can be overlaid on the processes and information flows in the value chain to understand where priority actions are needed to help meet the business objectives.
2 The use of activity-based costing is a natural corollary of value chain analysis to understand how costs accrue in relation to value-adding activities and processes. Hence activity costs can be allocated to the value chain to identify where IS might produce significant cost reductions.
3 An information model of the business can be constructed and used as the basis for a coherent and economical plan for building the new systems and data bases for the business. This is described in outline in the last part of this chapter.

INFORMATION ANALYSIS

Value chain analysis produces an overall, high-level 'picture' of the main external and internal business information relationships in the context of the main processes in the industry and the firm itself. Before proceeding to address the specific needs for systems and information resources, one further step of analysis is valuable to understand how specific items of information (entities) relate to the key activities. This will identify where items of data originate, are updated and used in the various activities and hence where responsibility lies for their management. The value chain produces a high-level flow diagram for the information which can be analysed in more detail using data flow analysis techniques described later in the book. **Entity/activity** analysis at a high level produces an information model of the business which can be used to ensure the information resource is created and maintained in the best way to ensure future systems can function effectively as a whole.

Entities are the fundamental things that the organisation needs to hold information about, e.g. customers, orders, products, personnel, finance. These can be structured and related to show what each entity contains and which entities affect one another, e.g. customer: account details, address, sales history, etc. (i.e. things that are unique to a customer); customer places order, pays invoices, etc., are entity relationships. These define the basic information structures and relationships, independent of the organisation or systems in the business. Entity models are simple depictions of the information in a business which form a framework within which systems and data bases can be built coherently: effectively an 'architecture' for business information. This enables data duplication and inconsistency to be avoided. A very high-level entity model for a business enterprise is shown in Figure 4.8. This can be broken down into a set of more detailed models for each component.

The next stage is to depict how the main information and data entities relate to the main activities of the business. There are four main ways an activity can relate to an entity item:

C – Create an entity, e.g. put a new order on the orders file.
M – Modify an entity, e.g. change the delivery date on an order.
U – Use that entity, e.g. read all orders for a product to prepare a production plan.
D – Delete that entity, e.g. delete an order no longer required.

Figure 4.9 shows a simplified entity/activity relationship diagram in the form of a matrix. If the activities are sequenced as far as possible in value chain sequence, it enables the matrix to reflect the flow of information amongst the major activities and processes and they tend to cluster together in related groups, which reflect the data bases that should be constructed to bring together the related items. Figure 4.10 shows a clustering of related entities, again simplified, and also how information flows forward and back in the business, as would be shown by value chain analysis.

This is intended to be a very brief overview of some aspects of information analysis, at a level that business managers need to understand. Such high-level models form a framework within which more detailed analysis and systems design can take place. Other aspects of information and data analysis are considered in Chapter 6.

APPLYING THE APPROACH TO A MULTI-BUSINESS UNIT ORGANISATION

In a large multi-business unit organisation there are many advantages to adopting a similar approach to developing information systems strategies. The extent of the advantages will clearly depend on how similar the businesses are in terms of products, processes, suppliers and customers and to what extent, if any, they trade with one another. If there is considerable inter-company trading or they operate in the same industry then mutual understanding of how IS is affecting the industry and the value chain could lead to many mutually beneficial options. In the example given in Box 4.3 the fact that the largest timber importer (International Timber) and the largest builders' merchant

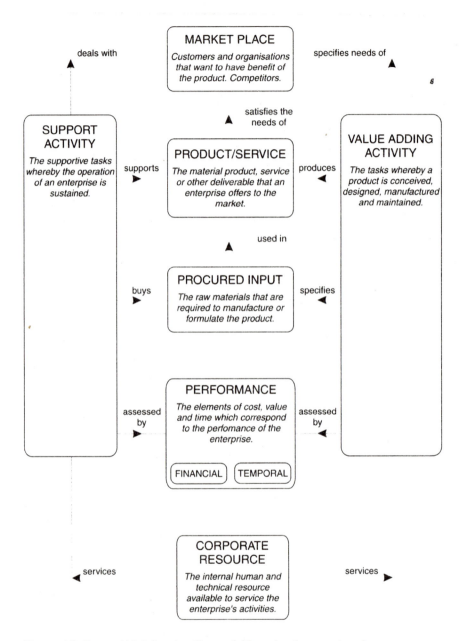

Figure 4.8 General high-level entity model for a business enterprise

Source: A. Bytheway and B. Dyer (1992) *Corporate Information, EDI & Logistics*, Cranfield School of Management.

Entities

#	Entity
1	Debit/credit
2	Incoming payment
3	Invoice
4	Financial contract
5	Outgoing payment
6	Incoming invoice
7	Client
8	Sales contract
9	Mailing
10	Order
11	Service contract
12	Delivered order
13	Client/goods registration
14	Article-package supplier
15	Supplier
16	Purchase order
17	Goods
18	Calculation algorithms
19	Depot
20	Receipt of goods
21	Education
22	Function
23	Employee
24	Department
25	Employee action
26	Time capacity
27	Time and cost registration
28	Employee payment

Business Activities / Entity matrix (columns = entities 1–28)

Business Activities	1	2	3	4	5	6	7	8	9	10	11	12	13	14	15	16	17	18	19	20	21	22	23	24	25	26	27	28
1 Financial registration	C	C	C	C			M	U		U	U						U		U					U			U	U
2 Incoming cash flow		C	C															U										
3 Outgoing cash flow					C	M						U		U	M	U				U								
18 Approval of incoming invoices				U		C						U		U		U				U								
5 Sales support			U				C	C	C		U												U	U				
7 Sales			U				M	C	M	U	U												U	U				
8 Order registration								U		C	U	U	U				M						U	U				
9 Order validation							U			M	C	U	U											U				
19 Order receipt and planning							U			U	U	C	C						U				U	U				
20 Service							U			U	M	C					U						U	U				
26 Advice										U	U	C					U	U					U	U				
15 Supplier's management					U					U			U	C	C	U	U	U						U				
17 Ordering of goods										U				U	M	C	C	C		U			U	U				
6 Product management						U							U	U	U						C						U	
12 Storing of goods										U				U	U		M		C	C								
13 Stock control																	M			M								
14 Stock taking																	M			M								
22 Personnel management																						C	C	C	C	C	U	U
24 Time and cost registration																									U	M	C	
23 Wages and salary administration																							U	U	U		U	C

(NB. Entities are usually deleted only by the activity that creates them)
C = created; M = modified; U = used; D = delete

Figure 4.9 Entity/activity analysis

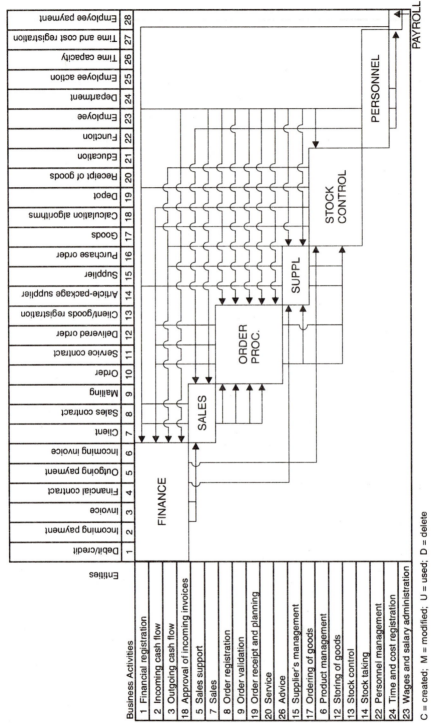

Figure 4.10 Entities, activities and information flows

C = created; M = modified; U = used; D = delete

(Jewson's) are both owned by Meyer International could lead to significant benefits from a jointly devised IS strategy.

If companies address similar customer needs and even serve the same customers, then common customer-related IS strategies could be beneficial. The case is comparable if similar or the same suppliers are used. If the nature of the products or processes is similar, say in a group of manufacturing companies, then it is likely that to some extent information systems needs (such as manufacturing resource planning or just-in-time supplies) are similar and much can be learned from each other. Even when the similarities are less obvious, it may well be that some of the critical success factors in each business have aspects in common and therefore the way IS can help achieve them can be translated from one business to another.

Unless similar tools/techniques or management processes are adopted across a group of companies, it may prove impossible at any stage to make a valid comparison of IS opportunities and threats. Whilst each company may have to implement the solutions in a unique way, the ideas may be easily transferred across the different units. For example, a company serving food retailers or DIY stores will be under some pressure to adopt EDI-based trading systems. Its experience and the benefits it gains from such systems may well help another group company take a more pro-active approach to using EDI with its less advanced customers or suppliers and gain considerable advantages over competitors. There is often much to learn from what others are doing, why they are doing it and how. Rather than have to wait for every business in the group to create its own opportunities, any transfer of knowledge that can speed up the learning process could lead to significant advantage. This aspect will be revisited later in the book when the supply-side issues are considered. At this stage it is worth looking at the 'demand-side' options to ensure opportunities available to more than one organisation in a group are not ignored or overlooked. The more similar the process for assessing the business IS options, the easier it is to compare them and learn across the group.

KEY LEARNING POINTS

- **There are a number of tools and techniques which enable business managers to consider the business and its strategy in information terms, in order to identify opportunities to improve business performance through better information and systems. These tools/techniques do not require a detailed understanding of technology.**
- **It is important that the tools/techniques used enable senior, functional and IT managers all to contribute to the development of the strategy and agree on the priority investment areas.**
- **In total the tools consider:**

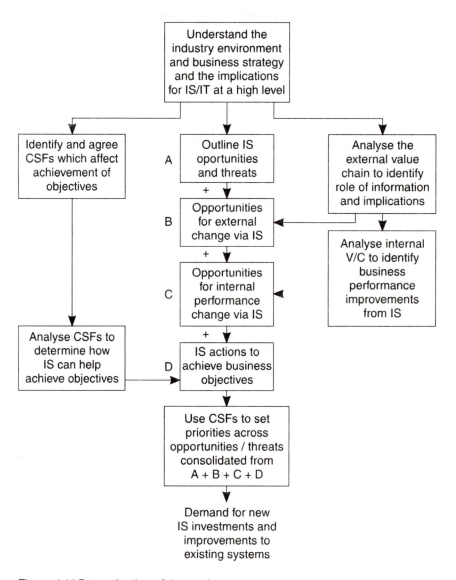

Figure 4.11 Determination of demand-summary

(a) **the role of information in the context of the industry – its products, services, processes and trading relationships – and in the business in relation to its activities, how it adds value and delivers that value to the customer;**

(b) **how the objectives of the business can be interpreted via critical success factors in terms of how better information and systems can contribute directly to the achievement of those objectives.**

- **These different views can then be overlaid and reconciled to identify priority investments in new information systems to either change how the business operates to advantage, or to improve the performance and control of the business to avoid disadvantage. How these tools and techniques can be brought together in a logical process is shown in Figure 4.11.**
- **It is important to have a comprehensive, well-understood process. Then when any parameter changes (e.g. the actions of a competitor, or a new business objective), that change can be introduced into the process at the appropriate point and the consequences for the IS strategy understood.**
- **It should not be necessary to challenge and change the whole strategy if any external or internal factors change – it should be possible to trace the change and its implications through the strategy and amend those areas it directly affects.**

The next chapter considers the ways and means of ensuring that the organisation achieves the required contribution from the requirements and priorities agreed within the IS strategy.

QUESTIONS FOR CONSIDERATION

1 Box 4.3 outlines the major components of the value chain for the timber industry and shows a number of areas where IS offers significant business opportunities. Attempt to describe the external value chain for a business with which you are familiar, showing the critical information relationships and dependencies. Identify any major opportunities where IS, perhaps in combination with business changes, could provide significant business advantages for that business.

2 Describe the main activities of your business in terms of the internal value chain and group them under the appropriate 'Primary' or 'Support' headings. Consider how demand information flows through those activities and identify potential problems that result where the information is not appropriately available. Do the same with supply information and identify where demand-and-supply mismatches cause problems. Discuss how improvements to the information systems could overcome those problems and also identify any factors which are preventing such improvements.

3 Select a few (three to five) of your organisation's business objectives and determine the Critical Success Factors (CSFs) for each of those objectives. Consolidate the CSFs and then consider how improved information or systems

could enable those success factors to be achieved and success or otherwise to be measured?

(N.B. it might be helpful for each of those questions to convene a small group of people to provide a more thorough knowledge of the business.)

RECOMMENDED ADDITIONAL READING

Cash, J.I. and Konsynski, B.R. (1985) 'IS Redraws Competitive Boundaries', *Harvard Business Review,* (March–April).
Ives, B. and Learmonth, G.P. (1984) 'The Information System as a Competitive Weapon', *Communications of the ACM* 27, 12 (December).
Porter, M.E. (1980) *Competitive Strategy*, Free Press.
Porter, M.E. (1984) *Competitive Advantage*, Free Press.
Robinson, D.G. and Stanton, S.A. (1987) 'Exploit EDI before EDI Exploits You', *The Executive Journal*, (Spring).

OTHER REFERENCE

Cash, J.I. (1988) 'Interorganisational Systems: An information society opportunity or threat?' *The Information Society* 3, 3.

Chapter 5

Managing the portfolio of applications

INTRODUCTION

The concept of the application portfolio was introduced in Chapter 3, as a way of understanding the contribution different types of information systems make to business success. It can be used to assess the current situation as described in Chapter 3, and also decide how future investments should be managed. It is a way of constructing a long-term management framework to enable the organisation to apply consistent and appropriate approaches to the management of its information systems and the associated IT resources. As a reminder, the basic portfolio model is reproduced in Figure 5.1.

Chapter 4 considered how the business and its environment can be analysed and interpreted in terms of its information and systems' needs. That process produces the 'IS strategy' and it needs to be continually reviewed and kept in line with the evolving business environment and strategy. But such a process is not the whole story. Many of the most innovative business ideas and also information systems are the result of 'informal' strategic thinking, arising from the creative skills of the people in the organisation. Organisations which capitalise on these ideas effectively often achieve greater success than those with rigorous, even excellent, formal strategic planning processes. The best organisations can do both. They foster and encourage creativity but within a management framework that enables winning ideas to be identified and exploited. In the context of the organisation's information systems, the application portfolio approach must cater for not just the results of formal IS/IT planning but also the less formal identification and satisfaction of information needs.

Whilst a 'one-off' planning initiative can produce a major step forward in IS development the process must become self-sustaining if the IS portfolio is to evolve in line with the pace and direction of change in the business. There does appear to be a pattern of behaviour around the portfolio in the more successful organisations. This is depicted in Figure 5.2.

The 'formal' approaches to IS planning described in Chapter 3 (based on Earl's classification), which should use the kinds of tools and techniques discussed in Chapter 4, will tend to identify needs for key operational and strategic

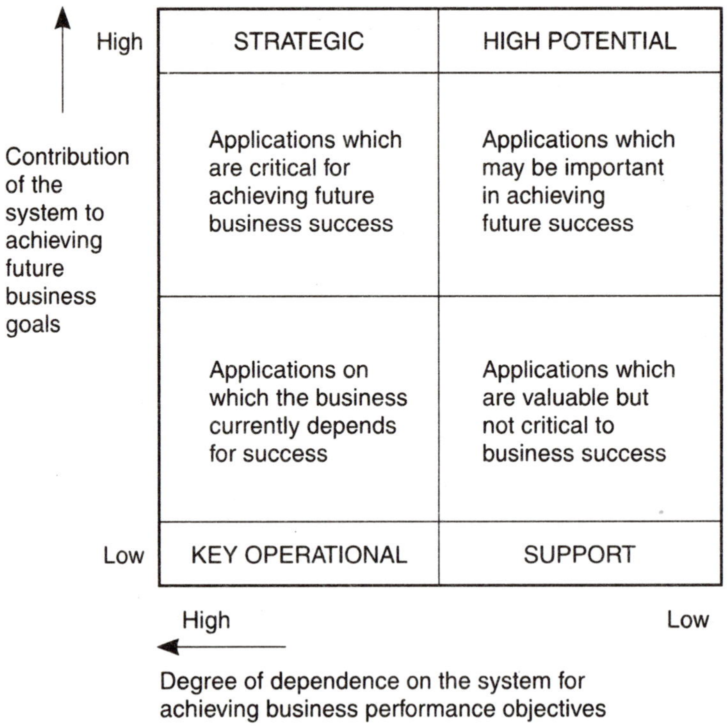

	STRATEGIC	HIGH POTENTIAL
High	Applications which are critical for achieving future business success	Applications which may be important in achieving future success
	Applications on which the business currently depends for success	Applications which are valuable but not critical to business success
Low	KEY OPERATIONAL	SUPPORT

Contribution of the system to achieving future business goals

High ← Low

Degree of dependence on the system for achieving business performance objectives

Figure 5.1 An application portfolio

systems primarily. Some R&D into high potential opportunities may be commissioned but few, if any, support systems should result from a top-down planning process. 'Informal' or bottom-up planning within the organisation will tend to produce a number of high potential ideas but also many more support systems to improve performance in that area of the business. All that is quite predictable, but what can also be observed is that organisations that have very effective key operational systems, also seem to be best at using IT in innovative ways, i.e. create more high potential opportunities. Whilst initially it may appear odd that those who are best at 'formal' planning are often also best at 'informal' thinking there appear to be two good reasons:

(a) if the key operational systems are good, the users and IT staff spend less time fire-fighting the day-to-day problems that poor key operational systems continuously throw up. Thus they have more time to be creative, and

(b) the well-organised information resource in the key operational base of systems provides the necessary sound basis from which to consider how that

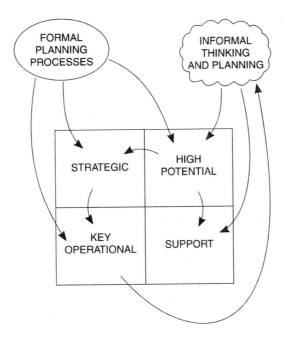

Figure 5.2 Routes into the portfolio

resource could be exploited further, with a degree of confidence that some of the ideas will be successfully implemented.

In essence the portfolio is the link between the **what** – what the business can and must achieve through its information systems – and the **how** – how those systems can be best supplied to the business. It thus encapsulates the link between the **IS strategy** and the **IT strategy**. So far this book has focused on **IS**, with little comment about **IT** and its management, on the simple premise that demand (IS) should precede and determine supply (IT). In subsequent chapters the focus is on managing the supply and this chapter forms the bridge between the two, using the application portfolio as the main framework for that bridge. It will be explored from a number of directions to show it provides that necessary management framework.

The IS strategy should be a business-driven statement of what is required, which can then be converted into a set of IT strategies and plans to supply the necessary resources and technologies to meet the demand. However, in most cases all the demand cannot be met immediately and priorities will have to be set.

Each investment will have to be funded and therefore justified in the context of the potential other uses of those funds in the business. Justification and priority setting of IS investments are discussed later in the chapter, as will the varying nature of the types of benefits to be expected and the issues in obtaining them.

Over time the contribution IS investments make to the business will change as the business and the industry in which it operates evolve and develop. Innovative IS investments of yesteryear have become the standard way of working today. Managing this changing role and contribution will be considered, along with the need to 'remanage' past investments to ensure they do not become liabilities, absorbing large amounts of resource for little benefit, rather than the assets they should be.

In large businesses there will be many application portfolios. Each business unit should 'own' its portfolio of systems, the content representing the consensus view of the business unit's management. There will also be a 'corporate portfolio' of the systems needed to run the overall organisation, and this will have an impact on the portfolios of the units to some extent. For instance a common general accounting system may be 'imposed' from the corporation on the units. In reverse there may be considerable potential gains from synergy between the systems in the units, if they trade with one another, or potential economies may exist from sharing IT resources. There are a range of options which will be discussed later in the chapter.

All of these and many other issues can be more readily resolved once the management implications of the different types of application are understood in terms of strategies which deal with the range of issues. That is the subject of the first part of this chapter. Some recent surveys (e.g. Price Waterhouse in 1991) have noted that despite enormous advances in IT in the last twenty years some things have not changed. As in 1971 – '70 per cent of all IS investments fail to deliver the benefits expected' – and it is usually because they were ill-conceived or badly managed. Earlier chapters have attempted to deal with the first of these; this chapter starts to deal with the second.

ANALYSING THE APPLICATION PORTFOLIO

At any one time the portfolio will comprise three different types of investment in IS:

(a) **existing systems** whose current and potential future business contribution needs to be agreed;
(b) **current** and **planned systems developments** to which resources are to be committed in the current budget or planning cycle (normally six to twelve months) and should deliver benefits in the near future;
(c) **potential developments** which are expected to be started in the next twelve to twenty-four months unless business priorities change.

It is important that the business managers update the content of the portfolio over time, so that it always represents a complete, agreed view of the role of IS in that business. It is also important that they understand the implications of that assess-ment and the obligations and responsibilities it places on them to deliver the total package of business benefits the portfolio content implies. This will be explained in detail below.

The principles of the classification have been explained earlier based on the definitions in Figure 5.1. However, it is obviously important that consistent criteria are applied by all involved and also over time to decide where an application belongs on the matrix. Table 5.1 suggests how that consistency can be achieved by posing questions which help clarify the contribution a system can make to the business.

It may well be the case that a system appears to satisfy several of the criteria and could be strategic **and** key operational **and** support all at once. Were it to go ahead on that basis many problems would ensue as will be seen later, given that different management strategies apply to the different segments of the matrix. This would lead at best to a confused approach to conflicting issues resulting in delays and overspending and at worst to complete failure to achieve any of the benefits. This is often exacerbated by the 'acronym' problem whereby a number of unlike components are bundled together and given a clever set of initials to describe the development **project** succinctly. In the process what business func-tion(s) the system is supposed to satisfy are obscured and ownership of the system passes to the IT department!

For example, a £3 million project in a company was called 'COMPASS'. The initials stood for Customer Order Management Production Accounting and Shop-floor Scheduling. By the time the PASS parts were delivered the budget had been exceeded and the project was a year late. When the project was broken down into its functional components and they were placed on the matrix it was clear that:

Production Accounting	=	Support
Shopfloor Scheduling	=	Key operational
Customer Order Management	=	Strategic

As a result over £3million had been spent to replace existing old systems with marginal benefit and no money remained to develop the strategic part, which could have provided a competitive advantage. The moral is to ensure that the business functions that the system performs (e.g. warehouse management or personnel records) should be used to describe the system, not some cryptic acronym. And if the system appears to fit in more than one segment it should be broken down a level and looked at again. Using a questioning approach as in Table 5.1 can help in achieving objectivity and consistency in agreeing the portfolio.

STRATEGIES FOR MANAGING THE APPLICATIONS PORTFOLIO

The application portfolio approach recognises the different contributions or **effects** the systems are intended to have on the business. It is therefore logical to put in

Table 5.1 Classifying the applications in the matrix

Question

If the development succeeds* will it:

(a)	Result in a clear competitive advantage for the business?	YES/NO
(b)	Enable the achievements of specific business objectives and/or critical success factors?	YES/NO
(c)	Overcome known business disadvantages in relation to competitors?	YES/NO
(d)	Avoid foreseeable business risks becoming major problems in the near future?	YES/NO
(e)	Improve the productivity of the business and hence reduce long term costs?	YES/NO
(f)	Enable the organisation to meet statutory requirements?	YES/NO
(g)	The benefits not yet known but may result in (a) or (b) above?	YES/NO

Interpretation

In answering the questions above the reasons for the judgement should be stated. The table below shows how the answers can be interpreted and the application classified based on whether or not any YES answers appear in a column.

If more questions produce a YES answer in any one column, i.e. the application appears to be in more than one category, then it should be reassessed by splitting it into its major components and considering each of them in the same way; i.e. the application should be broken down into subprojects – if this is not done the risks of failure will increase dramatically due to the mixed objectives and the confusion that it can cause once the project proceeds.

*For existing applications the question is 'Is the application delivering benefits which . . .'

	High potential	Strategic	Key op.	Support
(a)		YES[a]		
(b)		YES[a]		
(c)			YES	
(d)			YES	
(e)				YES
(f)			YES[b]	YES[b]
(g)	YES			

Notes:

[a]   If either applies, supplementary question is then 'Is it clear what the business benefits are and how they can be obtained?'   YES/NO
If YES it is STRATEGIC, if NO it is HIGH POTENTIAL.

[b]   to clarify which it is the following question should be asked: 'Will failure to comply lead to significant business risks (be specific about the risk)?' If YES it is KEY OPERATIONAL, if NO it is SUPPORT.

place the right management strategies or **causes** to achieve those desired effects. The reasons why so many IS investments fail to deliver expected benefits are:

(a) that the benefits were never achievable; or
(b) the benefits were achievable but the wrong strategy was used to achieve them.

The portfolio approach addresses these first through an understanding of the key issues that determine success and failure in the different segments of the matrix and then by matching available 'strategies' to those issues. Table 5.2 summarises some of those key issues under two headings:

(i) the **driving forces** behind the investment – **why** it is being done, an expression of how the success or failure of the system will be determined; and
(ii) the **critical requirements** which need to be met in order to succeed.

In the **high potential** segment the philosophy is R&D, i.e. controlled experimentation to identify the potential benefits and how they might be achieved in terms of cost, technology and changes to the business. The product is not a system but knowledge of whether the opportunity is strategic, key operational or support in nature and hence how to proceed, or whether further investment is not worthwhile. Whilst some high potential opportunities will derive from formal strategic planning, many others arise from individual's ideas or because a new technology is available, i.e. relatively informally. The high potential segment recognises the very risky nature of many IS/IT investments and the objective of the evaluation is to avoid the failure that risk implies. It also recognises that frequently there is a lack of knowledge about the types of benefits which are obtainable and effective evaluation should prevent the organisation chasing benefits that are not actually achievable.

Strategic investments should be driven directly by the objectives and success factors of the business, which in essence designate them as strategic. Less explicitly the application is driven by business imperatives which in themselves may be caused by the actions or perceived actions of the others in the industry. The over-riding concern is to gain some advantage through the investment and that implies a window of opportunity when that advantage will be available. Whilst it may be clear what the initial opportunity is, to achieve a sustainable advantage it is also very likely that business change will need to accompany the introduction of the new system if any advantage is to accrue. For all these reasons it is essential that the business management is in control of the development and the 'ideal' IT approach to the technical aspects of the system may have to be compromised.

Key operational systems in essence are to ensure the business is not suffering disadvantages. Unlike strategic developments, understanding what to do does not require a great deal of vision – similar organisations will have similar systems. To avoid disadvantage implies that the system is effectively implemented – how well it is done is critical. Whilst 'critical success factors' should drive the

Table 5.2 Some key issues in the segments of the portfolio

	Driving forces	Critical requirements
High potential	• new business idea or technological opportunity	• rapid evaluation of prototype and avoid wasting effort/resources on failures
	• individual initiative owned by a 'product champion'	• understand the potential (and the economics) in relation to business strategy
	• need to demonstrate the value or otherwise of the idea	• identify the best way to proceed – the next step
Strategic	• market requirements, competitive pressures or other external forces	• rapid development to meet the business objective, and realise benefits within the window of opportunity
	• business objectives, success factors and vision of how to achieve them	• flexible system that can be adapted in the future as the business evolves
	• obtaining an advantage and then sustaining it	• link to an associated business initiative to sustain commitment
Key operational	• improving the performance of existing activities (speed, accuracy, economics)	• high-quality, long-life solutions and effective data management
	• integration of data and systems to avoid duplication, inconsistency and misinformation	• balancing costs with benefits and business risks – identify the best solution
	• avoiding a business disadvantage or allowing a business risk to become critical	• evaluation of options available by objective feasibility study
Support	• improved productivity/ efficiency of specific (often localised), business tasks	• low-cost, long-term solutions – often packaged software to satisfy most needs
	• legal requirements	• compromise the needs to the software available
	• most cost-effective use of IS/IT funds and resources available	• objective cost-benefit analysis to reduce financial risk and then control costs carefully

strategic investments, it is the key operational systems which address 'critical failure factors'. Thirty years of experience with IS/IT has meant techniques and methods have been developed to meet this need – to ensure the system can be specified accurately and then perform to specification. This 'ideal' methodology should not be compromised for business expediency, even if it seems protracted and risk-averse in the extreme. The benefit of the careful approach to produce high quality, integrated systems and data will pay off every day the system works. Many organisations have the vision to develop strategic systems, but many fail because of the weak foundations of key operational systems and data on which they depend.

For **support** systems the issues are essentially about understanding the economics of the efficiency benefits that are achievable and then adopting an approach which ensures that it delivers those benefits at the lowest long-term cost to the organisation. The 'buy-not-build' philosophy should rule here, since:

(a) support systems' needs are very similar in many organisations and a wide range of package software exists to meet them;
(b) the ongoing maintenance costs of systems can be very high, often exceeding the development costs and these can be avoided by using packages; and
(c) in support-type activities it is always possible to change how things are done to use the software available rather than build or modify software to meet existing nuances of procedure etc. It is always worth asking – 'If the package is good enough for 100 other similar organisations, why isn't it good enough for us?'

Given the variety of factors which affect success in the different segments and the business consequences of success or failure, no single strategy for managing the variety of applications is likely to be satisfactory. Equally, adopting a unique strategy for each and every new development will lead to chaos and only by good luck will the right approach be used on each occasion. A limited set which meets the majority of the options needed and which is well understood throughout the organisation is more likely to lead to overall success.

Parsons (1983) described a number of generic management strategies, which when used in the right circumstances could be observed to lead to success. The strategies are behavioural causes of certain effects and these strategies can therefore be aligned with the effects required in the portfolio. Each shows quite distinct variations in the attitude and role played in the management of information systems of the three key and quite often distinct and separate parties involved, i.e.:

(a) executive management
(b) line management – functional management and users of the systems;
(c) IT specialists – in the organisation whether they are in the business unit or a central corporate group.

These are three of the 'stakeholders' in IS management as described in Chapter 2, and the three that have the most direct impact in turning plans into reality. In each of the generic strategies the balance of involvement of each varies and with it the decision-making processes which affect the outcome. Table 5.3 summarises the key roles that each group plays in the strategies, each of which is summarised below in the context of the portfolio. As will be seen later, there is to a large extent a correlation between these 'supply-side' management strategies to deliver the applications and Earl's planning approaches described in Chapter 3.

Table 5.3 Rationale and requirements for generic strategies

	Centrally planned	Leading edge	Free market	Monopoly	Scarce resource
Management rationale	• central co-ordination of all requirements will produce better decision-making	• technology can create business advantages and risks are worth taking	• market makes the best decisions and users are responsible for business results • integration is not critical	• information is a corporate good and an integrated resource for users to employ	• information is limited resource and its development must be clearly justified
Organisational requirements	• knowledgable and involved senior management • integrated planning of IS/IT within the business planning process	• commitment of funds and resources • innovative IS/IT management • strong technical skills	• knowledgable users • accountability for IS/IT at business or functional level • willingness to duplicate effort • loose IT budget control	• user acceptance of the philosophy • policies to force through single sourcing • good forecasting of resource usage	• tight budgetary control of all IS/IT expenses • policies for controlling IS/IT and users
IT role	• provide services to match the business demands by working closely with business managers	• push forward boundaries of technology use on all fronts	• competitive and probably profit centre intended to achieve a return on its resources	• to satisfy users' requirements as they arise but non-directive in terms of the uses of IS/IT	• make best use of a limited resource by tight cost control of expenses and projects. Justify capital investment projects
Line management and user's role	• identify the potential of IS/IT to meet business needs at all levels of the organisation	• use the technology and identify the advantages it offers	• identify, source and control IS/IT developments	• understand needs and present them to central utility to obtain resources	• identify and cost justify projects • passive unless benefits are identified

After Parsons (1983).

Business centrally planned

This implies that senior and executive management need to be fully aware of the development due to its potential impact on future business success. It is therefore most appropriate for **strategic** systems where the achievement of certain business objectives is dependent on the IS investment. Ensuring success in such circumstances demands the attention of senior management, to ensure that the objectives are met and that the necessary resources are applied to deliver the solution in the time required. Most strategic developments span a number of business areas and whilst the nature of the system can often be easily defined in outline, it will be its uniqueness and its close fit to the business strategy which will deliver the business advantages. To gain those advantages it is almost inevitable that changes to business practices and even organisation will be necessary.

To meet all of these requirements a 'task force' approach is best suited. Led by a senior business manager the team will need dedicated, usually full time, high quality business resources which represent the areas affected and with the authority to agree to business changes. Equally it will need good IT skills in the team to design the system and manage the technical aspects of its implementation. This dedicated team must have the business and IT knowledge to deliver success and have access to top management to resolve issues which will undoubtedly arise during the development. Subject to this senior management agreement the team has the authority to decide both what the system will do and how in business and IT terms that will be achieved.

Whilst the idea of a dedicated team is attractive, it is often difficult to implement successfully in many organisations. The people it needs are often the most valuable in their existing jobs and are not readily given up by their functional management for the duration of the project. But it is essential that they are. Even though it may not be the most efficient use of skilled resources, it is a very effective way to achieve clear objectives in a tight timescale. The need for key people dedicated to such teams may also limit the number of strategic developments that can be undertaken at any one time, since such key people are often in short supply. It is better to reschedule the projects based on the availability of key resources than to spread the resource too thinly or substitute lower calibre or less experienced people. This strategy addresses the needs of strategic applications most effectively but it could be used in certain circumstances to carry out a short, sharp, evaluation of a high potential opportunity or even attack a key operational development where the business faces the prospect of serious short-term disadvantage.

Leading edge

This implies that the organisation believes that by adopting technology which is leading edge in the context of its industry, it should be able to gain some business advantage. Senior management must endorse the principle, be willing to fund some experimentation to evaluate technologies and accept that not all the evaluations will succeed. Whilst the new technologies may be identified by IT specialists the evaluation should be in relation to some potential business need and carried out in conjunction with the business. The objective is not to understand the technology for its own sake. Alternatively the lead may come from the business, by seeing a technology in use elsewhere that may be applicable. Whilst that business 'vision' may be appropriate, the IT specialists must be involved in the evaluation, to provide an objective view of the capabilities of the technology and a view of the longer-term implications to the business of adopting a particular technology. This is essential to balance the often enthusiastic business user who has fallen prey to the sales pitch of a professional computer salesperson!

While the technology is 'brand new' to the organisation it should be confined to the **high potential** box for evaluation. It is very high risk to apply untried technology in any other segment of the matrix. Once evaluated it may well be that the technology has strategic potential for the business, and becomes part of a strategic application. Alternatively it may not and it would be prudent if the technology is only relevant to key operational or support needs to proceed more carefully in line with the pace of adoption of technology in the industry. If there is no advantage to be gained, it is perhaps best to let others take the risks!

Free market

The strategy that follows is 'monopoly' and before considering the free-market strategy in more detail it is worth clarifying the key difference between the two in terms of the decision-making roles of the three parties involved. Figure 5.3 attempts to clarify this.

The philosophy behind the free-market approach is that line managers are accountable for the performance of the business activities within their area of responsibility. As part of that responsibility, subject to their normal degree of authority, they should be able to make beneficial decisions about IS and IT and not be hindered in any way by another group in achieving their performance targets. Such a philosophy is very prevalent in profit centre-based organisations. The opposite view expressed by the 'monopoly' philosophy is that whilst line management decide what is needed, subject to senior management agreement to resource those needs, it is best if there is central co-ordination and control of how those needs are met. These two apparently opposing views can be reconciled by understanding how each satisfies the issues in different parts of the portfolio, since neither is an ideal solution in all cases.

The benefits of the free-market strategy are that business problems are resolved by IS/IT solutions close to the problem. This leads to strong motivation to make the system work, solutions that fit the problem better in terms of need, cost and time and in some cases a degree of business-driven innovation in the use of IT. This is very attractive to strong line managers with clear targets and objectives for their function, although the longer-term issues and costs of supporting the resulting

	'FREE MARKET'	'MONOPOLY'
DEMAND Who decides <u>what</u> is done and whether it is done – the IS decision	Line or functional management	Senior management based on needs agreed by line management
SUPPLY Who decides <u>how</u> it will be done in terms of the IT approach	Line or functional management with or without advice from IT specialists	IT specialists with endorsement of senior management (IT can veto 'unacceptable' solutions)

<u>NB</u> In some cases the MONOPOLY may be a combination of IT specialists and a particular function, e.g. for Accounting systems

Figure 5.3 Free market vs. monopoly strategies – key differences

systems are often overlooked in the drive to deliver short-term results. The downside is clearly that if everyone pursues such a strategy, integration of data and systems is extremely difficult at best and the organisation will acquire a wide range of often incompatible hardware and software. The long-term costs of such a situation can become unacceptable, but possibly even more critically the business overall may be prevented from gaining the long-term strategic benefits of IS/IT, which largely arise from the integration of systems and information resources.

Against that background the free-market strategy, operated within some limits to the types of technology 'permitted' in the organisation, is most effective in producing many of the **support** systems which are needed by the various functions in the organisation. It is also an appropriate strategy for some **high potential** evaluations – those driven by a business idea and which can be tested with limited IT help, to the point where the potential benefits can be understood. Outside these two areas it can be a dangerous and expensive strategy in the long term.

Monopoly

In many ways 'monopoly' is the converse of 'free market', whereby the influence of the centralised IT control of supply options will standardise on solutions which can provide integration of data and systems and control of the cost of technology to the organisation. This may well mean that the most expedient and perhaps ideal solution in each case has to be compromised to enable the long-term best set of solutions for the organisation to be achieved, at an acceptable overall cost. Each functional manager will not necessarily achieve the most cost-effective or timely satisfaction of his or her needs. This may cause resentment unless there is a general understanding of how the various systems of the organisations inter-relate across the functional areas. Often this is caused because the IT monopoly has gone beyond its brief and is setting priorities for what is done rather than optimising how best to achieve all that needs to be done. Senior management must set the priorities to make best business use of the IT resource available or, if that is unsatisfactory to line managers, increase the size of the resource.

The positive attributes of the monopoly strategy are that, if well directed in terms of business priorities and if users are competent in specifying their needs, high quality, integrated, maintainable systems are delivered in an overall cost-effective way. This is what is needed for **key operational** systems where a low-risk, controlled approach to the development process is essential to avoid systems failure and consequent disadvantage. The monopoly strategy can be adopted for support systems but may produce relatively high-cost solutions where cheaper, less comprehensive options would have sufficed.

Scarce resource

This is essentially a financial strategy which controls the spend on IT through a budget limitation, within which those investments which provide the greatest return for the spend will get priority. This means that each investment should be financially justified and the most cost-effective solution to deliver economic benefits should be selected. Expense will then be tightly controlled against the agreed budget to ensure the maximum net financial benefit is delivered. This approach tends to promote local specific solutions to meet the needs and miti-gates against flexible or integrated solutions which will always be more expen-sive. This drive for more economically justified use of IT is very appropriate for **support** applications and may produce effective key operational systems in the short term but at the expense of longer-term opportunities derived from inte-gration. It does not encourage innovative or speculative (high potential) uses of IT and precludes many strategic investments due to the demand for quantified financial benefits to be spelled out in advance. On the other hand, setting pri-orities on the basis of financial 'return on investment' criteria forces both users and IT to find the lowest-cost solution based on the long-term economics and hence encourages the buying of packaged software, which is normally available for most support applications. It is more cost-effective to modify business practice to use available software than to develop new software to satisfy non-critical tasks. The strategy does focus for good reason on the IT costs and it should be complemented by an equally strong drive to ensure all the claimed efficiency and economic benefits are realised. Often this is not the case and a full audit of many apparently financially justified investments would reveal a very poor actual return.

The above outlines are meant to describe the key attributes of each strategy sufficient to differentiate them and understand why they are most appropriate in particular segments of the portfolio. Figure 5.4 summarises that relationship. The rest of this chapter considers how these strategies can be used by business managers to help them in making appropriate decisions about IS/IT. The strategies are key concepts which offer considerable guidance throughout the rest of the book in how to address the range of supply-side issues that need to be managed successfully – they are important 'principles' to be understood and employed.

IMPLICATIONS AND USES OF GENERIC STRATEGIES IN IS/IT MANAGEMENT

The 'generic strategies' have primarily two uses in the process of developing the appropriate IS/IT management approaches.

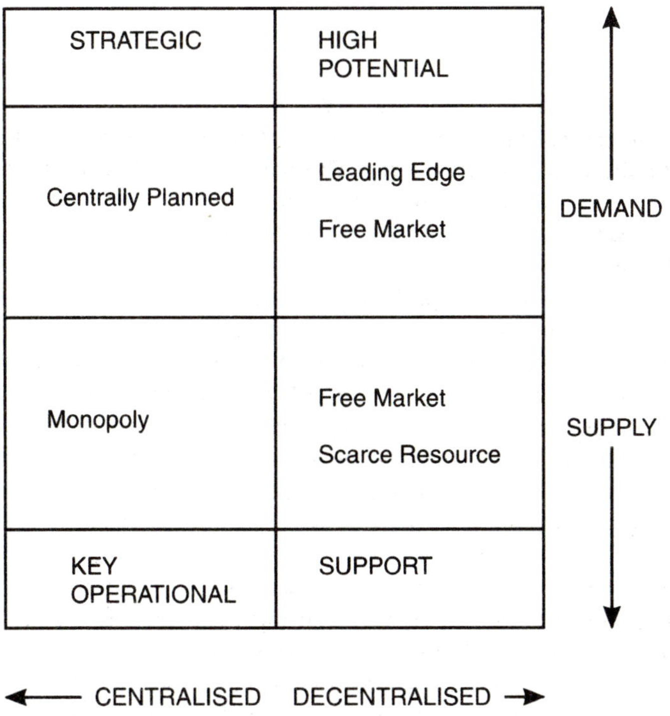

STRATEGIC	HIGH POTENTIAL
Centrally Planned	Leading Edge Free Market
Monopoly	Free Market Scarce Resource
KEY OPERATIONAL	SUPPORT

DEMAND

SUPPLY

← CENTRALISED   DECENTRALISED →

Figure 5.4 Relationship of applications portfolio and generic IS strategies

Diagnostic

They are a way of assessing the current situation and of understanding and describing the ways in which IS/IT is being managed. There is a strong correlation between the success of applications developed and the strategies adopted – a cause-and-effect relationship. The 'generic strategies' can summarise the apparent complexity of the existing situation, explain it and describe it succinctly. In analysing portfolios it is often the case that the majority of applications have been managed with an appropriate strategy. However, it is usual to find some that were developed in an inappropriate way and they will normally have a history of problems in the development process and have failed to deliver the required benefits.

The analysis is at two levels:

(a) for each system in place;
(b) as a pattern to demonstrate the overall match of current practice to the ideal mix.

Formulative

Once a future portfolio of applications can be identified and the strengths and weaknesses of the existing applications assessed, the generic strategies can be used to identify a migration path towards the required future mix. It is superficially attractive to say central planning is needed, but it might be an overkill and it is impossible to centrally plan everything. Allowing more freedom, using new technology or tighter, monopolistic control may be more appropriate in the short term. More rigorous scarce resourcing of support systems might yield resources to be deployed on strategic systems. Again, if the portfolio of applications required is changing, the mix of strategies adopted will need to reflect that new pattern.

No mixture can be prescribed for every situation but the generic strategies provide a limited number of basic options from which to select an appropriate set which matches the application portfolio requirements. This approach avoids the need to 'invent' the strategy entirely from the 'ground up' – it is easier to define the strategic approach by modification from proved approaches to suit the particular need and then identify the action necessary to achieve the migration path.

RELATING IS PLANNING APPROACHES AND THE GENERIC IMPLEMENTATION STRATEGIES

As was mentioned earlier in the chapter it would appear there should be some logical relationship between how an organisation plans for its IS investments, as described in Chapter 3, and the approach it adopts for the implementation of those investments. Whilst the two concepts of 'planning approaches' and 'generic strategies' are derived from different sources there are some clear connections that can be drawn and the evolution of the generic strategies used in many organisations can be reconciled with the evolution of IS/IT management shown in Table 3.2 and Figure 3.6. Table 5.4 suggests how the two are related. The correlation is not perfect and there are some anomalies.

(a) **Organisation-led** planning implies cross-functional views of IS to ensure investments are targeted on the business objectives and key themes implied by those objectives. It should obviously follow that the **centrally planned** strategy for implementation would best maintain that strategic view.

(b) **Business-led** with IS investments driven by the CSFs of the particular business areas should lead to uncovering high potential opportunities and in due course perhaps to strategic investments, but will also often lead to a plethora of support systems. This aligns closely with the **free market** strategy which is good for enabling innovation but also appropriate for support systems. In many cases, because of the functional view taken of the systems, the organisation fails to realise the full benefits and in practice only localised, support-type benefits materialise.

(c) The **administrative** approach to planning implies the main objective is budgetary control of IS/IT, which clearly can result in a **scarce resource** approach to implementation, when each investment is asked to justify a budget allocation via a financial case. Alternatively, one way of ensuring overall effective administration is to bring all the resources and costs together in one place and thereby be able to plan and control the whole investment programme through one budget centre – normally the IT department. This effectively creates a **monopoly** channel through which all investments are vetted. This does not imply financial constraints, merely centralised budgeting and monitoring of expenditure.

(d) **Method-driven** planning involves a highly analytical and structured approach to determining the needs for investment and it would seem prudent to follow through with the consistent, quality-based, highly structured implementation process that the **monopoly** brings. Both the planning approach and

Table 5.4 Relating IS planning approaches to generic implementation strategies

Planning approach (after Earl)	Portfolio segments involved	Implementation strategy (after Parsons)
A. Organisation led	Strategic	Business centrally planned
B. Business led	High potential (and support)	Free market
C. Administrative	Key operational and support	Monopoly or scarce resource
D. Method driven	Key operational	Monopoly
E. Technology led	Support or high potential?	Leading edge

implementation strategy are risk averse, careful and work well where a long-term plan to improve the performance of relatively stable business activities is needed and feasible, i.e. key operational applications.

(e) **Technology-led** planning and **leading edge** implementation approaches appear very similar but also seem anomalous when placed in the portfolio context. Reconciliation is not obvious given that Earl's work suggests that technology led is most relevant to identifying only support applications, whereas leading edge is best applied to high potential opportunities. The difference is one of perception and time. The technology-led approach implies an incremental adoption of technology as it is available and proved to enable technology efficiency to substitute for people's inefficiency – i.e. gradual automation through technology. Leading edge implies using a relatively new, possibly unproved, technology to discover whether it has strategic benefit to the business. For example, technology-led planning would lead to replacement of old inefficient software environments on personal computers (such as basic 'MS-DOS' operating systems) with new, more user-efficient front-end software such as 'Windows'. But leading edge would, for example, involve a completely new type of IT being evaluated, e.g. document processing technology. This difficulty in reconciliation in some ways reflects a traditional dilemma in terms of how much should 'technology-push' be allowed to influence an organisation's IS/IT Strategy.

In terms of the evolution of planning method shown in Figure 3.6 and Table 3.2, many organisations develop their mix of implementation strategies in the following way.

- **Stage 1** No coherent strategy – a mix of free market, monopoly, scarce resource and even leading edge – which is likely given the 'bottom-up' process.
- **Stage 2** A monopolistic strategy tends to prevail.
- **Stage 3** A combination of monopoly and scarce resourcing is common.
- **Stage 4** Users pursuing localised opportunities open up free-market activities in addition.
- **Stage 5** The use of the business centrally planned strategy occurs for the strategic applications.

This evolution can be observed in many organisations and those who succeed in the longer term are those that can accommodate the mixture of approaches most readily. This implies that no one 'force' – senior management, the IT function or the line managers – dominates the decision-making, but that a balanced set of approaches is adopted recognising the different roles each should play in different circumstances.

MANAGING THE PORTFOLIO – AN INVESTMENT MANAGEMENT VIEW

It is important that an organisation establishes some principles by which it evaluates IS/IT investments. Many organisations treat IS/IT investments like other capital investments and calculate 'paybacks', 'internal rates of return' or 'net present values' for the systems in order to determine whether or not to make the investment. This is satisfactory only when the costs and benefits can be predicted accurately over the life of the system. Otherwise the calculation is inaccurate at best, invalid at worst. In such organisations these 'rules' are often over-ruled or ignored in practice since many of the systems' investments cannot easily be appraised on financial grounds alone. Alternatively, false calculations are made to satisfy the 'rules' – the figures are invented to fit the purpose, in the knowledge that no one will ever check after the event. In effect this leads to inconsistent decision-making, and this can distort and even destroy the long-term strategy.

If the organisation was able to develop at any one time all the applications demanded, inconsistent evaluation would not really matter. The overall return on IS/IT investment might be very poor but at least the worthwhile would get done as well as the worthless! However, in most cases not all demand can be satisfied and priorities must be set. If no consistent justification approach is followed, the more beneficial applications may well be deferred, allowing those that are worth less to proceed. Assuming that does not mean an opportunity completely forgone, which may occur with delay, the resources and funds invested have provided a poorer return than could have been achieved, to the overall detriment of the organisation.

An obvious conclusion from the above is that the same principles and practice should govern the go/no go decisions for individual applications *and* deciding priorities across applications competing for resources. The only additional factor, assuming that systems are not sequentially dependent, is the amount of resource consumed. The limiting factor is normally people in quantity or quality (particular skills) but the same logic applies whatever the limiting resource – priority setting should enable maximum return from the use of that resource.

The discussions below consider investment evaluation first and then priority setting, assuming not all applications can be achieved in parallel and skilled staff are the scarce resource.

EVALUATING IS/IT INVESTMENTS

A 'technology' investment cannot strictly give a return on investment unless it replaces an older technology and carries out the same functions more efficiently. Most 'technology' investments are justified on the back of applications. Even if capacity on computers and networks has to be purchased in advance of the need, the justification should be based on systems that will use that capacity and the benefits they will provide. However, it is often difficult to associate all 'infra-structure' type investments with the subsequent benefits of using applications, even where sophisticated capital cost recovery accounting techniques are used. The arguments below will assume that reasonable cost allocations of shared resources can be arrived at – reasonable in the sense that:

(a) unused capacity is not 'free' – there is at least an opportunity cost of using it for another application;
(b) each application need justify only the incremental capacity *it* requires, not the next capacity increment which has to be purchased;
(c) where the technology is dedicated to an application the full cost is attributed to the application.

Issues of allocating and charging out IT costs are dealt with in a later chapter.

On the other side of the coin, quantifying the benefits of any system can be a difficult, even impossible, task. In the book *'Information Economics'* Parker *et al.* (1988) assess in detail the ways in which information and systems benefits accrue and how they can be quantified to help in justifying investments. They consider three main types of application:

(a) **Substitutive**   Machine power for people power – economics being the main driving force, to improve **efficiency**.
(b) **Complementary**   Improving productivity and employee **effectiveness** by enabling work to be performed in new ways.
(c) **Innovative**   Intended to obtain or sustain **competitive** edge by changing trading practice or creating new markets, etc.

They then identify the ways in which applications should be justified and define five basic techniques for evaluating benefits.

1   The traditional **cost/benefit analysis**, based on cost displacement by a more efficient way of carrying out a task. For example, preparing invoices by computer and transmitting them electronically via a data network is more efficient than printing and posting them, both for the sender and receiver.
2   **'Value linking'**, which estimates the improvement to business performance, not just savings made, by more precise co-ordination of tasks in different areas: being able to bill customers more accurately, due to immediate delivery feedback, or satisfy a greater proportion of customer orders direct from stock due to the precision of the stock records, are examples of value linking.
3   **'Value acceleration'**, which considers the time dependency of benefits and costs in other departments, of system improvements, e.g. being able to prepare invoices one day earlier or giving sales data to buyers sooner, giving them more time to negotiate with suppliers. This implies that the benefit will occur in another area of the business.
4   **'Value restructuring'** which considers the productivity resulting from organ-isational change and change of job roles, enabled by the new system. For

instance, departments can be combined, even eliminated, due to systems developed to carry out functions in an integrated fashion. Information-intensive tasks such as forecasting, planning and scheduling can often be rationalised and improved.

5 **'Innovation evaluation'** attempts to identify the value of new business or new business practices levered from IS/IT. The value may be in the application itself, e.g. the use of expert systems to diagnose machine faults, or in the image it creates for the company (e.g. home banking services).

The above categories of benefit are suggested to be related to the application types as shown in Figure 5.5.

By assessing costs and benefits using these techniques the overall 'economics' of an application can be assessed. The ideas are certainly more creative in interpreting information's long-term value than traditional views of systems investments.

Whilst it is important to quantify and express in financial terms as many of the costs and benefits as possible, it is not essential to convert all 'intangibles' to financial figures. It is simply not possible to express all the benefits of 'systems' in quantitative terms and it serves no useful purpose to develop spurious calculations to quantify the unquantifiable. If a new system will improve staff morale because at last the company has seen fit to invest in improving office functions and modernise the environment, how can that increase be financially expressed even after the event let alone before it has happened?

As has been explained earlier the rationale for developing applications or investing funds and resources in each segment of the matrix is different and therefore the evaluation process should be different. The arguments used to justify a prototype expert system to model customer buying behaviour are not the

	Substitutive (efficiency)	Complementary (effectiveness)	Innovative (competitive)
(1) Cost/benefit	***	**	*
(2) Value linking	**	***	**
(3) Value acceleration	*	***	***
(4) Value restructuring		**	***
(5) Innovation evaluation			***

The number of asterisks indicates the relative importance
of the type of benefit to the application type

Figure 5.5 Relationship of benefits to application types (after Parket *et al.* 1988)

same as those used to justify a rewrite of the general accounting system. Equally, response to a competitor's action and a decision to integrate applications via a data base require different approaches to evaluation. The risks of failure in the various segments are different. This can be allowed for by asking for a higher predicted rate of return where the risk is higher, although this may in turn merely lead to creative accounting for the benefits!

The application portfolio can be related to the types of benefits considered in the *Information Economics* rationale. The mix of benefits expected from any application development in each segment will vary according to the contribution it is intended to make. Figure 5.6 attempts to show this.

In the high potential segment the benefits are unknown and the purpose of the evaluation is, in part, to identify the types of benefits which might be achieved, and hence the nature of the system. Obviously if there are no benefits it should be rejected.

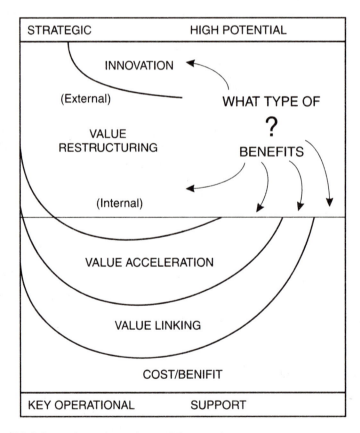

Figure 5.6 Information economics and the matrix

In the support segment the main likely benefits are of a substitution type – replacing a less efficient means of carrying out a set of tasks – although some may accrue from linking tasks together or by enabling faster or earlier completion of non-critical tasks, releasing resources for other more critical activities. Most of the arguments should therefore be based on cost/benefit, value linking or value acceleration logic. A little value restructuring may be possible if the system enables tasks to be centralised or decentralised to be carried out more appropriately. This might be true in a general accounting system for instance. Many of the arguments will be the same for key operational systems, although more emphasis will be placed on effectiveness through integrating activities, whereby the value linking and acceleration benefits should increase in importance. Such benefits from systems integration may also force some internal restructuring of activities in the organisation to ensure the benefits are gained.

The strategic segment is about change – change of business relationships and practices to gain advantages and achieve objectives. Hence the types of benefits will accrue by innovation and by restructuring both internal organisational processes and the relationships with the outside world, especially customers and suppliers. Accelerating business activities and linking them more proficiently will contribute to this, but basic cost/benefit appraisals will be difficult due to the degree of change involved. It is similar to carrying out a new promotion campaign or reorganising, where estimating payback is far from easy in advance. The portfolio approach and the *Information Economics* rationale suggest that:

(a) Quantified justification of applications is easier in the key operational and support quadrants – where all aspects of the application will be better known or can be determined and risks are lower and the rate of change is slower. High potential applications should be considered like other R&D investments rather than like key operational or support systems. Strategic applications may be difficult to argue quantitatively in advance and timing may be critical to the achievement of benefits.

(b) A singular approach to system justification will tend to produce one type of application to the exclusion of others. This argument is particularly strong where a deliberate scarce resource approach has been adopted and pure financial return on investment decides whether projects go ahead and also the priorities. This will clearly favour the key operational and support quadrants.

The arguments surrounding the appraisal of applications in the different segments are now considered in more detail.

Support applications

The main argument for such systems is improving efficiency, which should be possible to quantify and convert into a financial argument for investment. Additional arguments may revolve around system and technology obsolescence and improving staff morale and these may be difficult to quantify. If the application development requires the use of a 'scarce (central) resource', then in this segment it is reasonable to expect potential benefits to be estimated **before** resources and costs are incurred to identify the most economic solution within the benefits achievable. Again, if the application is contending with others for the limited resource, then a support application must show a good economic return for the allocation of a scarce resource.

If, however, the project can be carried out within the user department's control then it is reasonable that, since the budget or funding is under local control, the go/no go decision is made by local user management. The IS/IT investment is an alternative use of funds to other investments locally and is not competing with alternative use of scarce IS/IT resources. Hopefully, user management will expect the case to be argued in predominantly financial terms, but if not that is their responsibility.

In summary, assuming a scarce resource strategy is being adopted 'centrally' for all support applications, then any allocation of that resource should be argued on economic, return on investment, grounds primarily. At the same time, some discretion can, without great risk, be left to local management via a free-market strategy. The balance of scarce resource/free market in this segment will depend on how centralised or decentralised the organisation is overall.

Key operational applications

Whilst as far as possible all costs and benefits of a new development/redevelopment/ enhancement to a key operational system should be converted to a financial evaluation, this may not allow for all the arguments involved.

For support systems it was suggested that benefits should be estimated before any resource is allocated or costs determined. This is inappropriate for key operational applications where financial benefits are not the only driving force, and also the most economic solution may not be the most effective. This is the area for a strict 'feasibility study' to find the best solution from a range of alternatives, each with differing costs and benefits and risks.

The business success may be at risk if a system falls behind the business needs. It also might be worth spending more to achieve an integrated solution which meets a range of needs more effectively and upon which new strategic applications can be built. The relationship of the 'project' to other existing, proposed and potential systems must be included in the evaluation. Normally this will increase the cost and the 'intangible' benefits. Some of those benefits will be able to be related to critical success factors which by inference will, if achieved, lead to achievement of business objectives (and vice versa if they are not!). An argument often used here is 'What will happen to the business if we do not invest in improving key operational systems?' and therefore 'Can we afford the risk of not doing it?'

The approach that works best for key operational systems is 'monopoly' which implies a central control and vetting of all applications and enhancements.

This enables a standard checklist of questions to be considered in the evaluation of any new project. Factors that are important (other than economic return) from either a business or IS/IT perspective can be allowed for and, if necessary, changed over time. The centralised approach should also preclude solutions based on only economic expediency rather than business benefits, although it may mean a particular application may cost more in the short term.

In conclusion, it should be stressed that for key operational systems the business management should be the final arbiter. It is their business which will suffer by lack of investment and they should (provided they can afford to pay) be allocated the necessary resource to meet such systems needs, for whatever reason they feel the case is justified.

Strategic applications

The fact that an application is deemed strategic implies that it is seen as important, even essential, in achieving business objectives and strategies. Obviously, it is important to cost the investment and where possible put figures to the potential benefits, even if the latter are only orders of magnitude, not estimates suitable for a discounted cashflow calculation. However, the main reasons for proceeding are likely to remain 'intangible' – expressed as the critical success factors that the application addresses.

The most appropriate approach to managing in this segment is to integrate the planning of the systems with the business plans ensuring that IS/IT opportunities and threats are being considered along with the business issues and strategies. Hence, an application will get the go/no go decision based on whether it is relevant to the business objectives and strategy and likely to deliver benefits in those terms, not as a system in its own right. Whether this will actually happen is partly a question of luck (that the target does not move), partly of judgement (the quality of business acumen of senior managers), and partly good management of the application as and when it is developed.

The key issue is whether the management team, steering group or whatever body makes such decisions, is unified in endorsing the project and that the 'organisation' deems the investmently worthwhile. The critical factor is then re-sourcing the task sufficiently to achieve the objectives in the optimum timescale. This may need repeated senior management intervention to ensure both user and IT resources are made available. The budget for such investments and then financial control of actual expenditure should perhaps reside with the 'steering group' to ensure that progress and resourcing are centrally monitored as well as planned.

High potential applications

The very essence of high potential projects is that the benefits are unknown. The objective in part is to identify the benefits potentially available. It is the R&D

segment of the matrix and should be justified on the same basis as any other R&D and preferably from a general R&D budget rather than IS/IT central funds. In practice, where the money comes from (R&D budget or IS/IT or user budgets) is important but not critical. What does matter is not pouring money down the seemingly bottomless pit that R&D can become, if not properly monitored. The idea of 'product champions' to be responsible for such projects, given a budget against agreed general terms of reference, to deliver results or otherwise, is the most effective way of initiating and managing the 'high potential' stage in application life cycles. So whatever the source of the funds, once the project starts the 'champion' has control over the budget, and is accountable for its use.

The word **evaluation** is what the high potential box is really about – nothing should stay in it too long or have too much money spent on it. When initial allocations are used up, further sums have to be rejustified, not just allocated in the vague hope of eventual success. Clearly this means that the high potential applications being tested need to be monitored by the business management, both to control overall costs and identify those that have significant potential; so that they can be fully exploited.

The above approaches to application justification in the various segments may lack the precision ideally required. But this is no more than is true of other aspects of research and development, advertising, reorganisation, building new plant or facilities, taking on new staff or training people.

IS/IT investments should be considered just as objectively and just as subjectively as other business investments. The portfolio approach allows the balance to vary according to the expected contribution required.

Clearly, over time, applications can migrate round the matrix, as the business and IS/IT use evolves. High potential applications cannot be high potential for ever. They either have significant potential and become strategic, have no potential and should be rejected, or have limited benefits of a support or key operational nature. As they move, further investment should be appraised based on their planned destination. Strategic systems will over time produce fewer advantages, as others catch up, or the industry or business objectives change. As they become the established way of doing business, they essentially become key operational systems and may have to be reimplemented to be more appropriate to that role – this implies further investment of resources and should be argued from a key operational perspective. Equally some key operational systems eventually only fulfil a support role, as the business changes and hence further investment should be severely curtailed, or again the system reimplemented to provide a better economic return over the long term – by reducing support costs etc.

Hence over time an application will move at least partially round the matrix and as its contribution changes, so should the way further investments in the application be argued.

SETTING PRIORITIES FOR APPLICATIONS

As mentioned earlier, the mechanisms used to decide whether or not applications go ahead should also be used to set priorities across applications when all cannot be done in parallel. Some priorities are logical – project B cannot proceed before project A has built the data base etc. – but many more are independent of each other.

It is important to introduce some consistent, rational approach to priority setting if any strategy is to be implemented successfully. Short-term business pressures will change, projects will not proceed as planned, resources will not be available as expected, new opportunities and requirements will emerge. Each of these can change the priorities and unless a consistent rationale is employed, the short-term issues will over-ride the strategy. In that short term, resources are limited and must be used to maximum effectiveness. The main constraint is normally skilled IT people, often in particular skill areas.

Based on the earlier discussion of application evaluation it should be seen that setting priorities across applications of a similar type, i.e. support or key operational, etc., is not too difficult. Other than ranking them on similarly expressed benefits, the remaining parameter is to optimise the resource use. It might also be prudent to modify the final 'score' by consideration of the ability to succeed – the risk of each application – to ensure that not just high-risk projects are tackled, resulting eventually in no achievement! Risk can either be allowed for as contingencies in cost and resources or by reducing the potential benefits or, in some cases, both!

Hence, three factors need to be included in the assessment of priorities:

- what is most important to do – **benefits**
- what is capable of being done – **resources**
- what is likely to succeed – **risks**

Spadaro (1985) shows a matrix-based approach for assessing 'request factors against success factors' to identify a ranking for projects based on importance and risk of failure. How risk can be assessed is considered in the next chapter.

Priorities need to be set in the short term to enable the best use of resources within the acquisition lead time for further resources, assuming these are actually obtainable.

Within the **support** segment setting priorities should not be too difficult – those with the greatest economic benefit that use the least resources should get the highest priority. This will encourage users to express benefits quantitatively and look for resource efficient solutions, such as packages, to obtain a priority. Support applications will tend to be low risk but relative risks may modify the priorities to ensure an overall return is guaranteed.

Within the **strategic** segment the basic rationale is equally clear. Those applications which will contribute most to achieving business objectives, and use least resource in the process, should go ahead first. To assess this, some form of simple decision matrix can be useful in assessing the 'strategic contribution' or weighting of different projects. It produces a strategic 'score' or value for each application or project by explaining in terms of how, and therefore to what degree, it will help in achieving the various success factors. A simple 'high, medium, low' weighting can be used to give some useful perspective on which will have potentially the greatest business impact. Table 5.5 demonstrates the process.

All applications, wherever they fall in the matrix, should be assessed against such a 'strategic weighting' table to help decide or confirm in which segment they belong. **High potential** applications should demonstrate some, if as yet unclear, relationship to objectives, whereas **strategic** applications will be more obviously contributing. **Support** systems should show little strategic contribution, otherwise they are more important and **key operational** applications should relate to at least some CSFs.

Setting priorities amongst **key operational** systems is more problematic than support or strategic, where the basic rationale is clearer. The arguments for (i.e. benefits of) key operational systems will comprise basically:

Table 5.5 Strategic weighting via critical success factors

	APPLICATION CONTRIBUTION		
	HIGH (3)	MEDIUM (2)	LOW (1)
OBJECTIVE A: CSF 1 CSF 2 CSF3 etc.			
OBJECTIVE B: CSF 1 CSF 2 etc.			
OBJECTIVE C: CSF 1 CSF 2 etc.			
OBJECTIVE D: etc.			
TOTALS			

OVERALL
TOTAL

- economic
- critical success factors (CSFs)
- risk to current business
- infrastructure improvement

Each of these issues must be given some form of relative weighting to decide order of preference before looking at resource constraints.

In each case the cost/resources used by the project should be matched against its importance in each of the four categories to establish overall priorities. Economic benefits are relatively straightforward and business objectives are included via CSFs. The IT view of 'infrastructure' implies providing appropriate hardware/network capacity, implementing coherent architectures, increasing skills, improving the resilience or flexibility of systems, etc., i.e. investments which will avoid IT becoming a business constraint. Risk to current business could be assessed by describing 'what risks are run if the project does not go ahead'.

The types of business risks to be considered (due to poor product/service quality, process failure, loss of control, customer dissatisfaction, etc.) and the links to IS projects is argued in some detail by Peters (1988).

Applications scoring highly in all four categories are obviously higher in priority than those scoring highly in 1, 2 or 3 categories and those at each level in the ranking using less resources get priority. It is a subjective method but does allow for the strategic, financial, user and IT perspectives to be included.

Buss (1983), who proposed a similar approach, also makes an important observation concerning, as he says, the 'misconception' that 'computer steering committee can decide the priorities'. In general he suggests that politics may interfere, that representation in discussion will be unbalanced and the only common ground will end up as economics! He says the best way to set priorities is to make them the product of a formal planning process at corporate or business unit level. The mechanisms to be employed can be agreed by a steering group but it should not be implemented as a meeting-based process.

High potential applications are difficult to prioritise and will tend to be driven somewhat in the reverse of strategic applications – what resource is available to do it and then which application might best employ that resource? If, as is suggested earlier, high potential applications are 'individually' driven, normally a keen champion exists, it is the secondary resources that are the problem. Whilst it sounds wrong to suggest 'he who shouts the loudest', or 'has the most influence' will obtain priority in this segment, it may be the best way to allow priorities to be set because:

(a) the results will depend not just on the value of the idea, but also the force with which it is pursued;
(b) setting objective priorities on scanty evidence is not very reliable anyway.

If the idea potentially impacts many CSFs it clearly stands out from others and should be elevated above the general scramble for R&D-type resources. In the discussion below, high potential applications are not considered as being in competition for IS/IT funds, but are funded from R&D general budgets. But of course they may compete for certain key skills or resources.

The remaining task is to set priorities across the segments of the portfolio to decide how much resource to devote to the different types of applications. This is not simple since the rationale for investment in each is different, as shown above. However, the approach recommended for key operational applications can be extended out of the key operational domain. The problem is that strategic applications will score heavily on 'critical success factors' whereas support applications will score heavily on 'economics'. Management must decide the weighting they wish to attribute to each type of benefit and then rank the systems.

The relative weighting given to each will depend on a number of factors but in general the greater trust the management have in their own judgement relative to the need to be reassured by figures, and the trust they have in the user's understanding of the business and in IT in developing effective systems, the greater the weighting placed on the CSFs etc., relative to financial aspects. In a way this is a sign of maturity of the organisation and how it plans and manages IS/IT. It also tends to reflect on the strength of the company within its industry. The stronger the position the less IS/IT investments are expected (like other investments) to prove an economic case in advance, and a short-term payback, as opposed to providing long-term business development benefits and opportunities.

If the overall plan is developed and maintained in a priority sequence that reflects the ratio:

$$\frac{\text{Benefits to be achieved (adjusted for risk)}}{\text{Limiting resource consumed}}$$

then it helps both in short-and long-term planning decisions because:

(a) resources can be reallocated where necessary from lower to higher priority applications on a rational basis, with the agreement of users;
(b) appropriate resourcing levels for the future can be set, and action taken to obtain the right type of resources to meet the demands, expressed as a consensus view of the benefits available.

It is quite possible then to produce a 'planning system' which should keep the plans and resource utilisation up to date. It is important to 'report' the current plan to **all** involved to aid understanding of the reasons for the ranking of any particular user's project. Mystery or uncertainty are far more destructive of plans than the discussion and reconciliation of real problems.

Again the above arguments may lack the precision ideally required for setting priorities. Much subjective judgement is inevitably involved – but rules for the various factors involved can be sensibly established, rather than each priority decision be effectively made on a different set of criteria.

In both the evaluation of projects and setting priorities, one aspect must not be ignored – 'after the event'! Some form of review/audit (not a witch hunt!) must be carried out on a high percentage of projects to identify whether (a) they were carried out as well as possible and (b) whether the benefits claimed (and possibly different benefits) were achieved or not.

One of the factors that differentiates successful from less successful companies in their deployment of IS/IT, according to a survey by the Kobler Unit (1987), is the management resolve to evaluate IS/IT investments **before and after** they occurred.

However, evaluating the benefits of any system after it is installed is fraught with problems – since it will depend on the type of contribution expected, the timescale used and whether the system is viewed in isolation or in the context of other investments. These problems are described by Huff (1990) who concludes 'it appears as if we may never have a complete understanding of the entire costs and benefits of IT'.

In summary evaluating IS/IT investments is clearly not a simple task. It requires a combination of management perception of the overall nature of business improvements that can accrue, plus realistic appraisal of each investment, to ensure that maximum benefits can be realised at an acceptable cost. At the same time consistent criteria must be applied to both the evaluation of investments and the setting of priorities across the variety of investments.

MANAGING THE APPLICATION PORTFOLIOS IN A MULTI-BUSINESS UNIT ORGANISATION

So far we have considered the management of the applications portfolio for a single business unit. This is the most appropriate level to carry out the analysis to gain a consensus view of the managers in that unit – they 'own' the portfolio. However once this is done there are further benefits to be gained in a multi-unit organisation by considering the range of applications in all the units' portfolios. Few organisations consist of one business unit and there is a need to ensure that across the whole organisation maximum benefits are being obtained from IS and that IT resources are being used to maximum effect. Figure 5.7 summarises the ways in which benefits can be gained by developing an overall portfolio management approach in a large corporation. The benefits of such an approach are different in each segment and will vary depending on how diversified or otherwise the corporation is, as discussed in Chapter 4.

Before considering the implications of diversity the general principles involved need to be understood, and they can be summarised by the '4Cs' shown in Figure 5.7.

High potential – 'communicate'

Whilst the essence of the high potential segment of the matrix is degrees of freedom to innovate, there is benefit in informing others what the R&D project is trying to achieve and/or about the technology being used. It may well be that the

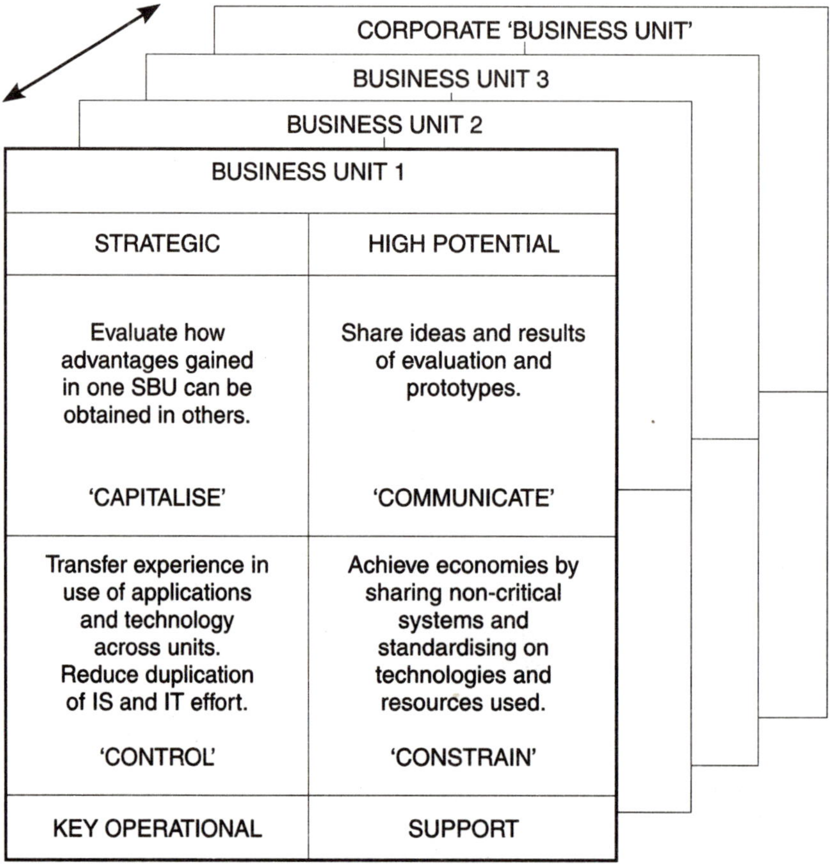

CORPORATE 'BUSINESS UNIT'	
BUSINESS UNIT 3	
BUSINESS UNIT 2	
BUSINESS UNIT 1	
STRATEGIC	HIGH POTENTIAL
Evaluate how advantages gained in one SBU can be obtained in others.	Share ideas and results of evaluation and prototypes.
'CAPITALISE'	'COMMUNICATE'
Transfer experience in use of applications and technology across units. Reduce duplication of IS and IT effort.	Achieve economies by sharing non-critical systems and standardising on technologies and resources used.
'CONTROL'	'CONSTRAIN'
KEY OPERATIONAL	SUPPORT

Figure 5.7 Portfolio management in a multi-business unit organisation

idea or technology is applicable elsewhere in the organisation and hence others will have a keen interest in knowing the results of the work. Equally someone in another business unit may well have tried a similar idea and knowledge of his or her success (or failure) may help the project or at least avoid repeated failure and waste of resources. The principle is to communicate, via some type of newsletter or electronic mail, possibly through the IT community, to enable ideas and experience to be shared.

Strategic – 'capitalise'

If one business unit has developed a system which is enabling them to gain a competitive advantage then the corporation as a whole should endeavour to capitalise on that development wherever it can. The managers of the other units should be **told** by the corporate executive to consider whether or not similar advantages are possible in their businesses and whether that type of application (not necessarily exactly as implemented) could deliver those advantages. They must be able to justify the case either way – whether they have a similar opportunity, or if not, why not. Many strategic applications are transferable, at least in concept, across quite diverse businesses.

Key operational – 'control'

The issue here is to minimise unnecessary IT cost to the organisation overall, whilst not risking disadvantage in any of the business units. Even in diverse companies some key operational systems perform similar functions (e.g. accounts receivable and payable) and the same software package or corporate system could be used in many of them. Where there is more similarity of business (e.g. all manufacturing companies) the rationale can be extended to other types of systems (e.g. MRP II software). To avoid unnecessary cost each new investment in key operational systems should be questioned as to whether existing systems, already in use (successfully) elsewhere in the organisation, cannot be used to prevent unwarranted proliferation of application software. The unit may have good reasons for rejecting existing systems, due to the particular nature of its operation, its size or the fit with its other existing systems, but the management requiring the development must demonstrate clearly why existing application software cannot be used. Control implies a corporate 'control' as each investment is considered, **not** an embargo on choice overall. Solutions forced by the corporate management on unwilling unit management usually fail to be implemented successfully. Minor problems can easily become major obstacles in the eyes of the unwilling!

Support – 'constrain'

As opposed to the control mechanism above this does imply a limited set of options from which the business can select its applications and supporting technology. The objectives of the constraints are to control costs, which is critical to overall success in the support segment. The choice may be very limited, e.g. the corporation may designate the general accounting package which everyone will use; or standardise on one type of spreadsheet or word processing package to limit the support costs. A list of approved software should be established from which selection can be made. Clearly it will not cover every type of support application but as new types are introduced (e.g. document retrieval) early standardisation will lead to the avoidance of huge costs in the long term.

The above explains the general principles involved and the reasons for them. However, there are clearly a number of factors which determine the value which will derive from management of the set of portfolios in a large organisation.

The starting point is to consider the degree to which the organisation is a 'corporation' of businesses which have some synergy, or a 'conglomerate' of disparate businesses which are managed as a set of financial assets. In the latter case the rate of change of the portfolio of businesses will also determine whether corporate intervention on IS/IT is to be of benefit. If businesses are continually being bought and sold there is little scope for even common support systems to be shared efficiently.

At the other extreme, in a corporation where many of the businesses trade with one another, there are potentially large benefits from optimising the trading systems across the businesses. Table 5.6 summarises the issues which should be considered across the business units to arrive at an optimum overall IS/IT strategy.

When considering to what extent corporate intervention is likely to provide net benefit to the organisation, there are three levels at which benefits can be achieved.

Table 5.6 Managing application portfolios in multi-SBU organisations

Factors which affect the benefits of corporate intervention:

1   Business factors (demand)
(a)   Conglomerate or corporation?
- the degree of diversity of the businesses and corporate acquisition/divestment policies

(b)   The similarity of the business units in terms of:
- types of products/services and processes
- markets and customers and suppliers
- scale of operation
- competitive position and strategy

(c)   The relationships between the businesses in terms of:
- inter-company trading and inter-dependency for success
- customers' views of the units and corporation
- ability/need to source products/services in different units

(d)   The geography of the business

2   IT factors (supply)
(a)   Economics of processing, communication and procurement: hardware, services and application software
(b)   Availability of technical skills and staff
(c)   Availability of technologies and quality of vendor services in different areas/countries
(d)   Existing IS/IT investments in the units – their effectiveness and costs

1 **Economic** To reduce expenditure on IT by exploiting corporate buying power and sharing technology and people resources. This essentially views IT as a commodity with limited value adding and is therefore appropriate for support applications and is the main benefit achievable in a diverse conglomerate. If this view dominates corporate thinking it is unlikely to maximise the IS benefits, merely minimise the costs of IT. It is a **technology-based** view that can often lead to the outsourcing of IT supply.

2 **Horizontal synergy and rationalisation** To exploit the benefits of similar systems in different units that have similar processes and reduce the costs of replicating support. This can enable the organisation to obtain earlier benefits by transfer of experience – it is an **application-based** approach which applies to both key operational and support systems.

3 **Vertical and horizontal synergy** To exploit inter-company relationships and the corporate information resource, especially where units trade with one another or deal with similar customers and suppliers. This is an **information-based** approach which is aimed at gaining advantages that competing organisations cannot achieve. It is most appropriate in a 'corporation' and can lead to cross-unit strategic systems but may also provide greater benefits from key operational systems. It is very difficult to achieve if the units are seen as 'profit-centres' since whilst the benefits to the corporation overall may be significant, each unit may have to compromise its ideal needs.

In many large organisations there is no coherent approach to managing the overall corporate suite of applications and whilst not exhaustive the options described here enable a more beneficial, structured view to be taken. In most organisations the approach is either driven by the centre, which is resented in the units, each of which ends up with a less than ideal set of applications, or it is purely opportunistic based on apparent similarity across units and short-term expediency to avoid costs or obtain early delivery of a system.

KEY LEARNING POINTS

- **The applications portfolio approach to managing the range of information systems that a business needs provides an overall framework within which consistent and coherent decisions can be made across the variety of different requirements.**
- **The concept is at the centre of any management process since it links the planning approaches needed to identify options for the implementation approaches which enable the delivery of the different systems.**
- **Since the portfolio recognises the different contributions made it offers clear guidance on how each application should be evaluated and consequently on how priorities amongst the applications can be set.**
- **At a higher level organisational/corporate management have an obligation to ensure that maximum net benefit from all IS investments and IT**

spending is obtained across the range of businesses it manages. The portfolio view enables situations and demands to be compared sensibly and cross-unit options to be assessed rationally.

- Many organisations have found that the portfolio approach has provided senior management with considerable new insight into the contribution IS/IT can make, and how they can play a constructive and valuable role in ensuring IS/IT is managed successfully to the long-term benefit of the business.

As will be seen in the next chapter, the same basic structure can be used to understand the different approaches that can be adopted to the development of particular applications, based on the contribution required.

QUESTIONS FOR CONSIDERATION

1 Based on the applications portfolio you derived for Question 1 in Chapter 3, describe as far as possible the generic strategies used to manage the systems. Identify any apparent anomalies in terms of the preferred strategies shown in Figure 5.4. Has this resulted in any notable problems regarding that system – if so, what are they?

2 From Question 1 above describe the prevalent strategies being adopted in your organisation for managing IS applications and consider the implications of this for the future management of IS/IT in the business.

3 Describe how IS/IT developments are evaluated in terms of gaining approval for investment expenditure. What techniques are used to evaluate the investments? Are the same techniques applied to all investments? If not, why not and do the techniques used relate to the different application types appropriately? If the same techniques are used what effect is that having on the nature of investments made?

4 How are priorities set across the range of IS development investments required? Explain the rationale for priorities and decide who in reality is setting the priorities:

(a) Senior management based on a clear overview of demand.

(b) Senior management based on projects as they arise.

(c) Line management – based on who shouts loudest or has most influence or power in the business.

(d) The IT specialists – based on their perception of business priorities.

(e) By consensus agreement of senior, line and IT management based on an agreed process which allows for demand-and-supply issues to be balanced effectively.

RECOMMENDED ADDITIONAL READING

Huff, S.L. (1990) 'Evaluating Investments in Information Technology', *Business Quarterly*, (Spring), pp. 42–5.

OTHER REFERENCES

Buss, M.D.J. (1983) 'How to Rank Computer Projects'. *Harvard Business Review*, (January–February).

Kobler Unit of Imperial College/Brunel University (1987) *The Strategic Use of IT Systems* (a survey).

Parker, M.M., Benson, R.J. with Trainor, H.E. (1988) *Information Economics*. Prentice-Hall.

Parsons, G.L. (1983) 'Fitting Information Systems Technology to the Corporate Needs: The linking strategy'. *Harvard Business School Teaching Notes* (9-183-176).

Peters, G. (1988) 'Evaluating Your Computer Investment Strategy'. *Journal of Information Technology*, 3, 3, pp. 178–88.

Spadaro, D. (1985) 'Project Evaluation Made Simple'. *Datamation*, (1 November).

Chapter 6

Managing the development of information systems

INTRODUCTION

The previous chapter described the applications portfolio and high-level strategies for evaluating and managing the whole range of IS applications according to the business contribution, i.e. expected benefits, of the different types of systems. This chapter deals in more depth with the specific processes to be managed and the roles and responsibilities of those involved, within the overall framework and principles described earlier. The emphasis is on the view of the business manager, who will reap the benefits or suffer the consequences of the development processes, and hence what he or she needs to understand in order to make an appropriate contribution to those processes. It is not the purpose of this book to provide an in-depth description of all aspects of systems development, this is eminently well satisfied by a wealth of books on the subject (for those who wish to understand the subject in more depth, see references).

This chapter will first examine and define the key differences between IS applications and the 'projects' that are put in place to deliver them. By classifying those projects the roles of the parties involved can be better understood and the critical parts each plays in the various stages in the process are considered.

During the last twenty-five years or so, much has been learned about the best way to develop and implement technology-based information systems, in order that they deliver the benefits required. The majority of that experience has been converted into methods and tools that enable the requirements to be converted into a working system. These will be described in outline within an overall structure that has been shown to be most effective in meeting the needs of key operational systems. For other parts of the applications portfolio those ideal methods have to be adapted, even compromised, to satisfy the different pressures and issues which determine success in those segments. Only a small part of twenty-five or more years of experience in developing systems has been translated into ways and means of ensuring that the benefits that were expected or hoped for are actually delivered. The benefits will always occur within the business, if they occur at all, and therefore it is the responsibility of business managers to deliver those benefits, assuming the system does what was intended. A structured approach to managing the benefits is considered later in the chapter.

Finally, much can go wrong with IS developments. Some, such as the notorious TAURUS system in the Stock Exchange, can fail totally after many millions of pounds have been spent. Others can succeed in part, others succeed but at much greater cost than expected and many are delivered late, causing business problems to be resolved too late or even so late that the business issues have moved on – some systems have been obsolete on the day they were implemented! As was said earlier in the book, some '70 per cent of all IS/IT investments fail to deliver the expected benefits'. Clearly IS/IT investments are risky! In the last part of the chapter a risk management approach is outlined which helps define those risks and their causes in advance, so that action can be taken to address them or the systems development process changed to avoid them. Since it is the business that suffers from any failure of an IS development, business managers must understand, and where appropriate, deal with the risks involved.

APPLICATIONS AND PROJECTS

So far this book has dealt with information systems and technology **applications**, which a business needs to be successful in terms of its business environment and strategy. For instance, it may need an order processing system, an employee records system, a general accounting system or a marketing information system. It will need such systems whether or not they are based on information technology. Orders need to be processed, records of employees must be kept for legal reasons, and in order to pay them, and accounts must be kept – all of which can be done manually. The reason for employing IT for such systems is to do things more efficiently, effectively or in a way that enables the business to outperform its competitors in some way. In every case the rationale for applying IT to the system is to provide business benefits, of one kind or another, i.e. **applications of IS/IT should deliver benefits.**

On the other hand, in order to develop and implement a technology-based system, changes need to be made to business practices and the new system has to be constructed in some way to carry out the tasks. Normally these types of processes are considered as projects – a set of activities which when finished will have delivered the required system. As such **projects incur costs**, due to the use of resources and the purchase of technology and services. The resulting system may or may not deliver the expected benefits. As has been observed 'the result of any IS/IT development is change, the skill of management is to ensure the change is beneficial!'

Whilst this argument might appear slightly semantic it is valuable to understand the differences between **applications** and **projects** as will be seen below. If the 'application' is a small spread sheet for allocating internal departmental expenses then the distinction is rather arbitrary – given that the 'project' may only take one person a day or two and the benefits can be seen in a week. But as will be seen in the risk analysis part of this chapter, many of the risks of IS/IT developments are due to one factor – the size of the development, however this is measured. The way of avoiding such obvious risks is to break the 'project' into smaller 'subprojects'. It is best to consider the 'application' as a new way of working which should lead to business improvements and to then consider the 'projects' that have to be carried out to achieve that new way of working. It should not be assumed at the start that an application is best developed via one project. But equally the various projects involved must be brought to fruition in such a way that the application benefits are achieved.

The purposes in splitting large application developments are:

(a) to maximise the chances of achieving the benefits of the application; and
(b) to ensure resources are used in the optimum way in achieving the whole application portfolio.

The main factors that influence how that is done are listed in Table 6.1.

Whilst there are many advantages to breaking a large, complex task into more manageable components, it does increase the co-ordination problem and an overhead for managing that co-ordination is introduced. However that is more than compensated for normally by having each project focused on a specific set of objectives and deliverables. Measuring progress against those deliverables and the associated time and cost targets is far easier when the tasks involved and

Table 6.1 Factors which affect how an application is subdivided into projects

(a) Size

The application is too big to manage as a whole given all the activities involved – the major cost elements need to be managed separately to keep control and to achieve effective quality assurance and testing of all components.

(b) Timescale

To minimise the time to implementation and hence stages of benefit delivery – to separate critical-path elements and ensure they are co-ordinated most effectively. Aspects of more certainty are done earlier and put uncertain parts into later phases, to clarify requirements (after completion of earlier phases etc).

(c) Control of resources

There are many subdivisions of this:

(i)   Resources of different types and skills need specialist management.
(ii)   Resources report to different parts of the organisation and/or are distributed geographically.
(iii) Responsibility for achieving certain CSFs or particular benefits.
(iv)   The role of outside suppliers in the application.
(v)   Different types of technology involved.
(vi)   Variety of different functions and data involved in the application.

scope of work are precisely defined. This immediately suggests that there are different roles to be fulfilled.

(a) **Application manager** (often called business project manager) – whose task it is to ensure the benefits of the application are identified, agreed and delivered. This must be a business manager **and**

(b) **Project managers** – who may be business people or IT specialists depending on the tasks involved and types of resources involved. Their task it is to deliver the necessary 'components' of the application to agreed specifications and time and cost targets.

As has been said for a small system these roles may reside in the same person but for a large system there may be several project managers, looking after separate teams, who 'report to' the application manager. This overall configuration is shown in Figure 6.1, and the details of the different roles will be examined further throughout this chapter.

The next stage is to consider the nature of the types of projects necessary to deliver a successful IS/IT application. One view which helps clarify the situation is to consider the types of project according to who needs to control them and the immediacy of effect they have on the achievement of the application benefits. Whilst it may sound confusing, each application can be broken down into a portfolio of projects as shown in Figure 6.2.

The different types of projects can be defined as follows:

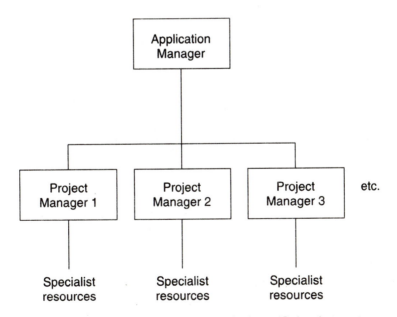

Figure 6.1 Application management structure for large IS developments

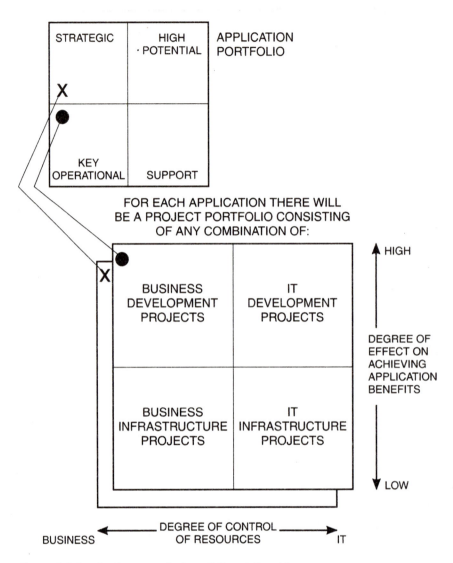

Figure 6.2 Application to project portfolio relationship

1 **Business development projects** – whose purpose is to change business practices and/or relationships to gain the benefits of the new information system.
2 **IT development projects** – which develop the systems using the technology to change how information is processed in the organisation, to gain business benefits.

3 **Business infrastructure projects** – which increase the ability of the business to devise and use IT-based systems and IT resources effectively.

4 **IT infrastructure projects** – which improve the capability of the IT resources of the organisation to deliver effective information systems.

The essence of the definitions is that 'development' projects are those that are particular to the application and 'infrastructure' projects are those which may relate to a number of applications currently under development or planned. Bear in mind that there will be a number of applications on the application portfolio and **each** will have a project portfolio. It will always make initial sense to combine some of the infrastructure needs of each application to avoid duplication of cost or inconsistency of approach. For example, if a number of systems require a new network or significant increase in computer capacity either centrally or in a department, it normally makes economic sense to enhance the infrastructure in one step to meet the total needs. Or if a number of systems require the development of new skills in the IT department, say in a new language, then this should be considered as infrastructure – to enable a range of future developments. Equally in the business, if a new customer numbering system is needed to enable several customer files to be brought together in a customer data base, this is a business infrastructure project.

Whilst infrastructure projects need to be related to development projects in terms of deliverables and timescale, it is often more cost-effective to combine them and it also enables the long-term benefits of an integrated approach to be realised.

It may, however, be the case that a particular priority application will be delayed if its infrastructure components are combined with those of other systems. That may be unacceptable, in which case it must proceed by considering its infrastructure needs as particular to the application, but a strategy needs to be adopted which will enable later integration of its infrastructure aspects with the overall requirements. It is clearly a matter of judgement as to whether a component project is 'infrastructure' or 'development'. But if a long-term IS and IT strategy is required both to maximise benefits **and** make effective use of resources and funds then each decision has to be taken with the longer term in mind, not just expediency for the sole benefit of the specific application.

The nature of infrastructure and the associated management issues are dealt with in the next chapter. Project management of infrastructure projects does not differ in any way from that of development projects – clear objectives must be set, deliverables agreed and then time, cost and quality parameters successfully managed. Infrastructure investments should primarily be justified on the basis of the applications that they enable and the long-term benefits of the application portfolio overall. This is not the whole story and further aspects are discussed in Chapter 7.

The rest of this chapter deals specifically with the development projects. As was stated in the introduction, frameworks and methodologies have been developed over the last twenty-five years to help manage developments, but they have focused mainly on the IT development component of the project portfolio. However, for an IS development to succeed work is needed to make necessary changes in the business to enable the system to work and hence obtain the benefits. The degree of change will depend on the nature of the application. Box 6.1 gives examples of the types of business development projects that might arise from three IS application developments.

Effective linking of applications to projects

Before considering the overall structure of managing an application development, which may consist of a number of projects, it is important to see how the

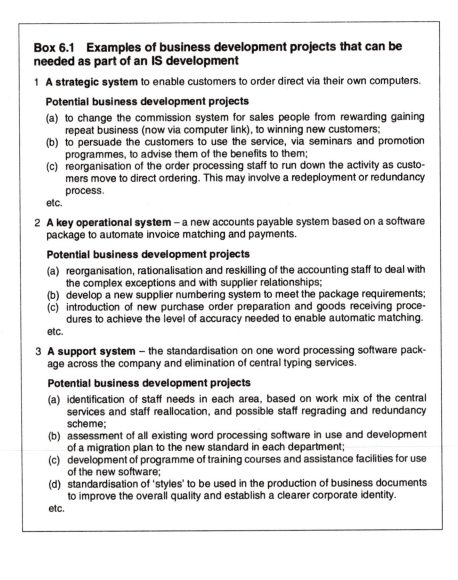

Box 6.1   Examples of business development projects that can be needed as part of an IS development

1 **A strategic system** to enable customers to order direct via their own computers.

Potential business development projects

(a) to change the commission system for sales people from rewarding gaining repeat business (now via computer link), to winning new customers;
(b) to persuade the customers to use the service, via seminars and promotion programmes, to advise them of the benefits to them;
(c) reorganisation of the order processing staff to run down the activity as customers move to direct ordering. This may involve a redeployment or redundancy process.
etc.

2 **A key operational system** – a new accounts payable system based on a software package to automate invoice matching and payments.

Potential business development projects

(a) reorganisation, rationalisation and reskilling of the accounting staff to deal with the complex exceptions and with supplier relationships;
(b) develop a new supplier numbering system to meet the package requirements;
(c) introduction of new purchase order preparation and goods receiving procedures to achieve the level of accuracy needed to enable automatic matching.
etc.

3 **A support system** – the standardisation on one word processing software package across the company and elimination of central typing services.

Potential business development projects

(a) identification of staff needs in each area, based on work mix of the central services and staff reallocation, and possible staff regrading and redundancy scheme;
(b) assessment of all existing word processing software in use and development of a migration plan to the new standard in each department;
(c) development of programme of training courses and assistance facilities for use of the new software;
(d) standardisation of 'styles' to be used in the production of business documents to improve the overall quality and establish a clearer corporate identity.
etc.

potential benefits required by the application can be translated effectively through to the projects. This is essential if the projects are to be focused throughout on the right deliverables, rather than become a set of vaguely related tasks pursuing incompatible objectives! A valuable technique to assist in this is critical success factor analysis, this time used at a lower level based on the application objectives. Figure 6.3 depicts the relationship.

The application objectives will be based on the target benefits, which will vary from mainly quantified, economic benefits for support applications to less quantifiable business performance improvements for strategic systems. The objectives themselves should if possible be measurable which will help later in identifying whether the benefits have been achieved. For each objective, critical success factors (CSFs) can be derived – i.e. those things which must be right if the objective is to be achieved. These can be consolidated and be used to derive the project objectives and in the process establish the correct set of projects required. Each CSF should be translated into objectives for one or more of the projects, in

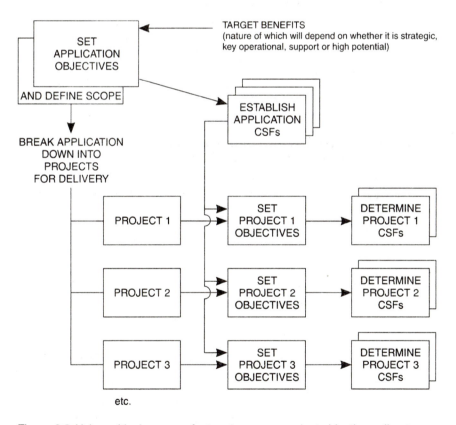

Figure 6.3 Using critical success factors to ensure project objectives align to application objectives

terms of the deliverables and constraints for each project. Then each project should be assessed in terms of the CSFs for meeting each of its objectives, so that once more 'what has to go right' in each project is known. Overall this provides through the cascade of objectives and CSFs a clear set of linkages back from each project to the original target objectives for the system. Even for a relatively small application, involving only one project this discipline is very worthwhile in order to avoid omitting some key aspect of the development process which will result in failure.

For a large, complex application this is bound to be an iterative process, since, as the objectives get broken down further, issues will arise that need clarification as to what the benefits are and how they can be achieved. It may well lead to the need to reconfigure some of the projects, to split some down further to make them manageable or even to the recognition that other projects are needed if the application is to succeed. By carrying out this process at the start of a major application development a number of benefits result.

(a) Throughout the development all those involved will have a clearer understanding of how their actions contribute to the overall success of the system. This should lead to better commitment of the various members of the teams to the overall objectives, rather than a limited focus on their project. As large developments rarely proceed according to plan, issues will undoubtedly arise about which a consensus is more likely to be achieved if these interdependencies are understood. Otherwise team members are likely to take a parochial view, based on ensuring that their part does not fail without considering the overall implications for the development.

(b) Once the CSFs are known, it is easier to identify who needs to be involved in the projects, in order that the CSFs can be addressed successfully. Often, as problems arise, new members are co-opted into the teams, but equally often, it is too late for them to address the issues which gave rise to the problems. If particular individuals are essential to deal with the factors which will affect the success or failure of the system, it is best that they become involved very early in the process rather than being coerced into co-operation when things are already going wrong. The process may also help identify both the nature of the projects involved and also the best people to lead those projects. Having the appropriate project managers as well as the right application manager (a subject which will be returned to) in themselves can be CSFs for the development.

(c) As will be described later, if the risks of an IS/IT investment are to be accurately assessed and then effectively dealt with, it is best done with a full understanding not only of the intended benefits but also with regard to the success factors. Risk analysis is essentially about understanding the factors which will lead to failure.

In the next section a framework for managing application developments is explained and the relationship between business and IT development projects is considered. But it is worth saying that many developments have the hallmark of failure stamped on them before they have barely begun, because the basic steps suggested above for 'initiating' the development have been ignored or glossed over. No methodology, however good, can hope to correct basic errors of judgement or misunderstandings made at the start of the process. They are at best difficult, expensive and time consuming to correct later, even if that is possible without substantially reducing the benefits that could have been achieved.

Box 6.2 demonstrates an example of benefits, objectives and CSFs for a large application development and the related projects.

A BASIC SYSTEMS DEVELOPMENT FRAMEWORK

One of the problems with information systems' developments is their intangibility. The product is eventually visible to some extent in terms of information on computer screens or printed documents. But that is only the tip of the iceberg and during the process of developing the system little if anything can actually be seen. Many systems cost millions of pounds – even tens of millions – and unlike other major construction such as a building or a bridge, there will be little visible to the potential user until it is finished. It is perhaps more like the construction of an aircraft, which is built in many parts, often in many places and then assembled and tested. The weakness in the analogy is that all of us know what an aircraft looks like, whereas few of us can visualise an information system! At best it

---

Box 6.2   The structure of a large application development

INTRODUCTION

The system required was a comprehensive order management system for an export agency in Scandinavia who market and distribute paper products on behalf of a consortium of paper mills. The main markets are in western Europe.

Application objectives

1 To reduce the cost of handling orders in sales offices, at the centre and in the mills*.
2 To improve the speed of order transmission and confirmation of delivery details to the customer.
3 To be able to answer customer queries regarding orders and improve the perceived service levels.
4 To reduce stock holdings at the mills and in the countries, without reduction in customer service*.
5 To avoid losing customers to more local suppliers due to poor service*.
6 To provide comprehensive sales order history by product and customer to assist in sales forecasting.

(* Specific figures and financial estimates of the benefits were made for these objectives in terms of cost reductions, and lost business prevented, etc.)

At the same time a new invoicing and accounts receivable system was being implemented to improve the collection of cash from customers, and this would rely on the order management system for order data.

Application critical success factors (sample)

- Provision of reliable and cost-effective computer links from sales offices to the centre and the mills to enable ordering from sales office to centre and/or direct to the mill.
- Dealing with the different types of product in the most cost-effective way:
  - commodity products (which any mill can make);
  - speciality products (which are made by only one mill).
- Accuracy of data capture of orders in sales offices.
- Availability of up-to-date stock data at point of order taking.
- Measuring improvements or otherwise in service times.
- Effectiveness of interfaces to new invoicing and accounts receivable system.
- Links to product and customer data bases and improving the quality of data they hold.
- Quality of exception reporting to highlight problems regarding customer orders, the reasons and recording action taken.

The application development was then subdivided into a number of projects

1 Order processing
2 Order tracking
3 Order history
4 Rationalisation of product code structure and data quality audit
5 Network development
6 Customer information 'Pack'

Looking at just two of these as examples

1 Order processing
(a) *Objectives*
  - To provide efficient capture and verification of customer requirements in the sales office.
  - To confirm order delivery details to customer within twenty-four hours.
  - To verify customer credit situation and approve order before delivery confirmation.
  - To determine reasons for lost orders (e.g. price, delivery, etc.).
(b) *Example CSFs*
  - Accurate stock data both in country and in mills.
  - Availability of production schedules in the mills.
  - Access to customer data base for credit approval.
  - Access to transportation availability and schedules.
  - Ability to establish new customer credit rating and discount terms quickly.
  - Up-to-date currency conversion data for costing delivery etc.

2 Network development
(a) *Objectives*
  - To provide a cost-effective, reliable set of network connections from all sales offices and all mills via the head office in Scandinavia.
  - To ensure response times will be satisfactory for the on-line order capture and verification.
(b) *Example CSFs*
  - Knowledge of data network services offered in all countries and their cost structures (to select the most effective mix).
  - Interfacing the in-house head office/mill network to the network services selected.
  - Accuracy of forecasts of order and associated transaction volumes to determine network utilisation and hence operating costs of options.

consists of a few inert boxes, some flashing lights and people trying to make sense of the gadgetry and images!

This preamble is trying to show that information systems developments are to some extent unique. It is vital that the design of the system and the process of development are well documented and well understood by all involved, since omissions or errors in communication may not be spotted until very late in the process, if at all. During the 1970s it became clear that although each information system is different, the process of designing and delivering a good system should be repeatable through good techniques and methods and the adoption of standard ways of doing and describing things. This need was more important as organisations were becoming dependent on their systems and could not afford them to fail – i.e. they were becoming 'key operational'. To meet this need '**methodologies**' were developed which blended structured analysis, design and programming techniques with quality management, project planning and control methods. These methodologies take into account the 'system's life cycle', i.e. not just the development phase, so that a system developed through such a methodology should be maintainable and able to be changed and enhanced as needed throughout its useful business life. Statistics show the life of most systems, especially core operational ones, is often much longer than planned for (often ten to 15 years, rather than the five to ten planned). Other statistics show that often much more money is spent changing the system once it is operational than was spent developing it. Whilst the cost of development must be managed the system must be designed, constructed and documented such that the costs of change and maintenance over an extended period are minimised. Again it is beyond the scope of this book to deal with the different types of methodologies in any detail, nor to describe in depth any of the techniques and methods which are commonly used. However business managers need to appreciate the main aspects of the process of developing systems to enable them to contribute effectively to the delivery of a beneficial system.

Figure 6.4 outlines the main stages involved in the application development process. It demonstrates that whilst there is obviously considerable work ('effort') required from IT specialists throughout the process, there is just as much business effort required in total during the development process. The diagram also separates activities which relate to the overall application (which are shaded) and where this may be sub-divided into specific projects. In this case it suggests that perhaps six separate projects were needed to be carried out and then the products of those projects brought together to produce the final business application. The purposes and products of each of the major stages in the development process are described in outline below. Then key aspects of the two halves of the model – 'above the line' (IT effort) and the often neglected 'below the line' (business effort) will be considered. The model will be described in general terms first and then in terms of how it may vary in the different segments of the application portfolio to provide the best approach.

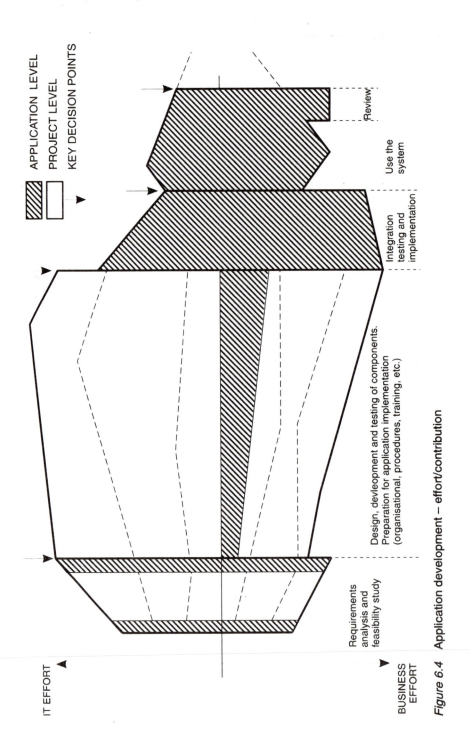

APPLICATION LEVEL
PROJECT LEVEL
KEY DECISION POINTS

IT EFFORT

BUSINESS EFFORT

Requirements analysis and feasibility study

Design, devleopment and testing of components.
Preparation for application implementation
(organisational, procedures, training, etc.)

Integration testing and implementation

Use the system

Review

Figure 6.4 **Application development – effort/contribution**

Requirements analysis and feasibility study

Given that a required application has been defined in the application portfolio the first stage is to define the objectives, target benefits and scope of the system as described earlier and shown in Box 6.2. This requires effort from both business and IT people to jointly agree what the application is intending to achieve. Not only do the outline requirements have to be determined but also any constraints which have to be taken into account must be understood. The objectives and target benefits must be analysed to define the business requirements which the system must satisfy. These should be classified or ranked into absolute **needs** which the system must meet or it is not worth proceeding, and **wants** which if met would be beneficial but are not critical.

Since these requirements have to be described then one or more projects should be undertaken to determine the feasibility of and consequent costs and timescales for satisfying the requirements. The purpose of the feasibility analysis is to determine which options, if any, are most appropriate to satisfy the requirements and normally to produce a justification for the investment. That justification may be a strict financial appraisal or a more general argument to justify expenditure depending on the expected contribution, defined by its position in the portfolio. It should always be a business responsibility to describe the overall case for the investment. Whilst the IT specialists have a considerable input to the process in terms of options and estimated costs, it is the business managers who have to believe in the benefits and ensure their delivery in due course.

Design, development and testing of components

This is potentially a very large and expensive component of the development process and for particularly large applications should be broken down into at least two stages – normally with a major review of the development plan and costs after the design of the system is complete. For other applications, however, it is more effective and certainly quicker to develop and even test some components whilst others are still being designed.

Once the feasibility of application is agreed and the investment approved, the application development should be broken down into appropriate projects as described earlier, each with defined deliverables and time and cost targets. Obviously how those projects are progressing towards the overall application delivery needs to be monitored and the plan will inevitably change as some components get ahead or fall behind schedule. Equally the costs as estimated during the feasibility study are unlikely to be very accurate and some revisions may be necessary. This may lead to reappraisal of the investment if the costs increase beyond acceptable latitudes. Normally a feasibility study would expect to estimate development costs within ±20 per cent, except for unusual or risky projects, but until the system is designed and its operational parameters are known better the operating costs of the system will be less certain. During this phase those estimates should clarify, as should the benefit details, and should either change significantly from the expectations of the feasibility study the investment should be reappraised. In reality this is rarely done until too late, i.e. the money has been spent.

The key aspects of this and the other stages in terms of IT and business activities are described later.

Integration testing and implementation

Once all projects have delivered and tested their individual components, e.g. hardware is installed, user procedures and training is complete, the software is tested, the whole application must be tested to ensure it works. This needs careful planning and design to ensure that the testing is both comprehensive and simulates the real environment effectively. It is often when problems are discovered and changes are identified, which have to be resolved before implementation. Very tight change control procedures are needed to ensure that making one correction does not cause further problems. It is a complex task which requires attention to detail by both IT and business members of the team. Often under time pressure that discipline is lost and the hope that 'it will be alright on the night' takes over. Problems which are ignored or covered up during this phase can return with greater severity once the system is installed.

Once the application has been demonstrated by testing to meet the requirement it should be formally signed off as acceptable to the business. Then it can be implemented and the necessary business changes made to obtain the benefits that were intended. There are a variety of ways of carrying out an implementation – a 'big-bang' change over from the old to new systems through to parallel-running two systems for a period of time – and the approach chosen will depend mainly on the risks to the business of the system failing. Once the system is fully implemented and the old ways of working have been stopped, the development process has been concluded.

Using the system

Few systems are free of problems as soon as they are implemented, and careful monitoring of its performance in both IT and business aspects of its operation is needed for a few months. During that time each problem encountered must be recorded and corrected if it stops the benefits being achieved. Strict control of the resulting changes is needed so that further problems are not caused. Once the system is installed it often becomes apparent how the system could be improved either to reduce costs of operation or deliver further benefits. Also business requirements may have changed since the system was designed some months or even years before, and this may require further changes to be made. The needs for both these types of improvements should be recorded but until the system is functioning satisfactorily according to the original specification, it is very risky to make significant changes. These should be considered in the review stage below.

Review

This is generally the most neglected stage of the process, either because it seems unnecessary if the system is working or because if there have been significant problems no one wants them exposed! However, the organisations that seem to succeed best with IS investments are those who systematically review the main developments after implementation. Most organisations have relatively rigorous prc-investment appraisal techniques in order to decide whether to proceed. Without an equally rigorous post-implementation review of what was or was not achieved, nothing can be learned about whether investments in IS/IT are actually worthwhile. Given that statistics quoted earlier suggest that '70 per cent of all IS/IT fail to deliver the benefits expected' we clearly have much to learn.

The review has three main purposes:

(a) To learn from the particular development in order that other developments can have more chance of success. This will involve an assessment of what was done and how to enable improvements to the development processes to be made.
(b) To evaluate whether the particular investment has delivered the expected benefits and if not, why not, and thence a set of actions can be established to correct the situation where this is possible.
(c) To determine what changes need to or can be made to the system to deliver further benefits and to develop a plan for delivering these benefits. There is a body of evidence that suggests 'second-order benefits', i.e. those that can only be understood once the system is implemented, are often far greater and require less investment than the 'first-order benefits' that justified the first development. Without a constructive review process these will not be identified.

When such a review should take place is difficult to prescribe, but normally three to six months after full implementation is sensible and it is probably worth repeating the process once a year thereafter to ensure the benefits have not decayed or depreciated. In all cases the review should not be seen as a 'witch hunt' to allocate blame for problems – that approach produces little of value to the organisation.

The above outline was intended to describe the main purposes of the major stages in the process, which will apply to all IS/IT developments. Obviously for small developments the timescale is considerably compressed but the main tasks should not change. For very large developments lasting years, managing the range of activities and resources involved is a complex task which must be carried out in a well-understood clearly defined framework. The next sections consider specific aspects of the 'above and below' the line processes (as in Figure 6.4) which are key to the successful management of IS/IT developments. For more detailed understanding of all that is involved, books on system development and/or the reference material for any well-known 'systems development methodology' should be used. They provide highly structured frameworks and detailed checklists for all the deliverables involved. What is covered here is intended to complement those methodologies.

In the last part of the chapter an approach to risk analysis is considered which enables business and IT staff to understand how and why a particular development may fail and how to deal with those risks.

MODEL FOR THE TECHNICAL ASPECTS OF THE SYSTEMS DEVELOPMENT PROCESS

The framework in Figure 6.4 suggests a linear or sequential set of stages in a process which would be converted into a series of detailed steps and controls in any methodology. It is actually easier to understand in terms of a 'V' diagram as shown in Figure 6.5. This framework is considered first in the context of key operational systems and assumes that the system will for the large part be designed and built to satisfy a unique set of business needs. Variations on a theme in the context of the applications portfolio are considered below.

Over the last twenty years considerable effort has gone into improving the efficiency and effectiveness of the technical processes involved in boxes 3 to 5 in Figure 6.5. Much progress has been made in providing CASE (Computer-Assisted System Engineering) tools to ensure the reliability **and** speed up these stages. Whilst those tools also help identify logical flaws in a user specification produced from Box 2 they cannot redress any failures to understand the business or its needs in that specification. In any development it is worth spending as much time as necessary getting the products of boxes 1 and 2 correct before moving forward. Whilst IT specialists can facilitate that process to produce a specification which they can satisfy, it is incumbent upon the business to define and communicate the requirements accurately. Hence in this section the focus is on ways of ensuring those stages are carried out effectively. Many major developments are doomed to fail at a very early stage, yet with a moderate investment of time and money at this stage, the waste of very large sums of money can be avoided.

TOOLS TECHNIQUES AND METHODS FOR NEEDS AND REQUIREMENTS ANALYSIS

Given that the overall purpose of an IS/IT development is to improve business performance in one or more aspects, the first stage is to determine what needs to be done and what needs to change in order to do it. If that merely means, for instance, printing invoices faster to improve the speed of customer payments, then the focus of the requirements is clearly on the processes that effect preparation of data for and then printing the invoices. Most systems are not this simple,

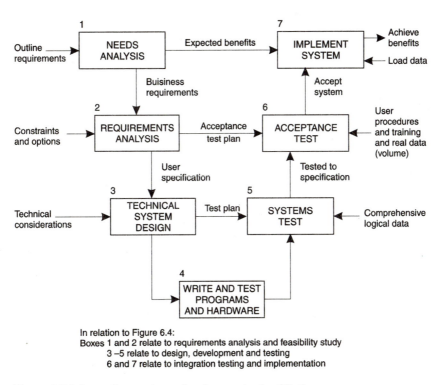

In relation to Figure 6.4:
Boxes 1 and 2 relate to requirements analysis and feasibility study
3 –5 relate to design, development and testing
6 and 7 relate to integration testing and implementation

Figure 6.5 Information systems development – the 'V' diagram

Source: This figure is adapted from work by Andy Bytheway and Rob Lamabert at the Cranfield School of Management

however. In a building society a system was installed in the branches to enable mortgage applications to be processed in the branch rather than by sending paperwork to head office for processing. Savings in staff were expected at head office, based on carrying out the work in the branches. In this case although the system essentially only affected branch staff, the benefits accrued elsewhere and the impact on head office activities had to be included in the examination of the system's feasibility.

To understand the requirements and implications of a system, two complementary approaches are needed. One set of tools and techniques is needed to examine the business and what it does from a logical point of view to define the most effective way of carrying out the business activities – this can be considered the 'hard' or rational approach. However, organisations are made up of people and behaviours which are not always purely rational and systems which treat people as an extension of the computer rarely work well. What is needed is to balance the hard logical approach with a 'soft' or organic approach which allows people to define how the system should work to enable them as individuals or as an organisational group to work effectively. This more 'holistic' approach to information systems which incorporates the role of the people in the system has been developed into a 'soft systems methodology' based on the work of Checkland (1981) and others. The best information systems are those which integrate the computer-based aspects of the system with the 'human activity systems' of the organisation. This aspect of IS is becoming more critical as technology pervades more and more aspects of working in organisations. Establishing a way of working which brings the knowledge and creative skills of the people who will be involved with the new system, to define **how** to achieve what is intended, should enable the following:

(a) buy-in by the people involved in the new system;
(b) a better system in terms of its fit with other aspects of the working environment;
(c) a better understanding of factors which will affect the success or failure of the development. This may enable the application scope or development process to be modified to focus on areas where benefits are more readily achievable;
(d) either a simpler system because changes elsewhere can simplify the problem or a more creative system which enables people to derive greater value from it;
(e) a more viable implementation plan for the system. It is often by forcing the business to think about the 'acceptance testing' criteria they would place on the system that possible flaws in systems design or how it can be introduced are uncovered.

Any information systems development will cause changes in what people do and how they do it. The soft systems approach enables a full understanding of why change will be of benefit, hence what the system does and how it does it can be aligned more closely to achieving those beneficial changes – both in business and organisational terms.

Returning to the more logical or rational approaches to understanding and analysing the business requirements, given that a number of people with different knowledge of the business need to input that knowledge and others need to understand it, a simple maxim applies – a picture is worth a thousand words. Every methodology incorporates some form of the structured analytical and descriptive techniques to enable people's knowledge to be depicted and describe what the system should do. In essence they enable the area of the business involved to be described in information terms so that the new system can be specified in terms that both user and IT specialist can understand. The techniques of data flow analysis and data entity analysis were introduced earlier (in Chapter 4) as high-level tools to be used in formulating strategy. Here they are used to define accurately how the system should logically work in order to achieve the business improvements. Often it is necessary to describe the existing way of working, using the same tools, before analysing how it can be changed. Figure 6.6 depicts the three key aspects of a system that have to be inter-related.

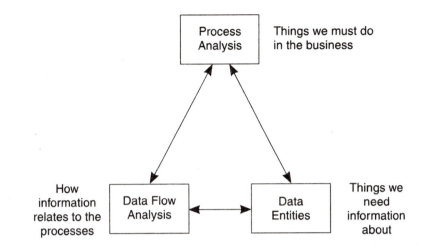

Figure 6.6 Core information systems relationships – modelling systems requirements

Analysis of the data entities produces an entity model which depicts how they are related for business purposes, as shown in the simple example in Figure 6.7. These relationships are normally very enduring in spite of changes in how activities are carried out and hence can be used to build data bases which are stable over the long-term.

An entity model is not dynamic, nor does it tell anything about how things are done. For instance in Figure 6.7 whether the customers pay by cash, cheque, have credit or pay by direct debit is not known – only that a customer payment must relate to an invoice which in turn contains invoice lines relating to products purchased by that customer. Obviously this is a trivial example but if the many types and elements of business information and their inter-relationships are to be fully understood a 'model' of the business in information terms is needed. Earlier in the book it was argued that many organisations' information resource is fragmented, unstructured and even incoherent. This normally results from a lack of effort spent deriving and using a basic model of information relationships when constructing the various processing and reporting systems. The second type of modelling that helps in defining and analysing requirements is the **data flow model** that combines the data entities with the business processes or activities that produce and use them. The first stage in the process is to analyse or 'decompose' the processes into the detailed components. For instance, the overall process may be to 'recruit new staff' which might consist of the following detailed activities.

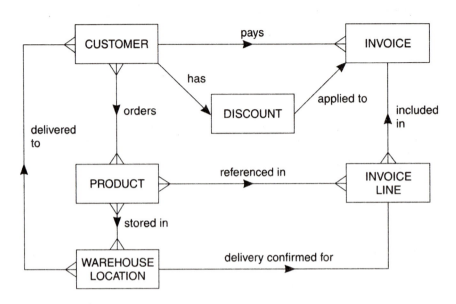

The 'crow's feet' ———< show that there are many of the entity
(e.g. a customer orders many products and a product is ordered by many customers)

Figure 6.7 An entity model

Recruit new staff: generate job description
                      agree salary range and grade
                      place advertisements
                      vet applications
                      interview candidates
                      take up references
                      offer job
                      reject other candidates etc.

These subprocesses can then each be described in some detail as to what is done, what information is input to the process and where it comes from, and finally what information is output from the process and where it goes to. An example of a data flow diagram is shown in Figure 6.8. (In Figure 6.8 a particular notation or set of symbols is used for the elements of the diagram. This varies in different methods, but all of them represent similar elements.)

Referring to Figure 6.8 the basic activities involved in a simple order-taking process are described. It is a logical representation, not a physical one. For instance whether the customer phones the order, sends a purchase order by post, faxes it or sends it direct from a computer via EDI is not included. The diagram

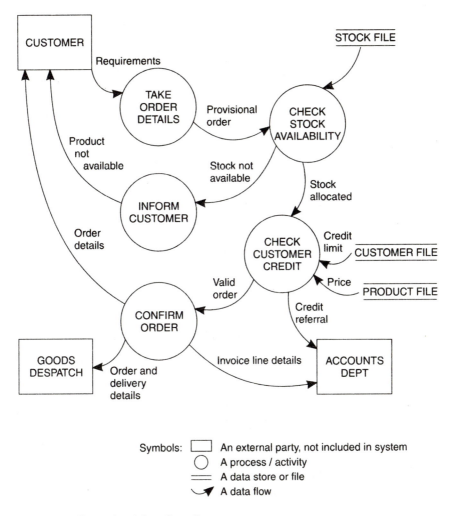

Figure 6.8 Example of data flow diagram

reflects either (a) what happens now or (b) what we want to happen. For instance, it might be decided that we wish to carry out the credit check before allocating stock to the order for some reason. The model can be used to describe in logical terms the processes and information relationships the system must address. Obviously most data flow models are very extensive and can become complex and most of the techniques have 'layering' features whereby processes are gradually broken down in more detail, but the cross-referencing is maintained. Each of the circular process symbols in Figure 6.8 may need to be broken down further for clarity of understanding. CASE tools, as mentioned above, can help in the drawing of such diagrams, checking them and keeping the relationships and cross-references explicit.

The result of such analysis is a specification of the logic a system must achieve – **what** it must do. By adding details such as volumes, time constraints, etc., the system's designer can determine **how** those processes etc. can be improved through technology. This description or model of the required information system is not only the basis for the technical design but will also drive a number of other activities in the overall development process.

(a) The testing and acceptance criteria for the system once it has been 'technically' proved against the specification. The model can be used to define what needs to be tested and can be converted into a logical testing plan and an implementation plan in the business. This will involve proving processes, checking the data flows are correct, verifying the data quality and the passing of information to outside parties and other systems. The model should ensure that no aspect of the system is left untested.

(b) The detailed analysis of the business improvements and benefits the system should provide will be understood in more detail. What they are and where they occur and what needs to be done to ensure they are delivered is more explicitly defined. This is a key input to the 'benefits management' process described later.

(c) The model identifies where changes to business processes and activities are needed to enable the new system to work effectively. This will enable user management to define activities which are needed to make those changes in terms of procedures, tasks, people's job roles and even customer/supplier relationships and organisation structures and relationships. These will need to be addressed in parallel with the IT development process. These changes become the 'business development' projects described earlier.

Overall the determination of the system requirements is the most critical stage in the process. The modelling and analysis techniques outlined above enable that to be carried out accurately and comprehensively **and** ensure effective communication between the parties involved in the development. This early understanding of what is involved and the agreement of what needs to be done is vital to the success of any IS/IT project.

The 'V' diagram model described has been developed over time to enable key operational systems to be delivered successfully, on the assumption that needs can be explicitly defined **and** that the software will be designed and built to meet those explicit needs. This is not always the case and the model needs to be modified to allow for both these issues which occur to different degrees with respect to applications of the four quadrants of the application portfolio.

VARIATIONS ON A THEME

The two issues raised above can be restated in terms of the following.

(a) **Uncertainty of needs and benefits** which is especially true in the high potential and strategic segments of the portfolio. Here the requirement is to simulate or prototype the system, or parts of it, to clarify what is needed and what is of real benefit before finalising the specification. This may also apply to some aspects of a key operational or support system though this is less likely, given these are normally well-known business activities. To achieve this the basic 'V' diagram needs to be adapted as shown in Figure 6.9 to include the prototyping stage to determine the details of what needs to be done.

In Figure 6.9 much is the same as before (as in Figure 6.5) except that the requirements analysis box has been exploded into three steps. The purpose is so that uncertain business requirements can be clarified or how they can be met can be simulated. It may be that the whole system (a high potential application) is to be prototyped via a small, 'string and glue' version or one aspect of the system needs evaluating in this way before requirements or feasibility can be determined. The prototype may be aimed at understanding the costs involved and/or how to get the benefits and/or to understand how potential users will react to the system. Thomson Holidays piloted in travel agencies a minimal prototype version of their TOPS system to evaluate all of these. A major building society prototyped a sales support system in a number of branches in order to do two things: (i) determine out of a list of more than eighty potential benefits which were most feasible to achieve; and (ii) to evaluate a software package against those potential benefits and its usability by staff. They eventually built their own system to satisfy those aspects of the system which could give them a competitive advantage – something a software package, available to all societies, could not do.

The prototyping process may be iterative and may mean that basic needs have to be revised. Only when requirements to be met can be agreed and a feasible approach determined should the development proceed. If, of course, this cannot be done the development should be stopped. This emphasises the point that prototyping is used to evaluate in a practical way what is to be done and how, and hence success must not be assumed. Management must be willing to write-off the cost of the prototype before starting. This is obviously true in the case of failure but it is also true if the prototype succeeds! The prototype is not the real system, it is a 'mock-up' which would not be suitable for full-scale operation. However, there is a great temptation amongst managers when they see a working prototype to want the same thing on a larger scale – immediately! It may well be the prototype has continuing value for training and simulation of the intended operational system, but the final system must be far more robust and supportable than any 'string and glue' prototype can be.

(b) **Purchase of application software packages** which should normally be the preferred option for support systems and is usually a possible option for key operational systems. Application software packages such as payroll and general accounting systems have been available for some twenty years, but

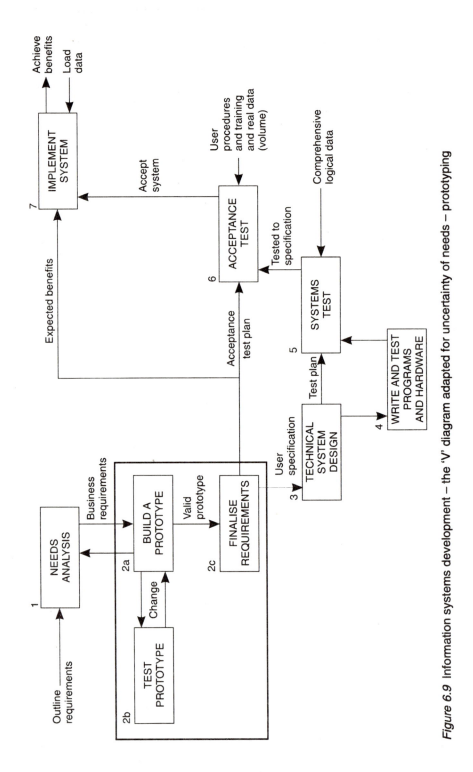

Figure 6.9 Information systems development – the 'V' diagram adapted for uncertainty of needs – prototyping

over the last ten years or so packaged software has been developed to meet a wide range of business activities. There is now also a wide choice available from a variety of software companies for most types of package. In general the functionality, quality and flexibility has improved significantly and some suppliers offer a comprehensive suite of packages which integrate with each other to satisfy many of the more standard needs of an organisation. At the same time 'packages' have been sold to business users and senior management as a panacea, low-cost solution to all the needs! The systems development process has been simplified in some managements' minds to 'buy a package, implement it and reap the benefits' and many have been greatly disappointed when this approach has been tried.

In practice the purchase of a software package can replace the most expensive, time-consuming and difficult part of the development process – technical design, construction and testing. However, to get the full benefits from purchased software most of the stages of the development process still need to be undertaken as shown in Figure 6.10.

The first two stages need to be carried out as before, except that the software available to meet the needs should be evaluated in both user and technical support aspects during the requirements analysis. A clear understanding of the constraints that the software must satisfy is needed against which to evaluate the packages. For instance 'it must run on an IBM-type PC' or 'it must be able to interface with our MRP II system' or 'it must be able to deal our customer account numbering structure' or 'it must be able to handle volume, value and speciality discounts', etc. These must be established as part of the requirements so that the suppliers can adequately prove that these fundamental needs can be met. Other apparent prerequisites may also need to be questioned. When one company was buying a general accounting package it stated that the package must be able to deal with 30,000 general account codes, as per the existing in-house built system. It was found that no package could cope efficiently with more than 10,000. Apparently no other major user of the package had a problem with this! and so the company decided to rationalise its account coding structure which had grown like Topsy to satisfy each and every department managers' whims. The saving through this rationalisation was well over £100,000 per annum in the costs of operating the general ledger without any loss of functionality.

This example raises an important general point regarding the purchase of software packages. No package will do exactly what is needed in the ideal way for any organisation.

The business has to decide amongst three options, all of which may be relevant to any one development:

(a) What are essential functions that must be met in a certain way – often because of other systems with which it must integrate?
(b) Where is the business willing to change what it does or how it does it, to the way the package works?

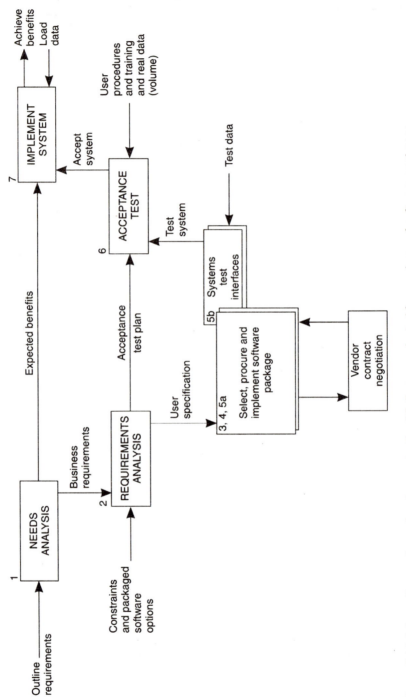

Figure 6.10 Information systems development – the 'V' diagram adapted for purchase of software packages

(c) Whether it is feasible and worthwhile to develop additional software to overcome the limitations of the package.

This assessment needs considerable thought during the requirements analysis phase before the specification is finalised. Neglect of these issues can result in many surprises and disappointments when it is implemented and also, very often, significant unexpected costs. The most dangerous option is to ask the supplier to amend the core software product to make it fit your organisation's unique needs (or even worse modify it yourself!). As later releases of the package become available there is likely to be a considerable cost in tailoring it each time. Or the improvements available will have to be forgone and the increasingly obsolete version kept.

In procuring the software, contracts for all aspects of the vendor's services will need to be put in place. Once the core package is implemented the interfaces must be tested and the users must prove they can operate the system satisfactorily as with any new system. These stages may be less fraught, due to the supplier's experience, than with custom-built software but they still need to be done. Again this is often overlooked on the assumption that the software must work. It is always vital when bringing in a software package to visit one or more other user of the same package to establish how well it works and learn from their experience of implementation about the potential problems and also how well the vendor's services match the claims in the glossy brochure. If the company intends to buy many software packages it is advisable to set up a standard check-list-based selection procedure against which users and technical staff must test and validate the software and supplier.

The overview given above of the 'technical' process of developing information systems is not intended to be comprehensive or detailed. It is intended to give the business manager an overview of what is involved such that he or she can contribute effectively to what is a complex and often difficult process. If the reader wishes to understand it fully, the books referenced at the end of this chapter (and many others) will satisfy that need.

What many of the books fail to address is one particular aspect of the 'below the line' activities: in Figure 6.4 that resides firmly in the area of business responsibility. An approach to this which complements all that has been said above is the subject of the next section.

BENEFIT MANAGEMENT

In each of the versions of the 'V' diagram in the last section the top line stays very much the same, i.e. analyse the needs in the outline requirements in terms of expected business benefits and then, once the system is implemented, achieve the benefits. This part of the process can be called 'benefit management', which is a set of tasks or even a specific project running in parallel with the IT development. Benefit management projects are 'business development' projects in the context of the project portfolio (Figure 6.2) and the responsibility for ensuring benefits are delivered from the investment lies in the business with the 'application manager'.

Considerable experience and thought has gone into devising methodologies which enable an IT development to be delivered with a better than even chance of working – but little intellectual or practical effort has been applied to establish management processes or techniques for maximising the benefits delivered by that working system. Only recently has any research been done into how benefits can be actively managed to fruition and one would expect coherent business-based approaches to be developed during the next few years. One reason for the current lack of knowledge is that very few organisations carry out an effective post-implementation review of whether or not expected benefits were delivered. If there were a substantial base of project reviews from which the reasons for success or failure in benefit delivery could be understood, it would be possible to produce at least checklists to assist managers in achieving the benefits.

One approach which has been developed in the National Health Service[1] enables the benefits of new hospital management systems to be identified and delivered. The approach includes some principles and high-level steps which apply to most systems developments in most organisations. Whilst the nature of the benefits may be different in each situation the overall process of managing for them can be very similar. An adapted version of the process is outlined in Figure 6.11 where it is aligned as necessary to the key stages in the IT development. Each stage is considered in overview from the viewpoint of the business management roles and responsibilities.

1. Benefits identification

This is the very first stage of assessing the reasons for embarking on the application development. Based on the outcome of the strategic planning processes described in earlier chapters, the overall need for a new or improved system is identified. The nature of the mix of target benefits will depend on whether the system is strategic, key operational or support, as described earlier. If the nature of the benefits and/or how to obtain them is unclear then the system should be put through the R&D process implied by the high potential segment until they are known. Hence the whole benefit management process does not really apply to the high potential segment, except that it is a way that the benefits can be identified.

Identifying the target benefits implies an iterative process of discussing what the system objectives are and the business performance improvements that it should deliver. In the National Health Service a checklist of potential benefits that might be available has been developed to assist this assessment. This allows managers to consider a wider range of potential improvements that a system might deliver rather than starting each time from a blank sheet and creating a list from scratch.

The list of benefits required must be agreed by the managers whose activities

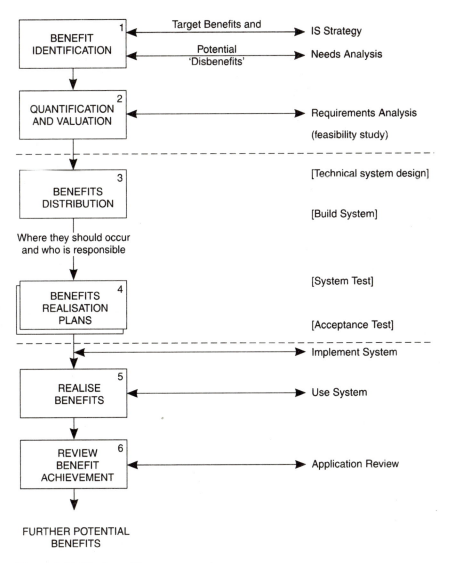

Figure 6.11 The benefit management process

are affected by the system. At this point the critical success factors for the application can be assessed and the appropriate projects set up to evaluate the feasibility of obtaining those benefits. One or more of those subprojects would be stage 2 of this process as described below. At the same time potential 'disbenefits' of the system should be considered, i.e. what adverse impacts on the business or organisation could it have? These may be deemed unacceptable and hence the objectives or scope of the system revised or actions should be put in hand to ensure those disbenefits are avoided. No one wants nasty surprises at the end of the implementation. So, as far as it is possible, these should be anticipated at the start of the development process.

2. Benefits quantification and valuation

All business performance improvements are measurable and hence so are all the benefits delivered by information system. Some can be measured directly in relation to the system, e.g. staff headcount reductions due to automation, decrease in product rejects due to quality control data, reduction in stock levels through a warehouse control system. Many of these can also be converted easily into financial values and where this can be done it should be, to enable an economic appraisal to be made. In other cases the measurement may be less direct. Better timing and control of deliveries should lead to more satisfied customers, which in turn may lead to increased sales or at least avoiding lost sales due to delivery problems. The level of customer satisfaction will need to be measured and some estimate made of the business benefits of improved delivery. These quantified benefits may not however, be suitable to undergo rigorous discounted cash flow calculations.

In essence every target benefit should be expressed in terms that can, in due course, be measured even if the measure will be subjective, e.g. customer or staff opinion. These measurable improvements will be reviewed in stage 6 of the process.

As an example, Frito-Lay, the snack food manufacturer decided to equip its sales/delivery force with hand-held computers and the prototype system showed that this saved about three to four hours' administrative effort each week. The sales managers were asked to decide what that time saving could deliver as a benefit. It was agreed that each sales/delivery person should be able to increase their sales by between 3 and 10 per cent per week given the increased selling time available and their different customer mixes. This became one of the target benefits to be delivered by the system and after implementation this was measured and an average of 6 per cent, over and above general market growth, was achieved.

3. Benefits distribution

The last point above also relates to this stage in the process, in terms of determining where in the business the benefits should occur and hence who in the organisation should be responsible for their delivery. This is often overlooked in bringing in new systems, but 'ownership' of the benefits and clear allocation of responsibility for delivery is vital to success. This is easy to identify if the system is essentially within one function of the business. But it is more difficult when the system crosses functions and especially when reorganisation and rationalisation of tasks across functions is essential to the delivery of benefits. Responsibility may have to be shared, but then this must be made explicit.

In all cases it is essential that a manager is made accountable for the delivery of each of the intended benefits and then, in conjunction with the application manager, he or she should put in place whatever actions are required to obtain them. The designated manager will be expected to measure the relevant business performance change and explain the results in the review stage.

4. Benefits realisation planning

The application manager should establish plans with each of the responsible managers for the delivery of each of the benefits. Some benefits will accrue immediately the system is implemented, others may be consequent on other tasks to be carried out after the system is installed. But just as an acceptance test plan should be prepared in advance of the system delivery, so should a realisation plan for each of the benefits defining what will be done and when. Often, of course, the benefits are interdependent. The application manager needs to reconcile each of the individual plans to ensure that the full range of benefits are achieved at the earliest opportunity and in the most effective manner. This reconciliation may take several iterations of planning to find the ideal overall plan of action which each manager involved can support and resource.

5. Benefits realisation

Some of the activities in the benefit realisation plans will have to be carried out before the system is implemented, especially where staff have to be trained to use the system. All of these types of activities should be completed ready for when the system is implemented, following satisfactory acceptance testing. It is difficult to be more explicit than saying that the benefit realisation plans should now be carried out in the timescale intended. But like any plans progress must be monitored and inevitably things do not always go according to plan! It is the application manager's role to monitor and control the implementation of the plans and where things go wrong to agree revised plans with the responsible managers, to overcome the problems, so that the majority of benefits are still achieved, even if not in the ideal way. Any problems which do occur should be analysed and actions agreed documented to enable the review process to be objective, comprehensive and constructive.

6. Benefits review

There are three main objectives to this stage in the process:

(a) To determine whether or not the benefits of the development have been achieved and if not, why not, and whether any further action can be taken to achieve them.

(b) To determine whether, now that the implementation is complete, there are any further benefits possible and to establish how they might be achieved by specific actions or by including those benefits as targets for other developments. It is often impossible to identify all the benefits of a system in advance. Further benefits often become apparent only when the system has been running for some time and the associated business changes have been made. If, as has been suggested earlier, more benefits are actually identifiable after the event than before it, if there is no review process then these will never be identified.

(c) To enable lessons to be learned for other developments, both in terms of the process of benefits management and in the specific issues associated with obtaining certain types of benefit.

It is worth repeating that any post-implementation review should not become a 'witch hunt', it must be an objective process with future improvements in mind, not a way of placing blame for past failures. If it is seen as a negative process, honest appraisal and a constructive critique of what has happened become impossible and the whole process falls into disrepute or is not carried out. There should be a complementary review of the IT development issues surrounding the application, again with a view to sharing knowledge and experience for the benefit of future systems. That is often in place in organisations but it tends to be held behind the closed doors of the IT department. This review is a business review aimed at maximising the benefits gained from the particular system and for all future IT investments.

In the 1970s it became clear that the activities involved in the IT aspects of IS development could be brought together into a coherent structure to improve the reliability and quality and reduce the costs of the process. Only in the late 1980s have many organisations come to realise that a similar structured framework is needed to address the other side of the investment equation – the benefits. Few organisations have any process in place that resembles in total or contains all the elements described above. Most organisations now recognise that to get 'value for money' from IT, they must actively manage the value component as well as the costs. Understanding of the full range of issues involved in achieving the benefits is incomplete. No framework is yet available that will fit the needs of all types of applications or the wide variety of benefits they can deliver or the different circumstances within which they must be achieved. Over the next few years such frameworks should materialise to help management.

RISK ASSESSMENT AND MANAGEMENT

The purpose of the final part of this chapter is to address a problem that the earlier parts of the chapter were trying to eliminate! In spite of all that can be done to bring structure and certainty to the process of information systems developments, they are often still inherently risky adventures at times. Much has been written about how to assess the risks involved, usually from a technical or IT viewpoint, but the approach described here focuses on the **risks of not achieving the benefits**. Whilst technical risks obviously affect this, there are many other risk factors, often within the power of business managers to avoid or manage. The whole point in assessing risks is to understand them such that the development scope or process can be changed to avoid them or action taken during the process to deal with them.

The risks of each development need to be assessed in order to improve the chances of success, but management need to understand the relative risks of all the developments in the portfolio in order to set sensible priorities, as mentioned in the last chapter. This means comparing the risks of strategic, key operational and support applications in a consistent way. (High potential systems are inherently very risky and the R&D approach is used to minimise the consequences of the risk in business and financial terms.) By reviewing a number of approaches to risk assessment, a synthesised approach can be produced which enables a common set of risks to be considered for every project, but whereby the potential impact of the risk is of different severity for strategic, key operational or support systems. A detailed scoring system and action checklist has been developed by the author (Ward 1993). It is beyond the scope of this chapter to explain that method in detail but the principles are important.

In considering how the benefits arise in the different segments of the application portfolio they are summarised as follows:

(a) *Strategic systems*   The benefits are the result of innovation and change in the conduct of business to gain a competitive edge. This normally requires restructuring of some business processes and/or changing the relationships with trading partners, and implies some uncertainty about the business implications of the system.

(b) *Key operational systems*   The benefits result from carrying out business processes more effectively overall, and normally result from rationalisation, integration or reorganisation of existing processes. The main objective is to avoid business disadvantages. Whilst the business issues are probably well understood, risks often arise due to the complexity of the system and its links to other existing systems.

(c) *Support systems*   The benefits mainly come from carrying out business tasks more efficiently by removing them, or by automation to reduce the cost of carrying them out. The business functions involved are normally stable and well understood and there is also a wide range of packaged software available to use. The risks arise from knowing how to implement such software effectively and so gain the available benefits.

High potential projects do not actually deliver finished, operational systems, and hence real benefits, and are dealt with as 'high risk' by treating them as R&D projects. Therefore they are not considered in more detail here. By limiting the budget for the high potential stage of any development, financial risks are minimised. The real risk is missing the opportunity available or deciding to invest heavily in a 'loser' – these are difficult to allow for in a structured risk assessment.

In considering the factors that affect the delivery of the required benefits of any IS/IT project, three are obviously key to its success.

(a) **Time**   When the business needs it.
(b) **Quality**   A system that does what it should.
(c) **Cost**   That is worth incurring.

In an ideal world all three should be achieved – a perfect system, when needed, at the optimum cost. However, being realistic, it is difficult to achieve all three on any IS/IT project. The evidence from the past is that in many IS/IT projects none of the three is achieved! That is mainly due to the risks being misunderstood and partly due to not understanding which of the three variables – time, quality, cost – was critical to the particular system's success. The criticality of each will vary in the different segments of the application portfolio. If perfection in all three is not achievable then for strategic projects **time** is often the most critical, otherwise the window of opportunity may be lost and associated business changes are infeasible or difficult: cost is less critical to overall success. That is not to say that cost should be ignored! In the other two segments: **quality** is most critical for key operational systems to avoid them failing the business, and **cost** is most critical in support systems, if economic benefits are to be maximised (see Figure 6.12).

STRATEGIC	HIGH POTENTIAL
TIME Quality Cost	(R&D PROJECTS)
Time **QUALITY** Cost	Time Quality **COST**
KEY OPERATIONAL	SUPPORT

Therefore risk factors must be considered in the context of how they affect:

	STRATEGIC	KEY OPERATIONAL	SUPPORT
TIME	***	**	*
QUALITY	**	***	**
COST	*	**	***

Figure 6.12 Balance of generic CSFs for different applications

The approach outlined here weighs the risk factors differently in the three segments, in order to accommodate the different impact they are likely to have on overall success. From the research risk categories and factors have been determined which individually or in combination have to be dealt with in order to minimise the chances of:

(a) not achieving the desired benefits;
(b) not achieving the necessary timing;
(c) using more resources than needed.

The effects of (b) and (c) will not only reduce the net benefits of the particular application but will also reduce the ability to gain the total benefits expected from all applications in the overall IS plan.

Risk categories, factors and potential impact

A search of the literature identified a number of major risk factor categories and within these a list of specific factors that can be demonstrated to reduce the likely success of IS/IT projects. There is considerable agreement on what those factors are and they are described below. The potential impact of the factors can then be considered against the key success factors for the different types of applications – strategic, key operational and support based the effect they have on the balance of the time, quality and cost parameters.

A simple impact assessment approach can be used which attempts to describe the impact if the factor is not satisfactorily addressed.

H – High risk   – the project is unlikely to succeed unless action is taken to deal with the risk before the project starts.
M – Medium risk – contingencies need to be considered in case the risk leads to project problems.
L – Low risk   – should have no effect in normal circumstances.

People issues

These relate to obtaining the appropriate commitment and involvement of senior management, ensuring the project team includes the right mix of business and technical skills, and that the communication between business users and system deliverers is effective. Weaknesses in any of these areas can cause misunderstandings at the earliest stages of projects which lead to major problems later. As can be seen from Table 6.2, each factor has a different potential impact, especially the first two. Senior management involvement in strategic projects is essential, but can lead to confusion and unnecessary interference in support projects.

Project size

It is almost self-evident that large projects are more difficult to manage than small ones, and since large projects are normally expected to deliver large benefits the consequences of failure are far more significant. Size can be best expressed as the number of total man-years' work required, but the problem is compounded by both the number of different individuals involved and the elapsed time taken – more things change over a longer time period including the project personnel. The definition of large or small projects will depend on the organisation.

Control of the project

This is a set of factors which describe how rigidly the time, quality and cost aspects of the project are to be controlled in terms of milestones, standards, methodology, budgets and change management processes.

To succeed with strategic projects requires a degree of flexibility in how things are done in order to achieve early delivery of the system, whereas for key operational systems quality should not be compromised for expediency. Support systems deliver mainly economic benefits, so managing expenditure is important, but timing of delivery is less critical – economic benefits are always available.

Complexity

Again it is obvious that the more complex the problem the more difficult it is to ensure a good solution. Complexity can arise in both the business and the technology and this is usually compounded by the number of different business functions which need the new system and the number of other systems with which it must be integrated or interfaced. As with the other categories the potential impact of complexity varies around the matrix. In the support segment achieving simplicity of systems functions will lead to low-cost solutions. In the other two, complexity will exist and must be accommodated in the timing and method of quality control.

Novelty

This concerns both the amount of business change needed to obtain the benefits and the novelty of the technical solution proposed. If both apply the risks become very high but in many cases, other than support systems, change or technical novelty are an essential ingredient if the benefits are to be obtained.

Stability of requirements

Again the more certain the future is, the easier it is to ensure the system will deliver the benefits. By careful definition of the project scope, certainty can be

Table 6.2 Risk categories and factors affecting success of IT projects

Category		Factors	Strategic	Key op.	Support
A. People issues	(i)	Degree of senior management involvement	H	M	L
	(ii)	Business knowledge in the project team	H	M	L
	(iii)	Technical skills and experience of project team	M	H	M
	(iv)	Co-ordination between business and technical staff	H	M	M
B. Size (specific figures need to be established for the organisation)	(i)	Man-years' work involved	H	H	H
	(ii)	Number of people involved	H	H	H
	(iii)	Elapsed time for the project	H	M	H
C. Project control	(i)	Use of standards and formal development methodology	M	H	M
	(ii)	Testing procedures and change control	M	H	M
	(iii)	Budgetary and expenditure control procedures	L	M	H
	(iv)	Constraints on project team re. innovation and change	H	L	L
D. Complexity of system	(i)	Business complexity of problem	M	L	H
	(ii)	Cross-functional business issues	M	H	H
	(iii)	Technical complexity of solution	H	M	H
	(iv)	Number of system interfaces	M	H	H
E. Novelty	(i)	Use of new technology (new to the organisation)	H	H	H
	(ii)	Change to business practices/processes	L	H	H
	(iii)	Change to organisation	M	M	H
F. Stability	(i)	Clarity of scope of system and its boundaries	M	H	H
	(ii)	Rate of change of business area affected by system	L	H	H

H, high risk; M, medium risk; L, low risk.

increased by tackling more stable areas and leaving others for later. However, other aspects of the business may be changing which could have a direct or indirect effect on the system. These need to be considered.

The brief overview above is intended to summarise the risk factors and categories. Detailed arguments about the rationale for each would take many more pages, as would explaining the questionnaire and the particular scoring system which can be used to operationalise it. The impact assessment is summarised in Table 6.2. It is based on the literature research, modified to map onto the matrix, by consideration of the nature of each type of application development.

This approach, which enables application development risks to be assessed at the start and again, as needed, as the development progresses, is just one of many available. It is important that every organisation has some form of risk analysis which is applied consistently across all the IS developments it undertakes. They are inherently risky and every organisation has, or knows of, systems that did not work and/or were implemented years late and/or cost orders of magnitude more than expected. The purpose of risk assessment is to:

(a) understand the factors that cause developments to fail;
(b) identify which of those factors are likely to impact a particular development;
(c) take action to deal with the risks that are likely to occur.

It is the responsibility of the application manager to determine the nature and degree of risk involved and ensure appropriate action is taken.

KEY LEARNING POINTS

- It is important for non-IT specialists to understand the key aspects of the processes involved in bringing the development of an information system through to a successful conclusion. A checklist of those aspects that a business manager must ensure are dealt with is summarised in Table 6.3.
- Whilst many of the tasks should be performed by others it is incumbent upon the business manager who is responsible for the system (in our terms the 'application manager') to ensure the tasks are carried out in a way that is appropriate to the nature of the development.
- Whilst this chapter has summarised some well-known approaches which any good methodology will include, it has introduced three aspects which are less traditional and are particularly important for today's large, complex IS/IT developments:

1   The need to consider the overall development as a number of inter-related projects which need to be dealt with separately by specialist resources, but which need to be brought together to complete the application successfully.

2   The introduction of the idea of 'business development projects', the

Table 6.3 Key tasks in IS/IT application/project management

- Set application objectives and establish target benefits
- Establish business requirements for system
- Agree CSFs for the application and projects
- Establish feasibility of meeting requirements
- Develop viable project plan – establish team/responsibilities
- Estimate resources/costs/timetable
- Understand the risks and deal with them
- Break down projects into phases, tasks and deliveries
- Quality assurance – application will meet requirements
- Manage resources – IT and business
- Make necessary business changes, new procedures, train staff for system implementation
- Control project with regard to time, quality and cost
- Test application
- Implement and realise benefits
- Review the success or otherwise of the application

focus of which is to ensure the full benefits of the investment are identified and realised. A deliberate and conscious approach to benefits management is suggested which should run parallel to and complement the IT development methodology.

3 The idea of 'variations on a theme' from a standard development methodology which matches the different issues in the application portfolio. This enables both prototyping of needs and the selection and procurement to package software to be included in a relevant way, rather than see them as different ways of achieving new information systems. Both have an increasingly significant role to play but neither is a panacea solution, nor a substitute for a consistent, coherent approach to systems development.

- The types of developments now being undertaken are more critical to business success and are often complex in business, organisational and IT terms. This implies that business managers must appreciate the risks involved and be able to take the necessary action to reduce the risks as far as possible.
- The evidence that IS/IT is being managed successfully is delivered through the relevance and quality of the systems that are implemented. Much has been learned in the last twenty years about how this delivery can be improved – but many developments still fail to deliver the expected benefits.

The next chapter considers a range of IS/IT management issues which need to be dealt with if the whole environment is conducive to long-term success with information systems and technology in organisations.

QUESTIONS FOR CONSIDERATION

1 For a major system development with which you are familiar attempt to:

  (a) describe it in terms of its objectives and factors which are/were critical to its success;
  (b) describe it in terms of the different types of projects (business and IT development, business and IT infrastructure) that are/were involved in or related to the development;
  (c) determine whether the combination of projects is/was both appropriate for the overall development (were any aspects omitted etc.) and whether the approach to the project dealt adequately with the critical success factors.

2 For the same or another development describe the benefits that were used to justify the investment. Attempt to determine, perhaps with the help of others, whether those benefits were actually achieved and if not, why not. Consider how well, if at all, the steps in the process described here for identifying and realising the benefits were carried out.

3 For each of high potential, strategic, key operational and support application developments describe three key factors about the involvement/role of each of (a) senior management, (b) line management/users and (c) IT specialists, that are appropriate for success in that type of application, i.e. the answer should look like:

	High potential	Strategic	Key operational	Support
Senior management	1	1	1	1
	2	2	2	2
	3	3	3	3
Line management users	1	1	1	1
	2	2	2	2
	3	3	3	3
IT specialists	1	1	1	1
	2	2	2	2
	3	3	3	3

NOTE

1 Acknowledgement: the ideas have been adapted from the benefits management process developed by the HISS Central Team of the Information Management Executive in the National Health Service – see references.

RECOMMENDED ADDITIONAL READING

Checkland, P.B. (1981) *Systems Thinking, Systems Practice*, John Wiley.
Checkland, P.B. and Scholes, J. (1990) *Soft Systems Methodology in Action*, John Wiley.
Gunton, A. (Ed.) (1993), *Information Systems Practice – The Complete Guide*, NCC Blackwell.
Hussain, D.S. and Hussain, K.M. (1991) *Information Systems for Business*, Prentice-Hall.
Osterle, H., Brenner, W. and Hilbers, K. (1993), *Total Information Systems Management*, John Wiley.
Ward, J.M. (1993) *Investment in IT – The Portfolio Approach*, CIMA Publications, Chapters 5 and 6.

OTHER REFERENCES

NHS Information Management Group (1993) 'Benefits Management – Guidelines on Investment Appraisal and Benefits Realisation for Hospital Information Support Systems' (reference IMGME D4001).

Chapter 7

Managing information system resources
Information and technology

INTRODUCTION

In the previous chapter a distinction was made between 'development projects' which deliver a new information system the organisation needs, and 'infrastructure projects' which improve the overall ability of the organisation to manage information and deploy information technology more successfully. In essence the overall management of infrastructure produces an appropriate set of IS/IT resources and the organisational ability to use them effectively. This in turn should enable relevant developments to be identified and each to be managed to success in terms of the business benefits expected. In the discussion that follows it should always be remembered that the ultimate purpose is to deliver business benefits from the changes that technology-based information systems can produce.

Each organisation must understand the long-term implications of information systems in its business and put in place the means of managing the range of resources it needs. Each development project cannot be dealt with in isolation from the others. At any one time an organisation will be living with a set of information systems which are a product of the past. It will have to live with many of them for an extended period and the ongoing consequences of having those systems have to be managed alongside the new developments it is undertaking. To succeed, the senior management must understand the issues involved and establish policies and processes to ensure appropriate resources are put in place, are organised effectively and utilised in the best interests of the business. Without that long-term management framework an organisation will not be able to invest in information systems with any confidence that it can obtain any real benefit. That can result in spending very little or spending too much rather than determine what it is worthwhile investing. A Kobler Unit Survey (1987) concluded that whilst there was no correlation between IT spend and business success, in some industries the least successful companies had either significantly lower or noticeably higher IT spend than their more successful competitors. It could be concluded that IT was one resource that they were not managing very successfully.

Whilst IS/IT resources have some unique aspects, mostly due to the rate of change of technology, for the most part they can be managed most successfully by adopting proved general management principles and concepts. The more IS/IT is perceived as peculiar or different from other business activities and resources, the less able business managers are to influence what happens.

The last chapter dealt with the issues associated with systems development; these next two consider the remaining key issues under four headings:

1 The **information management** issues – the principles involved in establishing effective processes to manage the organisation's information resources.
2 The **technological** issues – what non-IT specialists need to understand about managing the procurement and deployment of technology and the technology suppliers.
3 The **people** issues – the organisation of the specialist IT resources and their relationship with the rest of the business.
4 The **administrative** issues – where aspects of IS/IT need special consideration over and above normal approaches to business administration.

This chapter will deal with the first two of these and Chapter 8 the remaining two subjects.

These topics will be discussed in the context of all that has gone before in the book, but especially with regard to issues raised in Chapter 2 and the strategic management approaches described in Chapters 3 and 5. Before considering each of the topics in more detail it is worth summarising the requirements that senior management must ensure are addressed coherently if the organisation is to get the maximum benefit from its IS/IT investment (see Table 7.1).

Whilst senior management can consciously delegate these to appropriate parts of the organisation or to groups specifically set up to deal with them (e.g. policy/steering groups), they cannot ignore them or abdicate overall responsibility for them. It is often the failure to address these management requirements

Table 7.1 Requirements for senior management to undertake

* To ensure that IS/IT strategies, policies and plans accurately reflect business objectives and plans
* To ensure that potential business advantages available from IS/IT are identified and exploited
* To ensure that the business is not disadvantaged by its quality of information and systems
* To ensure that IS/IT investments are viable in terms of business risks and deliver the expected benefits
* To establish appropriate resource levels and set priorities
* To create the appropriate culture and working relationships between IT specialists and the business
* To achieve the appropriate balance between centralisation and decentralisation of the management of IS/IT and ensure that IT is sourced in the most effective way.

sensibly that leads to the problems that exist in organisations with regard to IS/IT, as were discussed in Chapter 2 (see Table 2.3). Each of these management requirements affects one or more of the information, people, technological or administrative issues that these two chapters address.

MANAGING THE INFORMATION RESOURCES

It has been said many times that information is a business asset/resource like any other and should therefore be managed like any other asset/resource, such as finance, people, plant, customers, products, etc. However, it was probably only with the arrival of information technology that information was seen as a specific resource, rather than something that was embedded in business processes. The earliest applications of the technology perpetuated this view, since they were focused on improving process efficiency. The data inputs and information outputs were organised and designed in the optimum way for that set of processes, not for the wider uses they might have in the business. For instance, when invoicing was first automated, it was more cost-effective merely to reproduce the existing invoices which contained a minimum of essential information for 'manual' processing efficiency. However, the invoice details could have been extended to provide useful information for sales and marketing management. The same was true of order processing and other operational systems. To be fair, in the early days, the cost of storing the data was very high and the analytical tools available were poor. Neither of these two constraints apply today and images can now be stored cost-effectively along with numbers and words.

This early process focus, followed by a general failure of centralised data bases to deliver satisfactory management information and the subsequent explosion in personal computer-based 'systems', means that most major organisations have evolved a fragmented information resource, as explained in Chapter 1. One of the key conclusions of the MIT 'Management in the 1990s' research programme was that the lack of coherent 'information resource management' in most organisations was a major inhibitor in terms of gaining the full benefits IT could deliver. With the increasing trend to decentralise the technology the difficulty of maintaining a co-ordinated information resource is likely to increase.

That is not to say that information resource management is a new concept or involves new ideas. Since 1980 many books and papers have been written on the subject (e.g. by Synott 1981, Holloway 1988, Watson and Omrani 1988). Most of these accurately assess the problems and issues and propose clear strategies and processes, both for overcoming the negative consequences of the legacy, and ensuring the future coherence of the resource. Unfortunately, when organisations attempted to implement these eminently sensible and logical concepts the amount of work involved proved enormous. One bank estimated it would take 100 man-years of effort to consolidate, rationalise and optimise its customer data, so that it could become customer focused rather than product focused! As anyone who uses a number of the services that a bank offers will know, the left hand often appears not to know what the right hand has done! That is because as far as the computer systems are concerned you are effectively as many different customers as the services you use. Some financial service companies have even asked their customers **to tell them** what products and services they use to help solve the companies' information problems! Until recently there was no automatic reconciliation of individuals across the various personal taxation classes within the Inland Revenue. There is still little cross-referencing of recipients of government benefits across the various divisions of the social services. Not only does this lead to major duplication of effort but also opens up opportunities for fraud and other abuses of the services. Similar problems, though on a much smaller scale, are probably occurring in many businesses due to lack of appropriate policies for managing information.

Some typical problems which occur are:

- inefficient methods are used to capture, process, store and disseminate information;
- many additional and unnecessary computer or manual processes exist to consolidate and reconcile information;
- considerable duplication in activities of data capture and storage: often leading to separate and different sets of data about the same thing;
- systems are plagued by data errors;
- information is used for inappropriate purposes or alternatively information which is available is not used, since it is not known about or it is in the wrong place.

Some of these problems lead to high costs and business inefficiencies, others can lead to major business problems and can prevent the organisation from responding appropriately to the demands of its business environment.

Information resource management (IRM) implies a set of management policies and operational disciplines covering the acquisition, maintenance, utilisation and dissemination of information in and by the organisation. The focus is on gathering, storing and providing relevant information of adequate quality, accuracy and timeliness, at an appropriate cost, together with the provision of appropriate access to the information. The approach should also enable a rapid response to changing business needs, i.e. provide flexibility in the use of the resource, which can only be achieved if the capabilities and limitations of the resource are well understood. A good filing system for documents, effectively indexed and cross-referenced, is a part of IRM, although here we are focusing on technology-based information.

There are in reality two parts to the problem, which can be related to the definitions of **information** and **data** given in Chapter 2. The first part requires that the business defines the 'finished goods' the **information** it needs and how that information will be provided and used. The second part involves the storage of the 'raw material' – the **data** – how it is organised and kept in order to provide it for appropriate use. In the terms used earlier, **information management** involves business and organisational issues and is part of the **IS** strategy: **data management** involves technical issues and is part of the **IT** strategy (see Figure 7.1). This may not be a theoretically sound way of defining the components but it helps in the practical world. Information management should be concerned with the **demand** issues – **what** information is needed; data management should be concerned with the **supply** issues – **how** it can be provided. The two together produce an overall approach to IRM.

The data management component of IRM has generally been understood by IT specialists for the best part of twenty years and effective processes are in place in many organisations. But as was said earlier this is much easier in a centralised IT environment and the responsibility for effective data management, as well as information management, will move towards the business user with the distribution of the technology. Some experts argue that it is vital that data management processes are recentralised to increase control, as technology is distributed. They believe that users will never adopt the necessary long-term disciplines and that information chaos will ensue. Others argue that only by placing that responsibility on the user will data and information be understood in terms of its value as a resource or asset. In the discussion that follows, the principles of information and data management will be outlined, rather than the organisational issues – which will be considered in the next chapter.

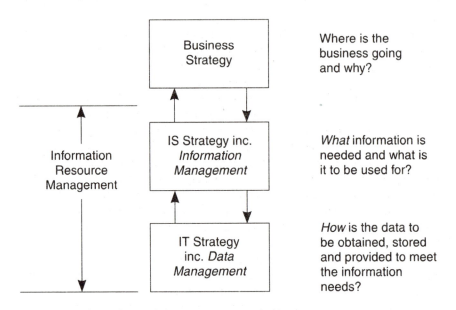

Figure 7.1 Information and data management in context

INFORMATION AND DATA MANAGEMENT

It is first worth establishing some objectives for these aspects of IS/IT management. Most authorities agree on the following objectives for IRM:

- to ensure appropriate quality and availability of information (right time, right place, right person, as well as right information);
- to provide coherent and consistent information to meet the current and future needs of the business;
- to effectively balance the cost incurred against the business benefit of the information.

Whilst not explicit in the objectives there is a clear need to relate the information management approach to the organisation structure as well as the business needs. Earl (1990) defines three parts to IS/IT strategic management – IS and IT strategy as defined here, plus information management strategy which he describes in terms of organisational relationships and management processes. Here his information management strategy is considered as a subset of the IS strategy, but the organisational dimension is as important as the business or application dimension.

In order to manage the range of information coherently, its business relevance and the inter-relationships and inter-dependencies of the various components have to be understood. This can be considered as the 'information architecture' of the business. It is a high-level description, or model, of the different types of information, expressed in terms of how they logically relate to one another and to the systems and business processes that use them. It can be thought of as the hub of the application portfolio as shown in Figure 7.2. It should be derived from the entity models which describe the information relationships in each of the applications and should describe where the various items of information are used in the systems. For instance, many applications will use information about customers, and in total they will define what information about customers is obtained and how it is used. The entity model for each application will provide only part of the picture, but a total view is needed to understand the full range of information about customers – in effect a high-level model or map of the information resource. This can then be used to ensure information is not duplicated, where responsibility for its validity should lie in the organisation and enable any new requirement to understand what is already in place that can be used. The model does not describe physically where the information is stored – that is part of the technical data management consideration below – but it provides a logical view of the information that the business has in relation to the main systems and processes of the business. Without such a description of the total information resource, significant effort will be wasted on each application development. Equally, the business is likely to waste considerable time resolving information problems, rather than obtaining the benefits from the information.

In order to understand the issues and components of information management it is probably easiest to start with data management which is better established

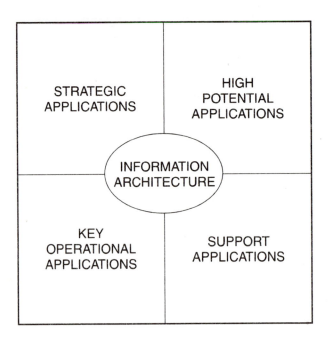

Figure 7.2 Information architecture

and more thoroughly understood. Effective data management implies that the following processes need to be in place, whether the data is managed centrally or physically distributed throughout the business.

1 **Data administration**   Involved the identification and classification of business information, including the data/information architecture, and the development of the processes and practices for defining any business information needs and the translation into data required to meet those needs. The data administration function should be involved in the development of all new applications.

2 **Data dictionary administration**   This involves developing and maintaining the data dictionary, where all the information components are defined, described and catalogued. It is the reference library for the information resource and it will also refer to where any item is physically kept.

3 **Data base administration**   Involves the design, development and maintenance of the actual data bases and files which are used by the applications, and the development of procedures and controls to ensure the correct usage, security and back-up/recovery are implemented.

4 **Access services**   Enable the provision of data to authorised users and ensure that the most appropriate data is employed for the particular purpose.

These four components of data management are shown in Figure 7.3.

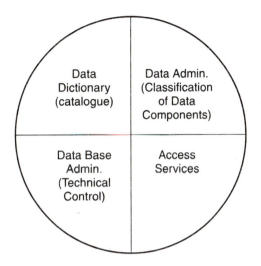

Figure 7.3 Elements of data management

Data management activities have a high technical content and traditionally have been located in the IT department. This made considerable sense when the majority of data resided in central computers and a limited range of data base software was in use. Nowadays this is perhaps less reasonable given the wide variety of data base software available on personal computers. The danger is that the data management function is seen by users as relevant only to the central systems, and hence it is not consulted or advised of developments in the business. Ideally, it should perhaps be located outside IT, but should still provide a central service to the users and provide a central control point with a clearly understood role within the business. In any case data management, in the terms used here, is only part of the task since it only covers how things should be done. There are a set of complementary tasks which have to be carried out by the business if data management is to be effective. Figure 7.4 expands the scope of Figure 7.3 to cover those related information management processes. The tasks focus on the two key aspects of managing information – ensuring its integrity for business use and defining the security needed to protect it from misuse or loss.

It is easiest to describe each of these briefly in the same sequence as the related data management activities at the core of the diagram.

1 The users of the data need to describe what it will be used for, what information they want in terms of data combinations and the degree of accuracy and
timeliness that are essential to the business use of the information. In essence,
the business users must define the information quality parameters and

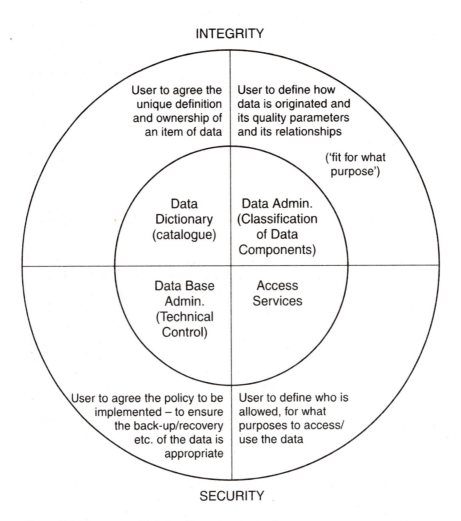

Figure 7.4 Elements of information management

relationships that will determine the classification, auditing and structuring of the supporting data. The term 'fit for what purpose' is useful to understand here. For instance, a first-cut sales forecast based on some simple market research may be valid for use in the marketing department but not fit for the purpose of production scheduling until it has been analysed in conjunction with existing, actual sales trends. Hence the production scheduling system should only access the 'approved sales forecast', not the 'provisional one'. This may sound obvious, but in many organisations data is used for purposes for which it is not valid due to a lack of control and understanding of what information can be genuinely derived from the data sources. Those parameters and relationships must be defined by the business people who understand the context and limitations of the information – technical IT people cannot do this.

2 Any effective data dictionary requires an agreed, unique definition of each item in the catalogue and, to support (1) above, a clear statement of who in the business is responsible for the integrity of that item. This would normally be the person who originates the data. If there is any question as to whether the data is fit for a particular purpose or can be made available to a new system or user, the 'owner' of the data item should be consulted and in many cases they may need to give permission for its use. In many companies, now, each item on a data base is accompanied by the name or job title of the originator or owner of that item.

3 The business 'owner' of the item of data must also define the security parameters for that item, based on the business uses of it. There are really three aspects to security:

(a) How confidential is the information, and therefore to what extent should access be allowed by others, or how carefully protected must it be? Normally this is dealt with by 'levels' of security which then result in appropriate procedures being implemented. The owner should be able to define which level is appropriate and why for any particular item.

(b) Recoverability – how quickly in the event of a system or computer failure does the data have to be available to avoid major business problems? This could be minutes in the case of the customer data supporting order taking, or hours in the case of customer account data, or even days in order to analyse customer sales. For any item the most business-critical use of the item will determine how quickly it must be recovered. Again several levels of recovery speed may be provided depending on the degree of damage that results, and to ensure priority is given to the most business-critical activities.

(c) Back-up – how frequently should the data be copied and how long do the copies need to be kept? Some items may need to be kept virtually for ever for legal reasons, others for periods of years and some may have an effective useful life of only hours or days. Once again a set of rules governing the frequency and life cycle of back-up of data is normally prepared, from which the user selects the one that is valid for the item.

4 Finally, in conjunction with all the above, the owners of the data items must define the basis on which others can have access to the item, so that the access services function can take appropriate steps when access by a new user is requested. Again a set of policies can be defined to govern the ability to provide access – from the extremes of 'under no circumstances outside the department' to 'any one can use it', via 'with my personal permission on a daily basis', to 'yes, provided I know who is using it', etc.

These, in brief, are the complementary business activities which are needed to match the better known, and often better established, data management processes, if coherent management of the organisation's information resources is to occur. The extent and range of the information being stored and processed by information technology is expanding at an exponential rate and hence the problem of managing that resource will increase. Equally, the dependence of businesses on that technology-based information to carry out its processes is increasing and hence the consequences of mismanaging the resource will become more severe.

It is possible to relate the issues in information management to the management of other business resources. Finance and personnel functions in organisations have specific, often legally defined, responsibilities for the control and management of money and people, yet every line manager and individual has personal responsibilities to discharge with respect to both. These are defined by the policies and procedures of the organisation, which are normally set up by the function with prime responsibility for others to carry out. This is the same for information resources, where the prime functional responsibility appears, today at least, to rest in the IT function. There is no real reason why a similar approach to responsibility for information management cannot be developed to match the better developed management approaches to money and people.

A PRACTICAL APPROACH TO IMPLEMENTING IRM

As a last part to this section on information management it is worth a brief consideration of the most realistic way to achieve most of the benefits of IRM, without deterring the organisation from any action by the apparent enormity of the task and to avoid suffering the worst consequences of poor IRM. The main problems to be dealt with are:

(a) overcoming the fragmented legacy derived from the old systems;
(b) dealing with the rapidly expanding information resource;
(c) matching the business benefits with the increasing cost of the work involved;
(d) getting agreement on data definitions across the business.

To offset the increasing extent of the task, modern data base and packaged software normally provides good facilities to assist in the work. Hence, as organisations migrate from custom-built systems to packages and employ more sophisticated and user-friendly data base software, there is both a need and an opportunity to define data and document the information architecture. This process of migration should be used to bring in the whole range of disciplines associated with IRM and then to ensure that procedures and policies are updated and enforced. This approach is most effective when a range of related packages are acquired, either from one supplier to cover many basic functions, or by selecting packages which can use one data base management system (DBMS) product. The latter approach is probably the best and many companies have adopted one DBMS (e.g. Oracle, Ingress, Sybase) and then only procure packages which can use it, rather than introduce additional proprietary DBMS's which are inherent in the packages.

Another approach derives from the application portfolio which suggests that quality, integration and non-duplication of data are most critical in the key operational applications, and hence IRM effort will provide the most immediate benefits there.

The greatest risks in terms of immediate disadvantages occur because of the inability of the key operational systems to meet current business needs. The IRM effort should first focus on avoiding the disadvantages that can accrue from a lack of discipline in managing the data used and information produced by key operational systems. Any new developments in this area should be subject to the full rigour of IRM.

Most strategic applications will rely at least in part on data from the key operational systems and so the primary focus above should assist here. However, most will also involve the introduction of new information and thus it is best to introduce the IRM disciplines as that information is obtained and used, rather than retrospectively. Most strategic applications will in due course become key operational and the up-front effort will pay dividends over the life of the system.

In the other two segments of the matrix, high potential and support, the benefits of IRM relative to the cost are less certain. Whilst an application is in the high potential phase, effort to structure, define and control the information is rather pointless, it is best left until the business role of the system is known (if it has one!). In support applications there are normally two separate types – those that are used in one department or function and those that are used by many, if not all the functions of the business. There are also usually very large numbers of support systems, when all those running on PCs are taken into account. The rationale for all support systems investments is economic so any investment in IRM activity here should show a financial return, normally in terms of current or future cost avoidance. This is likely to be justified where systems are cross-functional or have many users. Any system which is classified as 'support' is not critical to the business and therefore information quality does not normally need the same degree of care as elsewhere. Whilst it is worthwhile extending the disciplines of IRM to most new investments in this area, where the costs involved are small, it is probably unrealistic and uneconomic to attempt to impose the procedures retrospectively. This should also be the area where the replacement by packages of old systems over time offers the best opportunity to get the information rationalised and better managed. Figure 7.5 summarises these points.

MANAGING THE TECHNOLOGY RESOURCES

It is beyond the scope of this book to cover in any depth the management of the computer and communications technologies that comprise IT. Nor should business managers become excessively involved with the details of the technology – it is changing very quickly and even dedicated technologists have problems

	STRATEGIC	HIGH POTENTIAL
New	Ensure new data/ information is designed to fit information architecture and provide flexibility of structure to respond to business developments. Strategy: Central Planning	Keep information separate from the core architecture until its nature, value and role in the business are understood and the destination of the application is agreed. Strategy: Free Market Leading Edge
Information focus	Clearly defined information architecture and coherent information management processes to ensure effective use of integrated data and prevent business risks and disadvantages. Strategy: Monopoly	Rationalise and integrate information when economically justified. Introduce IRM as new software is introduced. Audit use of information to eliminate storage of obsolete/unused data. Strategy: Free Market Scarce Resource
Current	KEY OPERATIONAL	SUPPORT

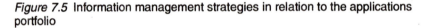

Nature of the information

Integrated resource ← → Localised use

Figure 7.5 Information management strategies in relation to the applications portfolio

keeping up to date. However, there are a number of general management issues for which principles need to be established, to enable the organisation to make appropriate decisions about the procurement and deployment of IT in both the short and long-term. Otherwise the management will become incapable of relating the specific requirements for spending on IT to the business and information systems implications of approving, or otherwise, the revenue or capital expense.

It is also a responsibility of business managers to ensure that **any** new development in the business environment, including technology, is understood in terms of the implications for the business and its strategy. That is not to say they must understand the technology and how it works, but they should appreciate what effect it may have on the industry and what it could achieve for the business.

Four other aspects require business managers to understand sufficient to make reasoned judgements about IT.

1 In the future an organisation will be affected by the IT investments of others, its customers, suppliers and competitors in particular and it needs to understand the implications for the business of those investments.

2 The IT product and service suppliers will represent a significant part of the expenditure budget of the business and each supplier will attempt to influence the senior management to spend it to its benefit. Unless the business managers can ask sensible business-based questions, they are likely to be confused by the advice of the suppliers and their own IT specialists, who each have a vested interest in the outcome. A typical debate might be as follows:

> *Supplier*: 'Unless you adopt open systems and a client-server architecture you will not be able to cost-effectively downsize and take full advantage of new packaged software . . .'

> *IT Dept:* 'We have such a high investment in PCs and mainframe systems and proprietary software that the cost of migration would be prohibitive and at present the range of software available on UNIX does not satisfy all our needs.'

What does it mean? Box 7.1 explains some of the terms, plus a few others that are in common usage. It is easy to say that suppliers and IT specialists must explain things in a jargon-free way that the business people can understand. However, if they do not, ignorance is no excuse in the eyes of the shareholders!

3 Management will have to make other decisions about IT-related resources, especially people. It is very topical in the early 1990s to talk about 'outsourcing' IT, by buying in, from normally one supplier, a whole set of services to support the use of IT, instead of employing significant numbers of IT specialists. Outsourcing or sourcing options are considered in the next chapter, but decisions about sourcing of skills and people are related to the issues associated with the technology itself.

4 Many decisions about the procurement of technology are about 'infrastructure investments' involving the spending of money now with the promise of benefits from the IS investments it will enable. Unless management can sensibly question those investments they can never be sure whether it is the best way of achieving the benefits and satisfying the business needs, or merely what the IT department wants to spend money on! One senior executive in a public utility, when presented with an £8 million cost for a new network, argued on the basis that 'without it none of the planned systems can go ahead' asked a simple question – 'what do I get for half the money?' The answer in reality was 90 per cent of the application benefits and the likelihood of spending less in three years' time to achieve the rest, if they were still relevant. On the other hand, well thought-out infrastructure investments can not only ensure that planned application developments deliver their benefits at a lower total cost, but also provide the capability and flexibility to meet unplanned and even unexpected needs earlier or at a lower cost.

Box 7.1   An explanation of some current IT terminology in common usage

1 **4GL (fourth-generation language)/application generator**
High-level programming languages, i.e. more like structured English statements, which enable people with little technical knowledge to produce computer pro-grams. They normally contain many features to simplify the work and enable faster development and testing of applications – e.g. report writing, enquiry facilities, data base access, etc. Whilst they produce inefficient program code, this is less import-ant on modern computers – the trade-off relative to saved man-hours is usually very beneficial.

2 **Client/server**
This describes the splitting of the computer resources between the end-user workstation or PC at the desk ('client') and a central shared capability ('server') – these are linked together via a network. It enables the user to have access to data and applications elsewhere but with the computer power on the desk to use them. It also enables the sharing of other expensive technologies, such as high-quality or high-volume printers amongst many occasional users.

3 **Document image processing**
This is a combination of technologies for scanning documents and 'pictures' and storing the images on optical discs. The technology enables vast amounts of paper-based information to be stored very cheaply. The main problem at present is how to index the contents of the documents to enable accurate, comprehensive and efficient retrieval of what is stored.

4 **Graphical user interface**
This describes the way in which the user gets access from the desktop PC or workstation to the various applications and facilities available. Instead of typing in words the screen displays a range of icons from which the user selects, via a mouse, the application or data or facility (e.g. printer) they wish to use. The approach was introduced by Apple in the 1980s but now is becoming standardised to some extent by the increasing use of Microsoft's 'Windows'.

5 **Open systems**
Open systems is a 'concept' or 'principle' not a technology. It implies the ability to communicate between all types of computer and to transfer application software from any computer to any other ('portability'). It also means that an application could run on different sizes of computer ('scaleability'). The consequence is that applications and data bases become hardware independent enabling the organis-ation to buy from a range of vendors rather than be tied into one because of its 'proprietary' operating systems. For the concept to be fully realised, and at present it is only partly realisable, standards such as OSI (open systems interconnection) for communications have to be adopted universally and hardware and software vendors must also provide standard operating systems. UNIX is the first of these. Versions of UNIX are now available from most hardware suppliers – but they are not all the same! Open systems will gradually become more of a reality over the next ten years, and most organisations need to plan to migrate to an open systems environment as older systems and technology become obsolete.

Before considering how these and other issues can be dealt with, it is necessary to define which technology components are involved and summarise the way in which those technologies are evolving. Whilst it appears that IT is evolving faster than ever before it is probably not the case. The power/£ ratio has been improving at about 25 per cent per annum for thirty years and the new capabilities of the technology have been changing just as fast. **But**, until probably the last five years this rate of change was only apparent to the IT specialists since it did not directly affect the user's desktop computer or terminal. Also the modern user friendly operating systems such as 'Windows' have meant that suppliers have developed excellent new software to work via these easy-to-use front ends. The number of suppliers of hardware and software has risen significantly over the last five years or so and therefore the choice of suppliers of similar products is now greater, giving the appearance, at least, of a wider range of different options – all presented via glossy brochures as the latest, best and cheapest!

In the context of this book the 'technologies' that need to be considered here are:

(a) **Hardware**, for entry, storage, processing and output of information at the centre and distributed both to a location and to the desktop.

(b) **Communications networks** – both the transmission medium (cable, microwave, fibre optics, etc.) and the hardware and software that enables connection to and use of the networks. Networks are often described as of three types – *local area* (within a building or site), *wide area* (connecting sites together) and *global* (offering international data, image and voice communications). It should not be forgotten that the most significant growth area of communications technology has been facsimile transmission (fax) and recent developments have enabled faxes to be input directly to company's internal electronic mail systems by optical scanning or reading the digital transmission signals.

(c) **Operating and 'environmental' software** which enable the computers to run application software and facilitate its use and development. This does not include application software packages which are to satisfy specific business activities and processes. However, it does include the general-purpose software such as spreadsheets, word processing and graphics packages, and application programming languages and generators (or 4GLs).

In overall terms there has been a major change in the nature of the products available as well as their power and capability. Until the mid-1980s the emphasis, based mainly on IBM's strategy for twenty years, was on proprietary hardware and software which tied the buyers into one or at best a few suppliers. Switching vendors often involved major redevelopment of existing systems and many companies underestimated both the time and cost involved, i.e. they often stood still in systems terms for some years at great cost. Most recently the power in the IT industry has moved from hardware to software suppliers who clearly want their software to run on as wide a variety of hardware as possible. Hence the philosophy of 'open systems' and the development of general rather than proprietary software standards. The term 'open systems' is usually used in the context of operating systems software based on UNIX, to provide transportability and scaleability across different types of hardware. However, the philosophy of open systems includes the ability to transfer data between different computer environments via a range of network types based on agreed international open systems interconnection (OSI) standards. It has also come to imply the ability to run the applications via a common user interface at the workstation on the desk, and the 'Windows' environment provided by Microsoft is becoming the *de facto* standard.

In general, therefore, time is on the side of the purchaser since the various suppliers are being forced to conform to agreed or *de facto* standards if their products are to reach a large market. In the process the hardware components of computer and communication systems are becoming commodities which can be purchased based on unit price performance. Software is gradually becoming hardware independent and will be able to be used across a variety of machines without any extra work. In addition, the development of **client/server** environments where the **client** on the desk can make use of resources and capacity elsewhere in the network **(servers)** means that capacity and software does not have to be replicated many times over throughout the business. What is happening and where it is happening are transparent to the user, to whom it appears all the resources he or she needs are on the desk (or at least close by).

Overall, therefore, the risks of making an inappropriate decision will reduce and the incremental costs of investments should also reduce – even if the number of options available increases. A key component of any IT strategy should be the migration plan towards an open systems environment and away from the existing set of proprietary hardware and software already in place. The migration plan should demonstrate when major reinvestment in either systems or technology is expected so that all significant spend will be directed towards the newer, more flexible and cost-effective technology options of the future.

JUSTIFICATION OF TECHNOLOGY INVESTMENTS

The purchase of technology either as capital items or procurement of capacity such as network resources should be justified in a number of different ways depending on the nature of its contribution to the business performance. Overall the expenditure should, over any two to three year period, be offset by the benefit stream which is delivered by the application developments, though in any one year this may not be possible given the need to procure technology in advance of its use. The rationale for investment can be considered under five headings.

1 Application-specific procurement to provide the technology for a specific system being developed for which benefits have been identified. Here the technology costs can easily be included in the application investment justification. It can also be argued that the resulting technology may contribute to improvements under (4) below, but the cost should be recoverable in full against the primary application. A pharmaceutical company has provided its technical representatives with portable PCs to reduce administrative and com-

munication costs. The cost can be justified by the short-term savings due to efficiency improvements but in due course the same equipment will be used to improve the ability of the representative to analyse customer needs and hopefully increase sales.

2 Some technology purchases are made to reduce the costs of running and supporting existing systems, due to more efficient technology now being available to meet the needs. This is often important in systems which involve significant amounts of data acquisition, storage, transmission and dissemination where significant improvements in cost per unit have arrived over the last few years. These justifications will often include some redevelopment work across a number of existing systems in order to take advantage of new capabilities. The justification of these costs will depend on the remaining business life of the applications. These changes should not be confused with user requested changes or enhancements to any system for which any new technology cost should be weighed against the benefits of the enhancement.

3 In some cases technology becomes obsolete in that it will no longer be supported by the vendor, or even worse the vendor goes out of business! Before jumping to the conclusion that the technology must be replaced, the value of any application using the technology should be assessed to see whether or not it can be discontinued. Assuming some or all of the applications are still needed then alternative technology that meets the application needs will have to be obtained. The appraisal of options should consider both the pure cost of the technology and the amount of work required to transfer the applications to the new technology. In addition it might be sensible to consider whether:

(a) aspects of the application could be amended or even redeveloped to use a more cost-effective type of technology. This might be particularly important if further benefits are available if the system is enhanced.

and

(b) existing technologies, those already in use in the organisation, could be used to increase the degree of standardisation, even if the technology is not ideal for the particular application.

4 Looking longer term and beyond the existing systems and current developments, technology infrastructure should be seen as an enabler of achieving the business strategy. However, it is too vague to argue that as a general principle. Any such arguments for such technology investments should be related to issues affecting the business environment or the strategy. For instance, Weill (1992) considers a particular case where IT infrastructure investment was aimed at increasing the speed to market of new products because new technology would speed the analysis of existing product components and their reconfiguration, where appropriate, in the new products. Product design and development times would reduce significantly. A second instance, again quoted

by Weill, is to enable the faster development, probably at lower cost, of future applications which would enable IT to respond faster to changing business needs. Equally providing a degree of flexibility in the technology infrastructure and in the capacity available can be justified when IS plans do not, in reality, cater for the majority of the applications which actually arise. It can be argued that the IS planning should be improved, but this is not always possible and patterns of previous demand can often be established to provide a guide to the nature of future demands. If demand is not actually predictable due to business uncertainty a more flexible, responsive infrastructure is essential.

5 Lastly, a factor which is often overlooked until the last moment is the need to provide technology capacity to support the growth in business activity, either in overall terms or to meet the changing mix of activities and resulting transaction needs. For example, a distribution organisation whose overall volumes and income were static failed to recognise the fact that order patterns were changing. More frequent orders were being placed, for smaller quantities each of which was of lower value and eventually the warehouse system became incapable of processing them in time to meet the promised delivery time. It was only when the customers started to complain that further investment was (urgently) made.

Overall the justification of technology should be seen in the long-term perspective of what the organisation is trying to achieve **and** the changing supply situation, if the organisation is to strike the right balance between the expenditure and the resulting, if indirect, benefits the technology will deliver.

TECHNOLOGY MANAGEMENT IN THE CONTEXT OF THE APPLICATIONS PORTFOLIO

In the previous section technology management issues were considered with limited reference to the applications which use the technology. Yet it is the applications that deliver business benefits, and the decisions about technology should be seen in relation to the types of applications, the benefits they offer and the risks incurred. Therefore it is worth considering the relationship between the technology strategy and the application portfolio.

At the highest level – the general relationship between IT evolution and business need – a useful way of classifying technologies from a business perspective was developed by Arthur D. Little Inc. (1981). They define four stages of technology evolution in the context of to what extent it is being employed in an industry. These stages are overlaid on the applications portfolio in Figure 7.6 to show where they would be expected to fit with the business's systems. The stages are:

1 The technology is not in use in the industry but is under development by suppliers or in use in other industries and it may have a future in the industry – **emerging** technologies – an example might be the use of CD-ROM 'catalogues' to replace traditional glossy printed catalogues by mail-order companies.

2 Technology leaders in the industry are using the technology, normally on an experimental basis to discover its relevance and potential – **pacing** technologies – an example today might be work flow management software in the financial services industry.

3 The leading organisations in the industry are implementing systems which use the technology – **key** technologies – for example the use of geographical information systems in public authorities and gas, electricity and water companies.

4 The technology is widely used in the industry – **base** technologies – there are many examples that could be used here: automatic telling machines (ATMs) in banks and building societies being perhaps the most obvious one.

There should perhaps be a fifth category – **obsolete**, – for those technologies being phased out in the industry as newer ones replace them. Continued use by the organisation would leave them further and further behind the main competitors. Equally it may be technology that is being phased out by the vendors. Figure 7.6 does perhaps need a little more explanation in terms of the overall management approach.

Emerging

Monitoring of vendor's developments and the early stages of the use of the technology within the industry or outside it is important. Even if no action is taken, implications should be drawn and 'trigger-points' for more careful

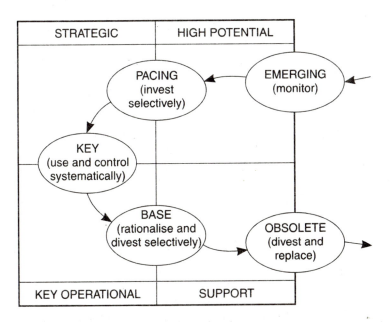

Figure 7.6 Technology maturing in relation to the application portfolio

assessment decided. Any action should be initially to test, evaluate and perhaps prototype the use of the technology, with the help of the supplier, on an application idea. This clearly fits with the leading-edge strategy that applies to the high potential segment of the portfolio.

Pacing

If the organisation's overall posture is to be a technology leader, then it should invest via a prototype or R&D evaluation in any technology that appears to offer benefits. A technology follower on the other hand would wait, but should monitor others' experiments and also open up a dialogue with potential vendors. It will be the general management attitude to these pacing technologies which will determine its overall technology strategy approach. This should normally reflect its attitude to all technology, not just IT.

This 'pacing' strategic choice will probably be reflected in the number of different vendors the company uses – the greater the leadership sought the greater the variety. The choice of major vendors is a business procurement decision not a technical one. Often a particular pacing technology will be provided by a limited number of vendors initially. The focus should be on identifying where, if at all, the technology offers business advantages which more than offset the risks of employing a relatively unproved technology – i.e. strategic applications.

The window of opportunity to gain major advantage from utilising new technology is in this stage during which other organisations still have much to learn, although their cost of following could well be less. With success in one or two firms the vendors will be quick to sell the technology to others in the industry. It is important that the senior management is kept informed about its position *vis-à-vis* its main competitors.

Key

These form the main operational technologies in use in the industry by the company and its competitors, and the company that fails to master their use will fall behind. There will undoubtedly be a number of vendors offering broadly similar and (no doubt claimed) compatible products. Restricting the number of vendors, unless the compatibility is truly seamless, is often the wisest course even if optimum functionality is sacrificed. As a technology is more widely used, its cost will undoubtedly reduce and make more and more applications able to use it economically. Equally it will become more reliable and the associated skills will be more readily available, making it suitable for key operational systems, where any degree of technology risk should be avoided.

Base

Well-established, even ageing technologies do need to be managed positively, not just allowed to continue to be used – they may inhibit further technology development and/or freeze the skills in the past. A strategy for selective divestment of the obsolescent or incompatible technologies must be established. Undue consumption of scarce skilled resources could be a prime reason for divestment. Again, monitoring the discontinuation of technology use in the industry or elsewhere is advisable to anticipate and avoid problems. It is often more difficult to get rid of a much loved, if inadequate technology than to bring in a new one!

Based on the discussion above, a number of simple principles about technology management, from a general management viewpoint, can be aligned to the segments in the applications portfolio. These are summarised in Figure 7.7.

KEY LEARNING POINTS

- **There are many organisational aspects of managing IS/IT resources which general managers often see as specialist tasks for the IT management to deal with.**

STRATEGIC	HIGH POTENTIAL
– avoid high risk new technologies unless tested in High Potential or a clear advantage is available – focus of technologies which speed the development process and/or provide flexibility of solution – develop the necessary skills to exploit the technology	– monitor new vendor offerings – technology interception planning – identify potential areas of application and invest limited £ in tests prototypes – evaluate both the use and also the potential limitations, economics of the technology
– incremental change within overall technology architecture, based on proved technologies – low risk – careful technology selection to ensure application integration not reduced or prevented – ensure all necessary support skills are available	– evolutionary technology – introduce based on the economic benefits that can be demonstrated – rationalise, standardise to reduce long-term support costs – 'approved' list – disinvest and subcontract support for old technology
KEY OPERATIONAL	SUPPORT

Figure 7.7 Some overall guidelines for technology management strategies around the portfolio

- To some extent this is valid for technology, but the management of the information resources cannot be delegated to technical specialists. Information is a business resource like any other. The role of the specialist is to provide expertise to support the business managers in ensuring the resource, in this case information, is marshalled effectively, does not decay and can be used to maximum advantage.
- To abdicate responsibility entirely to the IT specialist is perhaps similar to saying to a warehouse manager 'not only should you operate the warehouse efficiently – you should decide what we store in it and who we sell it to . . . '. Clearly that is not normal practice! But in many ways the data management role in IT is similar to the warehouse manager, in this case managing the 'information warehouse'.
- In most organisations the information resources have evolved without much conscious or concerted management, in spite of protestations by the IT specialists that long-term problems will ensue. Consequently the quality of the resource is extremely variable and it is often very fragmented. The situation will get worse as more and more information is captured, processed, stored and distributed via the technology.
- It is important that business managers understand the issues and the potential consequences and begin to take the necessary action to avoid them.
- With regard to technology management the situation is more mixed in terms of general management involvement in decisions about technology development and investment. Undoubtedly many managers are technology averse, and some even pretend that is a virtue! Others have dabbled with aspects of the technology and have some knowledge albeit from a limited perspective. Most have heard the horror stories about expensive failure of IT investment and would rather avoid blame by association in their own organisation.
- Business managers do not need to understand how the technology works, but they do need to know what it is capable of achieving for their business. This implies an understanding of how the technology can change the products and services of the industry and its effects on business activities and the economics of the business.
- Customers, suppliers, competitors and potential new entrants to the industry are all likely to be using IT in some way to improve their competitive position. Like any aspect that threatens the success of the business, the implications of those uses of IT must be assessed and responded to as necessary.
- It was once said that 'war was too important to be left to the generals': IT is too important to be left to technologists! There are a number of key aspects of technology management which non-IT managers should appreciate and be competent to influence decisions about.
- Whilst information technology is developing and changing rapidly many

of the management issues are relatively constant – except that as technology is more distributed or 'diffused' throughout the organisation, line managers in all functions will be closer to the issues. By understanding certain principles by which to address the issues, they should be able to discharge those responsibilities in the long-term best interests of the business.

QUESTIONS FOR CONSIDERATION

1   For three different items of business information with which you are familiar and are produced by computer systems, attempt to describe each in terms of its security and integrity attributes as shown in Figure 7.4. Then identify whether the existing policies/procedures in place for managing them and the supporting data are appropriate for the information's attributes.

2   Your chief executive has been approached by a major IT company with an offer to take over all the functions currently performed by your IT department. Write a brief summary of what you see as the short-and long-term pros and cons of outsourcing the various functions. What criteria should the company use to decide (a) whether to outsource at all and (b) how to select an appropriate supplier? Also identify the activities that will be required to be retained or put in place in the organisation if the majority of IT activities are outsourced.

RECOMMENDED ADDITIONAL READING

Appleton, D.S. (1987) 'Information Asset Management' *Datamation;* 1 February.

Earl, M.J. (1990) *Management Strategies for Information Technology*, Prentice-Hall, Chapter 6.

Weill, P. (1992) 'The Role and Value of Information Technology Infrastructure', Chapter 24 of *Strategic Information Technology Management*, (Ed. M.A. Mahmood), Idea Group.

OTHER REFERENCES

Arthur D. Little Inc. (1981) 'Strategic Management of Technology', Report to European Management Forum.

Holloway, S. (1988) *Data Administration*, Gower Technical Press.

Kobler Unit of Imperial College/Brunel University (1987) *The Strategic Use of IT Systems* (a survey).

Synott, W.R. (1981) *Information Resource Management*, John Wiley.

Watson, B.G. and Omrani, D. (1988) *Information Resource Management*, DCE Information Management Consultancy.

Chapter 8

Managing information systems resources

People, organisation and administration

INTRODUCTION

The previous chapter dealt with the management of two of the main components of information systems – information and technology. This one covers the other two.

(a) The **people** issues – the **organisation** and management of the specialist IT resources and how to ensure they enjoy an effective relationship with the rest of the business organisation.
(b) The **administrative** issues – the key aspects of IS/IT which need specialist consideration within the general business administrative processes.

Both of these are affected by the extent to which the organisation employs its own specialist IS/IT resources or buys them in and the degree to which those resources and the control of them is centralised in the IT function or devolved to the business functions.

The way IT resources are organised and the administrative policies which govern the acquisition and use of those resources will affect the whole 'life cycle' of IS/IT management – from forging effective planning links with the business strategy to the eventual reaping of the benefits from the IS/IT investments. Much has been covered in previous chapters which gives guidance on 'best practice' for managing IS/IT in organisations, and those threads will be pulled together in this chapter. As was explained in Chapter 2 the environment for IS/IT management in most organisations is becoming 'complex' as described by Sullivan (see Figure 2.1). Complex in the sense that two pressures are forcing businesses into a more challenging environment, over which they exercise less and less direct control. These pressures are:

(a) the external competitive pressures which increase the criticality of IS/IT in achieving business success, due to the actions of others, as well as the organisation's own IS/IT investments; and
(b) the internal organisational pressures which demand the distribution of information, systems and technology to the functions of the business due to the increasing capabilities of the technology and the ever decreasing unit costs.

Managing in such circumstances requires some organisational and administrative flexibility to reflect the varying nature of the role IS/IT fulfils and the different contributions it makes to the business.

A singular, rigid approach, such as many organisations adopted in the early years of data processing, does not accommodate the variety of issues that need to be understood and managed. Equally, a 'laissez-faire' attitude to controlling the use of IT will lead to significant waste, duplication and potential long-term chaos and even business disaster. A balance has to be found that provides sufficient degrees of freedom so that innovation and exploitation of IT options are not inhibited but also that large sums of money are not wasted on inappropriate or failed IS/IT investments.

PEOPLE AND ORGANISATION – THE IT DIMENSION

The focus of this section is on what needs to be done to ensure the provision of appropriate systems, technology and services to the business and considers the staffing and organisation of IT resources as a whole. Later the options for positioning and sourcing of those resources will be considered in more detail. It is worth reflecting on how IT organisations have developed over the last thirty years to understand what is now required, in relation to the current context and the legacy from the past. Most organisations have to manage their current and future information systems **and** remanage that often extensive legacy which was produced when the IT environment was very different. A good way of describing the evolving role of IT organisations was put forward by Zmud (1984), the essentials of which are very relevant today. The traditional role of IT was seen as a **manufacturing** one, where the objective was for IT to design and build a product to a specification and then maintain that product through its life. This led to a structure of functional specialists within IT, so that each set of activities was carried out by skilled specialists. The developing product was passed from group to group, (a) to ensure proper quality control and (b) to enable multiple projects to be run in parallel, very much like an engineering function. Systems analysts would work with the users to agree the business requirements and convert these to a technical specification, which would be passed to designers and programmers to construct. This in turn would be transferred to a technical services or operations group to run on the computers and they would schedule and control the system in 'production'. Maintenance and upgrades to the system would follow an equally tightly controlled set of change management steps, at least in principle.

To the business user much of what went on behind the closed (and often locked!) doors of the IT department was a mystery – and in many companies still is! The user's role was often seen by the IT people as simple – to specify what they needed, justify the expense and then use the resulting system properly. In essence a manufacturing- or product-based environment.

In Zmud's words that IT role has changed to one primarily of **distribution** which implies a service-based approach which facilitates the use of technology in the organisation. In essence the IT department has become one, and only one, of the channels of distribution that the IT suppliers have to the users. If that channel of distribution is ineffective then either the users or the IT vendors will bypass it. In some cases that channel will still involve a manufacturing process to build the systems – but that is a secondary aspect, not the primary reason for the way the IT department is structured. The IT function should be able to satisfy the majority of service needs of the rest of the organisation, or enable more direct liaison between the users and the vendors where this is more effective. It is often more expeditious to exclude the IT specialists from the link between the user and the vendor, but the loss of overall control of the types of hardware and software purchased may lead to systems incompatibility and excessive cost.

Figure 8.1 (adapted from Zmud's structure) shows an activity-based structure for the IT function, designed to be a distribution focused organisation, whose prime task is to provide services to satisfy the user's needs. Its secondary roles are to develop an architecture or blueprint for the management of systems, information and technology, to work with suppliers to plan for and introduce new technology and to support the general management processes of the business.

The main activities of the subfunctions are listed in Table 8.1. All of these activities need to be performed in a large organisation and most will need

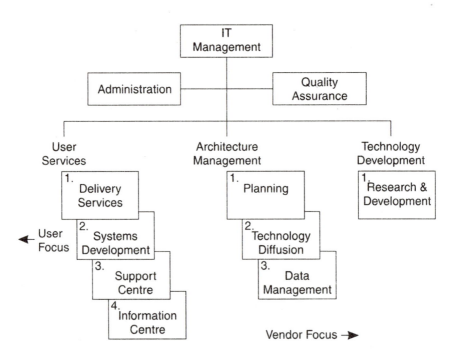

Figure 8.1 A possible structure for all the roles in the IT function

Source: Adapted from Zmud (1984)

attention in a small firm, although various subfunctions may be combined and carried out by one person. In a large organisation with several business units the 'user services' functions may to a large extent be distributed to the units. The architecture and technology management functions will probably be kept more centrally to enable effective co-ordination and control of relationships with vendors and also increase the buying leverage. There are also significant technical economies of scale to be gained, and avoided risks of lack of expertise, by keeping the very specialist technical resources at the centre. Replicating them throughout the business can be very expensive. As the technology becomes easier to use and the trend towards user development of applications is facilitated, more and more of the user service activities can migrate into the user functions. That is, of course, provided user management understand in full the long-term responsibilities involved, and establish an appropriately professional approach to discharging them.

This approach to structuring the IT function is compatible with the approach to managing applications described in the applications portfolio. The different user services will be more or less appropriate to the approach required to the development and ongoing support of the applications in the different segments of the portfolio. Figure 8.2 summarises the expected best fit based on the key aspects of the service required to match the core requirements of high potential, strategic, key operational and support systems. It will not be an exclusive relationship but the number of asterisks shows the degree to which the service generally meets the needs.

The other subfunctions are essentially at the hub of the portfolio supporting the applications management processes to a greater or lesser extent dependent on the size of the system, degree of integration required or the extent that new technology is being introduced by the applications.

The history of IT in many organisations can be described as a power struggle for control, which at various times has led to the centralisation or decentralisation of resources. It has seemed that control over the technology and associated resources has been the prime concern rather than using the technology in the best interests of the business. IT has often been a political football! The net result of overcentralisation and complete decentralisation is rarely satisfactory. The implications of the extremes have been known for many years. Table 8.2 summarises the problems, listed by McFarlan and McKenney (1983), which result when the IT function or the users dominate the decision-making. Clearly the long-term trend is to increasing degrees of user self-sufficiency enabled and enhanced by specialist technical skills. The general approach being adopted today in most organisations and described by a number of writers (La Belle and Nyce 1987 and Von Simson 1990) usually involves the centralisation of the core, vendor facing, technology-based activities and the decentralisation of the application-based activities. The key to achieving the right balance is to have in place appropriate **IS planning** activities in the business which can determine the demand, and appropriate **IT planning** processes which orchestrate the supply. If these are

Table 8.1 The roles of the IT function

Subfunction	Activities
User services	
1 Delivery services	Computer operations including job scheduling, etc. End-user facility operations support Telecommunications support Maintenance (hardware, systems software and applications software) End-user liaison and quality control for production systems
2 Systems development	System design and software development for production systems, for critical systems, for sensitive systems, for corporate-wide systems and for software tools
3 Support centre	Internal consulting service for organisational analyses, modelling, feasibility studies and systems analysis Broker for packaged software, external data services, word processors and personal computers End-user and systems personnel training
4 Information centre	Internal consulting service and support facilities for end-user applications development via micro-computers, decision support systems, modelling languages, data inquiry systems and automatic applications generators
Architecture management	
1 Planning	Overall information systems and technology planning Liaison with business strategic planning Overall evaluation of organisational use of information systems Establishing information policies Capacity and resource planning
2 Technology diffusion	Develop organisational infrastructure Investigate potential for applying new technologies within organisational areas Plan and manage new technology implementations and migrations Plan and manage pilot studies
3 Data management	Data dictionary Data base design and administration Access service control
Technology Development	
1 Research & Development	Monitor technical developments Develop technical infrastructure Technological forecasting
General	
1 Administration	Budgeting Personnel management Document management
2 Quality assurance	Standards development Evaluation of adherence to controls

Adapted from Zmud (1984).

PORTFOLIO SEGMENT / USER SERVICE	HIGH POTENTIAL	STRATEGIC	KEY OPERATIONAL	SUPPORT
1. Delivery Serices	–	***	***	**
2. Systems Development	*	***	**	*
3. Support Centre	**	*	*	***
4. Information Centre	***	*	*	***

Figure 8.2 Relationship of user service to the applications portfolio

working effectively, and mechanisms for doing this are described later, the actual distribution of resources in the organisation then becomes less of an issue. If there are no planning mechanisms, control of resources becomes the focus of the arguments.

THE PEOPLE RESOURCE – STRATEGIC ISSUES

So far this chapter has taken a logical view of the IT-related activities and functions that need to be structured, organised and managed. Clearly the activities have to be appropriately organised, but a further key factor in success is how well the people in the organisation perform those activities – their knowledge, skills and experience and the ability of the business to obtain the greatest contribution from high quality, well-motivated people. The organisation's ability to obtain, develop and retain highly skilled IS/IT resources, will determine in the long-term how much benefit the business gains from IS/IT. Well-qualified, capable IS/IT staff are in short supply and in great demand and this is especially true in areas of newer technology – such as the use of EDI, the application of expert systems, client-server technology, etc. There are essentially only four ways in which the skilled resource can be obtained. These are:

(a) Training new recruits from school or university, which is expensive. Also people early in their careers are more likely to move on within three to five years.
(b) Training existing non-IT people – especially in application skills in user areas.

Table 8.2 Effects of excessive dominance of . . .

IT Department	User Departments
• Forcing new systems to fit existing data structures – integration and tailored systems focus • Little innovation with new suppliers, technologies or services • Insistence on feasibility and cost/benefit studies in response to all requests • IT organisation based on technical specialisations, not user need • 'Maintenance' absorbs bulk of resources – up to 80+% • Users frustrated, senior management often not involved; 'secret' growth of user machines and staff	• Short-term problem focus, growth of incompatible systems • Hidden maintenance overhead due to proliferation of services/suppliers • Lack of quality control of data • Lack of experience/skill transfer duplication and differential rates of development • Little cost/benefit analysis or objective justification of systems • Rapid growth in (duplicated) technical staff • Central IT group degenerates

(c) Recruiting experienced IT people from other organisations.

(d) Buying-in external resources, for specific aspects of the work.

Whilst training is initially expensive, using external resources is potentially a higher long-term financial commitment unless it is to deal with a known and controllable peak load. Such 'outsourcing' options are considered below. Recruiting experienced staff can be expensive and whilst 'fresh blood' is often a healthy stimulant, they need to learn a lot about the business before they are fully effective.

Consider the following scenario which has become increasingly common. The existing IT staff are 'bogged down' in key operational and support systems, mainly maintenance and rewrites. A new major strategic development is conceived, but cannot be resourced internally in the time required. Decision: bring in external resources to develop the strategic application. What are the potential long-term consequences?

1 An open-ended contract with the external supplier to meet an ever-changing requirement for the strategic development.

2 No one in the IT department is capable of understanding and supporting it in due course, nor is there any real motivation to do so.

3 What will the external supplier do with the valuable knowledge gained? Undoubtedly 'sell' it elsewhere in the market place – perhaps indirectly to a competitor.

4 Demoralised staff who have to do the 'boring old work' which does not improve their skills while others get the 'good jobs'. They often leave – sometimes to join the external supplier! – and the situation worsens.

It can become a vicious circle. By referring to the rationale of the applications portfolio it should be clear that the one area that must not be handed over to outside parties is that which provides the future business advantage! Equally, the one area that can be handed over the purely economic consequences is the 'support' quadrant or much of what it contains. Outsourcing or facilities management can be employed in order to release resources to use elsewhere. If the organisation is to develop its capability **and** provide an attractive environment to its skilled people, its own resources, IT and user, must be deployed on the challenging strategic or high potential systems as well as keeping the key operational systems up to the business needs. If anything, it is more appropriate to pay outside resources to deliver key operational systems to a clear contractual specification rather than use scarce internal resources. Quality control could be maintained by a strong quality assurance process applied to the subcontractor.

It may of course be necessary to buy in some special skills that the organisation does not have to help evaluate a high potential idea or even assist in developing a strategic application. This resource should be bought with the objective of extracting that special knowledge for the benefit of the organisation, by using it not just to deliver results but also to train internal staff. In every case the organisation should ensure it gains more than the external supplier does from the arrangement.

The long-term aim is to move resources out of the support quadrant by finding less resource-intensive means, and whilst ensuring key operational systems are adequately resourced, develop a capability to carry out strategic and high potential projects. These ideas in terms of the applications portfolio are summarised in Figure 8.3.

Whilst it is obviously important to ensure that good 'hygiene factors' exist for all staff, the fact that IT staff are generally young, relatively well educated and good ones are in short supply means they are generally mobile. Hence retaining the best ones is not always easy – they often equate their career development to the 'IT profession' (whatever that is!) rather than the organisation that employs them. Their career opportunities will therefore depend to a large extent on the experience they can gain on a variety of applications using a range of modern technologies. One could therefore take a negative approach and use the most potentially mobile staff on limited types of systems using old technology! However, this would be counter-productive since

(a) they will leave anyway, dissatisfied with their lot; and
(b) the organisation's technical skills will be fossilised in the base of older technologies.

The long-term solution is normally to establish specific pay and reward schemes for the IT specialists, which match the types of people, age, marketability, etc., and provide good internal career development options. These can be best achieved in a large IT department, where management opportunities and a wide variety of

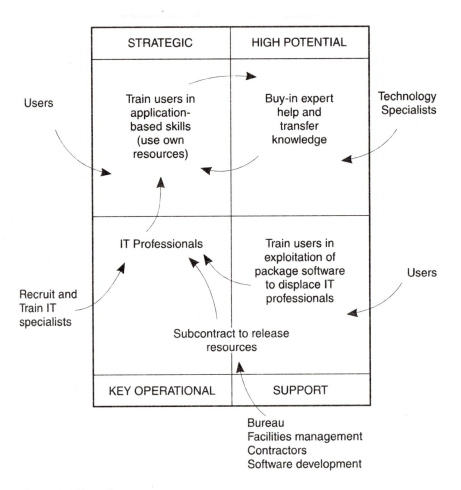

Figure 8.3 Use of resources

experiences can exist. It is difficult to achieve when IT specialists are dispersed in small groups throughout the organisation.

Alternatively, people who commence their careers in the IT function are also candidates for jobs in other parts of the business, where initially at least their IT skills are valuable. Often IT staff move into business areas with the intention of broadening their general experience and opening up new career prospects, only to find they are really employed as a general IT support person, doing what they did before but with less prospects for the future. Any such move should be considered as part of the organisation's personnel development policy, not as a way of solving users' short-term IS/IT problems. Inevitably, as time goes by more general managers will evolve from the IT function, and IT is often a good training ground given the disciplines involved and also the breadth of contact IT staff, especially systems staff, will have with the business. This, if coupled with a good training programme in business and management subjects, can ensure that the best IT staff are retained and developed in the best long-term interests of the organisation.

The corollary to this is that as more businesses become highly dependent on IT-based information systems for success, can they afford to have general management teams who do not have experience in managing the increasingly critical resource? It is not just a question of promoting the person who manages the bulk of the IT resource to board level – having an 'IT director'. This can help but can also be counter-productive if the other board members assume, wrongly, that he or she will now deal with all **IS** and **IT** issues. It is every director's and senior manager's responsibility to ensure that the information systems are meeting the business needs, the IT director can only be held accountable for the supply-side of the equation. In some large organisations, notably financial service companies and even in government, where the only business technology is IT, promotion to a senior management position requires some time spent in managing IT. One major leisure group requires all IT specialists to have spent time in the business before taking up an IT management post.

These transfers between business and IT functions can only serve to improve the general management's ability to deal with IS and IT as a normal part of 'managing the business' – rather than treat both IS and IT as a peculiar, mysterious even threatening aspect of modern business. The concept of the 'hybrid manager' has been discussed extensively over the last few years – 'hybrid' having a particular meaning with regard to a person's ability to manage a business activity and its IT component at one and the same time. Whilst in the general sense everyone is to some extent a hybrid in that they may be a marketing manager but have to manage people, it is worrying that the term has been applied particularly, even exclusively, to IT. If nothing else it perpetuates the myth that somehow IT is abnormal. At any one time, every manager is responsible for the quality of the information and systems in their area of the business, just as they are for the people in that area, or the budget they have. If they are technically literate, or at least not technology averse, they will be able to contribute better to the discussion of supply-side issues and options. But if their technical knowledge is, as is likely, incomplete and out of date, over-involvement in supply-side decisions can be disastrous. It would seem difficult for any senior manager to sustain comprehensive knowledge of both business and IT over any extended period given the rate of change in both. Other means have to be put in place to bring together and reconcile the demand and supply issues. These are considered a little later in the chapter.

TO INSOURCE OR OUTSOURCE? THAT IS THE QUESTION

It may not be **the** question but it is **a** question that many senior management teams are wrestling with today. The question is really – how many of the IT supply-side activities, as described earlier in the chapter, should be carried out in-house and how many are better supplied by external organisations? Some of the issues have been discussed earlier, but a more overall, strategic view of sourcing options needs to be considered. Much has been published recently on the subject of outsourcing and there are many well-documented case studies of both success and failure. Almost every organisation outsources aspects of IT but some rely exclusively on other parties to provide the whole gamut of IT services it needs. Buying a software package is outsourcing, in that the development process has been outsourced. At the other extreme, one oil company has outsourced not just its accounting systems but the majority of its accountants with them! Others no longer own or operate any of the computers or software that they use. Outsourcing is essentially a question of the degree to which the organisation can rely on outside parties to meet its needs and whether it is more beneficial and cost-effective in the long-term to satisfy those needs internally or externally.

Taking the example of buying or building a system for which a package is available, some of the more general issues of outsourcing become apparent. Once the business needs are defined and the potential benefits known then the decision to buy or build will depend essentially on the future certainty that those needs and benefits will not change significantly, i.e. on the stability of the situation. If it is likely that the needs will not change and therefore the system will need little if any amendment in the foreseeable future then the buy option is likely to prove less risky and more economical in the long term. If however the needs for the future are uncertain and the system will need continuous and major change to meet the rapidly evolving business needs, then the build solution is likely to be best, giving the business the ability to change it to any extent needed. Buying a package may preclude future changes entirely or they may only be possible at very significant cost. The business effectively may have to forgo future benefits and that may even lead to real business constraints.

The same basic issues have to be considered with regard to outsourcing where the short-term economics must be seen in the context of the long-term flexibility/ stability of the business needs. In general the more stable the business IS needs are, the more appropriate it becomes to use external suppliers to deliver the necessary IT products and services. It is far easier to define and manage a service 'contract' when all the factors affecting the contract are well known and unlikely to change.

Unfortunately the recent almost headlong rush into outsourcing by many organisations, especially in the public sector, has been based on short-term cost issues and in the public sector the policy of competitive tendering for all services. The outsourcing vendors can easily package up the services and contracts in such a way that they offer short-term cost reduction against existing needs, whereas the contract is less specific about the longer-term cost of meeting, as yet unknown, requirements. By serving a number of clients the vendor can achieve economies of scale that a smaller dedicated IT function can never achieve.

Whilst the above discussion may have appeared cautious, even negative, about outsourcing it is because, on a large scale, it is a relatively new way of meeting the range of supply-side needs and there is little experience of the long-term effects. To be more positive when used as part of a clear IS/IT strategy it can be very effective. A leading builders' merchants had developed its IS/IT strategy and was actively implementing its branch management and control systems throughout its 150-branch network, when the company took over a rival with sixty branches. The acquired company had its own systems based on totally different and incompatible software and hardware. The support of these systems was immediately outsourced to a third party, to enable the organisation to continue to implement its strategy without distraction. In due course the strategy was extended to those of the acquired branches that were retained and after three years the old, acquired systems ceased to run and the outsourcing contract ended.

In summary, outsourcing is a valid partial strategy for sourcing IT in most organisations and to some, especially smaller organisations operating in stable environments, it may provide a total solution. Some large organisations, however, leapt to almost total outsourcing because they were dissatisfied with the performance of their own internal function. Management may have overlooked the fact that **they** may well have been the main cause of the apparently poor IT organisation, and merely changing the source of supply will not necessarily produce better results.

GOVERNING THE INFORMATION SYSTEMS AND TECHNOLOGY OF THE ORGANISATION

In the 'complex' IS/IT environment described by Sullivan, when the business is developing and operating a comprehensive application portfolio, merely establishing appropriate organisation structures and resources is often not sufficient for long-term success. When reconsidering the 'strategic management requirements' or objectives listed in Table 7.1, it is clear that some cannot be met simply by policies, procedures and structural allocation of roles. This is especially true of the strategic parts of the application portfolio where the initiation, planning and delivery require the consensus of view and commitment of top management to achieve success – the environment within which Earl's 'organisational' (theme-based) approach to planning and the 'centrally planned' approach to implementation require a 'coalition of thinking' amongst senior executives, IT and line management. Hence the term used here: governing the whole range of IS and IT activities that need to be co-ordinated to achieve success in this 'complex' environment.

If some mechanism is not established over and above the normal organisational structure many of the really strategic issues which affect the long-term success of IS and IT in large organisations will not be dealt with. Most organisations understand and attempt to address these issues via some form of steering group of senior executives who meet at regular (if not frequent) intervals to address them. Extensive lists of reasons are often given as to why such groups are established but there are always two reasons which are not easily satisfied any other way. Both relate to the centralisation/decentralisation of control of IS demand and IT supply. If IT resources are highly centralised there is a need at a senior level to assess and prioritise demand and then set an appropriate resource level. If the IT capability is highly decentralised then there is a need to co-ordinate the applications planning: (a) to ensure that incompatible developments are not undertaken and IS/IT does not actually create business problems, and (b) to ensure that the IT resources are actually employed where there is business benefit to be obtained. Overall, the role of the steering group is designed to bring together the executive management regularly to ensure that the programme of IS/IT investment is linked clearly and coherently to the business strategy they are pursuing.

If the steering group is established for any other reason or set of reasons, i.e. reasons not related to the strategic role and direction for IS/IT in the business, it is likely to fail. And many do fail to contribute anything over and above what can be achieved by the normal processes of management. Some even introduce a new and unpredictable variable to those normal processes, resulting in contradiction and confusion! Unless there is some distinct value to be added to normal manage-ment processes by the steering group it is likely to be a liability not an asset! The lack of a clear value-adding role is usually the reason why they fail or at least degenerate to a talking shop attended by the executives' nominees rather than the executives themselves.

Even if the right people can meet to discuss the right subjects at the right time there is a further problem to overcome. There is a need for a supporting infra-structure of review and discussion which ensures the right agenda is put before the executive and also that its decisions are implemented. Given that the group is likely to meet, say, four to six times each year for some two to three hours at a time, they can have little effect on the many man-years of activity that occur between meetings unless there is a clearly focused agenda and the means of converting decisions through revised plans to appropriate actions. In essence the steering group must formally agree the IS/IT strategy overall on the basis that it fits the business strategy for the foreseeable future.

There are two further levels or stages required to achieve success with any strategy, as shown in Figure 8.4.

(a) What needs to be done, when and by whom to achieve the direction and targets set in the strategy has to be **planned** by the managers of the relevant resources and activities using their particular expertise and knowledge.

(b) Those plans have to be carried out successfully if the strategy is to be **implemented,** and again operational expertise and skill are essential.

Balancing this top-down approach there has to be a feedback and control mechanism. Once the implications of the strategic direction have been converted to plans, there are likely to be issues of resourcing or timing which will affect the achievement of the strategic objectives. These may have to be referred back to

FORMAL STRATEGIC PLANNING

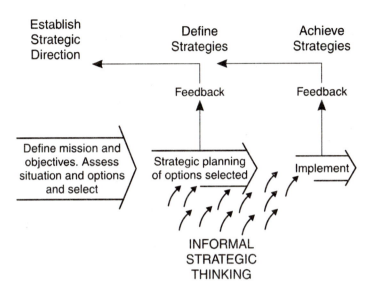

Figure 8.4 Strategic management processes

either accommodate them in the strategy or approve the increase of resources or reassess priorities. Equally plans are not always implemented as expected and when problems occur they can require either replanning of other activities or in some cases a reappraisal of the strategy. These relationships and feedback and control mechanisms need to be put in place to deal with changes or consequences in both demand and supply, i.e. in the business and IT domains of responsibility. Figure 8.5 describes an outline structure of activities which need to be carried out and continuously reconciled if a coherent strategy is to be developed and achieved.

This is a simple structure which may need adaptation or extension for larger organisations but the main purposes and functions of each are summarised below; a more detailed checklist of the suggested responsibilities is shown in Table 8.3.

To understand how the groups should work and inter-relate it is probably easiest to start at the **demand** side of Figure 8.5, i.e. with the 'business IS Planning' and 'Application Management Groups'.

Business (or functional) is planning groups

Depending on the organisation's structure, these may be established for each business unit or major function (or both if the organisation consists of both units and service functions). In a one-unit business this role and the executive steering group will clearly overlap.

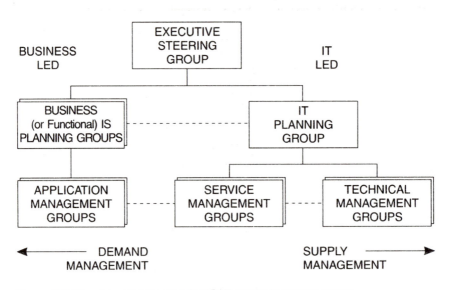

Figure 8.5 Steering organisation for IS/IT strategic management

Ideally, the representative of the business area on the executive steering group should 'chair' the IS planning process, although ideally, business IS planning should be part of the agenda for whatever business planning process exists. Either way the senior line managers involved in the business should be directly involved with the IS planning group. Their job is to produce a valid IS strategic plan that will deliver maximum benefit to their business area.

Whilst the obvious responsibilities include ensuring business priorities and requirements are reflected in the planned application portfolio for the area, it is also this group's responsibility to ensure that the plans inter-relate with plans in other business areas and are understood by the IT planning group. Where mismatches occur, problems should be resolved amongst the planning groups if at all possible rather than be escalated to the executive steering group.

In structural terms the planning group is the key link between the organisation's executive and the systems that the business has, and it must have a clear understanding of both the business strategic direction and the role that systems fulfil.

Application management groups

As was described in Chapter 6, application management is a business responsibility, since it is the business that has to define, use and get benefits from the systems. For each large system there should be an application manager, as described in Chapter 6, whose task it is to establish the needs of the business area and ensure those needs are satisfied by the system. The application management

Table 8.3 Responsibilities within the IS/IT steering group structure

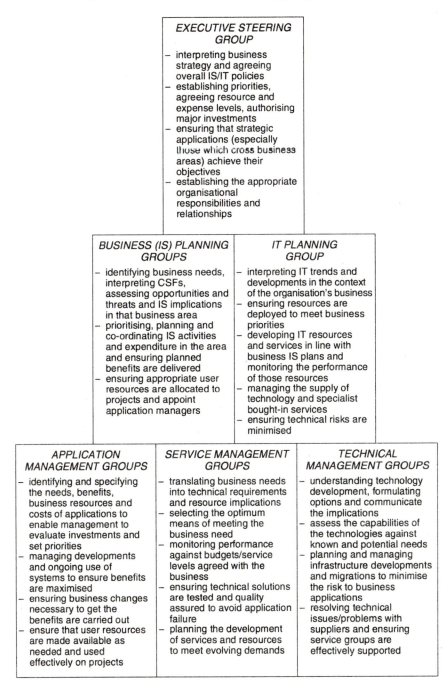

EXECUTIVE STEERING GROUP
- interpreting business strategy and agreeing overall IS/IT policies
- establishing priorities, agreeing resource and expense levels, authorising major investments
- ensuring that strategic applications (especially those which cross business areas) achieve their objectives
- establishing the appropriate organisational responsibilities and relationships

BUSINESS (IS) PLANNING GROUPS
- identifying business needs, interpreting CSFs, assessing opportunities and threats and IS implications in that business area
- prioritising, planning and co-ordinating IS activities and expenditure in the area and ensuring planned benefits are delivered
- ensuring appropriate user resources are allocated to projects and appoint application managers

IT PLANNING GROUP
- interpreting IT trends and developments in the context of the organisation's business
- ensuring resources are deployed to meet business priorities
- developing IT resources and services in line with business IS plans and monitoring the performance of those resources
- managing the supply of technology and specialist bought-in services
- ensuring technical risks are minimised

APPLICATION MANAGEMENT GROUPS
- identifying and specifying the needs, benefits, business resources and costs of applications to enable management to evaluate investments and set priorities
- managing developments and ongoing use of systems to ensure benefits are maximised
- ensuring business changes necessary to get the benefits are carried out
- ensure that user resources are made available as needed and used effectively on projects

SERVICE MANAGEMENT GROUPS
- translating business needs into technical requirements and resource implications
- selecting the optimum means of meeting the business need
- monitoring performance against budgets/service levels agreed with the business
- ensuring technical solutions are tested and quality assured to avoid application failure
- planning the development of services and resources to meet evolving demands

TECHNICAL MANAGEMENT GROUPS
- understanding technology development, formulating options and communicate the implications
- assess the capabilities of the technologies against known and potential needs
- planning and managing infrastructure developments and migrations to minimise the risk to business applications
- resolving technical issues/problems with suppliers and ensuring service groups are effectively supported

group should comprise that manager and the key users of the system. For a small system the 'group' may be one person, and the group may meet very infrequently – but how well the group process works will be a critical factor in the development and exploitation of large, cross-functional strategic systems where the 'central planning' approach to implementation is needed. The two groups so far are in combination responsible for managing demand. There are three groups involved in the management of supply.

IT planning, service management and technical management groups

The IT limb of the structure consists of three parts, two of which have been discussed earlier in the chapter. Overall resource and technology planning and development is the responsibility of the IT management team, but must also include or allow for IT resources not directly under their control. The head of the IT organisation should be a member of the executive steering group, but in that role he or she is first a senior manager and second an IT professional. The IT planning group is required to support the executive team's planning and produce the organisation's IT strategy.

The IT planning group should consist of the IT senior management team plus, if appropriate, senior user managers who control significant IT resources. This group will bring together the resource implications of the IS plans as well as determine the main aspects of technology development and capacity. It should direct the activities of the service and technical groups which are effectively the IT organisation as described earlier in this chapter, but once more Service Management should include any IT services which are located in the business areas.

One responsibility it must undertake is to interpret the implications of IT developments and trends for the executive steering group in relation to the business and its strategy. Some advantage will accrue by being technically advanced provided it can be exploited in business terms, and the executive must be aware of the potential opportunities and threats for IT innovation.

The effectiveness of the relationship between business-biased application management and IT-biased service management groups will determine not only how well applications are managed during development, but also whether the best application development approach is adopted in the first place.

The ability of service and technical management groups to work together will determine whether technology is employed on the basis of what it does for the business rather than just what it does! Technical specialists have a very important role in the organisation, but they and business-oriented users often fail to communicate. The service groups are the interpreters in both directions, capable of understanding the language of business and technology.

The executive steering group

This group is as critical to the whole structure as the keystone is to an arch. If the planning groups are responsible for developing demand-and-supply strategic plans then one key role of the executive steering group is to ensure these are in balance. This will involve reconciliation of demand vs. supply issues through a process of priority setting or by authorising changes in the resource level. Priorities within a business area should be resolved by the planning groups but priority setting across functions (marketing vs. logistics, say) or amongst business units will need to be resolved by the executive group. Ideally those IS/IT issues should be incorporated in the normal executive meeting process, but initially at least special meetings on IS/IT may be necessary. One further responsibility that cannot be discharged at a lower level is to understand and then action the potential synergies or cross-unit/cross-functional IS opportunities, where some strategic advantage can be obtained or disadvantage avoided. Policies can be put in place as described in Chapter 5, but ensuring that no cross-business opportunity is forgone will require some active intervention by the executive steering group. Lower-level views may become blinkered, even parochial, leading at best to duplication of effort and at worst to incompatible and mutually destructive IS/IT investments being made!

It is not just what the steering group does that is important, but the way that it does it. Its process should be open not secretive; its decisions should be communicated quickly and widely; it should demonstrate both its willingness to consider ideas from the planning groups which require such attention, and it should be quick to redelegate trivial non-strategic matters. These are all aspects of establishing an appropriate business based culture with respect to managing IS and IT. Finally, it should ensure that IS/IT successes as well as failures are recognised!

In summary this governing structure addresses some key facets of IS/IT strategic management:

- top management involvement where it is most useful;
- business and IT balance in determining strategy; supply-and-demand management;
- strategy, planning, implementation requirements;
- exploitation of ideas generated from anywhere;
- an ability to learn from and transfer experience;
- command and control in effecting policy decisions;
- consistency over time in developing and implementing strategies.

From using the model to assess the management of IS/IT in many organisations it is clear that if one or more of the functions is missing, or is ineffective, or not linked properly to related functions, then either strategies are not being developed or they are not being implemented. Many organisations need and use variations of this basic model – variations which allow for the size and diversity or otherwise of the business, the degree of corporate control exercised and the stage of IS/IT development, as determined by the nature of the application portfolio.

ORGANISATIONAL POSITIONING OF THE IT 'DEPARTMENT'

During the last twenty years the position of the manager whose sole responsibility is IT (hereafter called the IT manager), has gradually risen in the organisation. That is not to say the incumbent has always risen with the job, since as the role has been seen to be more important, so the managerial skills required have become greater. The best technician rarely makes the best executive, although until the 1980s most IT managers had a profoundly technical background.

According to all that has been argued before, information and IS applications pervade the whole business and their management is the responsibility of every line manager and their co-ordination a collective executive responsibility, i.e. essentially demand-side management. However, there are many aspects of pre-dominantly supply-side or IT management which need to be managed together, often centrally. Whether that department should report to the chief executive officer (CEO) or through another executive is a matter of debate and should really depend upon both how critical IT is to long-term business success and how similar service groups within the organisation report into the executive structure.

In a bank, for instance, IT is the technology of banking and an IT director would seem logical, not that an IT specialist should necessarily fill the job. In a high-technology company where IT is one of a number of technologies, it might well report to a technical director. Where IT is primarily seen as a commercial weapon, critical to the future of the business, such as in retailing, IT is likely to report through a commercial or business development executive. If IT is still only (or seen to be only) an administrative support tool then it may well report through finance (as was often historically the case), or some other essentially administrative/ services executive.

Normally as the application portfolio matures and the business dependency increases, so the IT manager migrates up through the hierarchy. At the same time, it is increasingly likely that the person filling the job will come from the business rather than from the IT department. A word of caution is worthwhile here. A study by Earl and Feeny (1994) of the role of chief information officers and IT directors suggests that the most successful IT directors are those with a sound IT background. In addition they must possess a set of attributes required in any top executive – integrity, loyalty plus good coaching and communication skills and an openness to new ideas.

RECONCILING THE CULTURE GAP BETWEEN IT AND THE BUSINESS

In spite of all that has been said earlier in this chapter about how the IT activities can be organised and governed to provide appropriate services to the business, there often exists in many organisations a gap in understanding and attitudes between the business functions and the IT community. This can be considered as a 'culture' gap, the effects of which are summarised in Figure 8.6. No one is trying to create the gap and each group is normally pursuing 'excellence' in its own way. Historically the gap, or even a chasm of misunderstanding, developed due to the technological 'mysticism' often cultivated by IT staff combined with the technological aversion of the average business manager. Early attempts to bridge the gap were through process improvements – the design of methodologies where the roles of the business manager, user of the system and IT specialist were clearly defined and a structured process defined how and when each would interact. Aspects of this were discussed in Chapter 6. Whilst this worked to an extent and improved the probability of success in well-structured projects, the long-term relationship between the business and IT staff rarely improved significantly. In effect it enables key operational and support applications to be developed and supported more successfully.

However, as the types of applications evolved into those of a high potential or strategic nature the gap tended to widen once more because the 'methodological' solution became less appropriate to those types of development. This problem was analysed by Crescenzi (1988) who studied thirty-four strategic application developments of which only four could be deemed wholly successful.

He used the McKinsey seven-S structure to analyse the differences between the successful and less than successful developments. A summary of the analysis is shown in Table 8.4, which shows that aspects of each of the seven-S's which are characteristic of failure and success and how they clearly differ. In most cases the attributes associated with failure are common characteristics of the methodological approach which is appropriate to key operational applications or the 'job shop' approach which is effective for support systems.

The characteristics of success relate in essence very well to the 'organisational' approach to planning and the 'centrally planned' approach to implementation

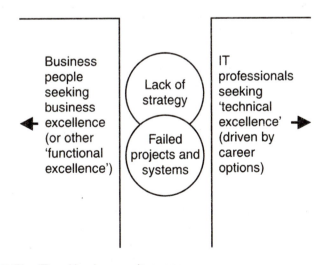

Figure 8.6 The IT and business culture gap

Table 8.4 Strategic information systems – success and failure by the 'seven Ss'

Success	S	Failure
Top-down management. Focus on business goals. Evolutionary development	Strategy	Focus on systems and technology
Team	Structure	Hierarchy
Selling and education. Accepting ambiguity	Skills	Technical only. Structured/inflexible approaches
Reward risk taking. Intuitive justification	Systems	Discourage risk/creativity. Financial justification
Loose, flexible	Style	Specified duties and roles
Visionary/champions. Accommodate different views in small team	Staff	'Superstars' not teams – different views not accommodated
Unselfish – share ideas and power. Accept imperfection	Shared values	Separation of user/IT. Technical excellence of systems (perfection)

After Crescenzi (1988).

described earlier. The key is a joint team in which the experience and skills of each member are respected, valued and exploited to enable the project to succeed. This implies greater flexibility of working on behalf of the IT specialists than perhaps they would ideally like or are used to. Most strategic applications require the team members to deliver more than the sum of the component skills if they are to create a unique system which by definition is ahead of others in the industry. Looking at the problem of managing each of the different types of application in the portfolio from a slightly different perspective, one can determine the essential characteristics required of the application manager. By comparing the ideas of the application portfolio with those developed about the Boston Consulting Group version of the product portfolio ('wild cats', 'stars', 'cash cows', 'dogs') then appropriate management styles for the applications can be defined. As the application moves round the portfolio during its business life, then the style of management, and often the application manager, will have to change if the system is to be managed according to its business contribution.

1 **High potential** applications require a similar style of wild cat-products, namely **entrepreneurial**, to champion the application through phases of doubt or decide to stop if the potential is not realisable. Entrepreneurs are strongly personally motivated, expecting recognition of their personal success. At the

same time they recognise that they must not be judged to have failed by others, and will either be adept at avoiding failure or be the first to decide it is not worth proceeding.

They also do not obey the rules and hence will cause change and innovation which implies changing preconceived ideas or ignoring or bypassing accepted custom and practice. This mode of operation is very appropriate for the high potential situation, but would be wholly inappropriate elsewhere in the matrix.

2 **Strategic** systems require more nurturing, to gain organisational acceptance through demonstrated contribution to the achievement of organisational goals and objectives. A style of **'developer'** best describes the type of manager required. A developer is someone who will acquire and develop the resources necessary to achieve the task or business objectives. Other terms to describe this are 'organisational climber' – someone whose career ambitions will be met by being related to the achievement of organisational success – or 'empire builder' – a much maligned term! A developer is a planner who achieves results through others, a team manager who moulds the resource to match the needs of achieving the strategic objective, and will be flexible to changing circumstances – adapting the means to achieve the end result.

3 **Key operational** systems require a different style of management entirely. 'Controller' is an appropriate term. A controller is risk averse, wanting everything to be done correctly and failure never to occur. Assurance of success implies reducing risk to a minimum via quality control, strict adherence to procedure and standards and building an organisation structure and mentality which is self-checking and control conscious. The best way of achieving quality control is to build it into the organisation by cross-checking procedures.

The controller approach is essentially inflexible, resistant to change, since change causes confusion and error. Within clearly defined parameters the status quo will be defended and ideas carefully scrutinised and evaluated before changes will be allowed. This is a critical requirement if key operational systems are to be managed to avoid disadvantages due to failure.

4 **Support** applications are ideally best managed with a **'caretaker'** approach. Caretaker managers get their satisfaction from achieving 'the impossible, with no resources, repeatedly' and have to be congratulated for it! It is a reactive, problem-solving approach where planning and resource management are less important than getting the job done expediently and efficiently to the satisfaction of the client. This implies a multi-tasking, flexible approach to achieving results which are not of any strategic impact but which will cause a major distraction from strategic objectives if not dealt with in a timely and adept manner. Support systems have no great future potential impact but will be a constant source of irritation if mismanaged.

An entrepreneur is impatient to achieve results to demonstrate his or her personal capability, whereas a developer has longer-term career aims of achieving success through the organisation. A controller wants to prevent the failure of the organisation and a caretaker wants to be recognised as an effective user of limited resources in solving problems. The nature of these management styles reflects the generic strategies required to manage the various components of the portfolio:

- an entrepreneur is a free marketeer, who pays little attention to established procedure;
- a developer is a central planner, close to the organisational goals who builds resources to achieve results;
- a controller is a monopolist, uncomfortable with anything outside his or her control;
- a caretaker is a scarce resourcer – proving he or she can achieve as much with less!

If the strategy is to be achieved then the appropriate management styles must be adopted and the strategy will not be achieved by managers who are 'square pegs in round holes' – a 'developer' managing support systems will develop ever larger, more significant versions of relatively inconsequential systems; a 'controller' expected to develop a high potential opportunity will never take the first risk! And so on . . .

The cultural web of the IT function

A technique, somewhat similar in concept to the seven-S structure, which has proved valuable in understanding the cultural aspects of business performance is the cultural web (Johnson and Scholes 1993). Normally it is used to assess the inter-related components of a whole organisation's cultural attributes in the context of its business environment and strategy. But it is also useful in describing the 'subculture' of any function and how that influences its relationships with the rest of the business. The basic model as shown in Figure 8.7 shows the interacting features of the organisation.

At the core of the model, the 'paradigm' or 'recipe' of the organisational unit, summarises the core set of beliefs and assumptions which actually fashion an organisation's view of itself, its environment and purpose. (This is similar to the 'shared values' component of the seven-S model.) Around this revolve three 'hard' and three 'soft' components of the culture through which the organisation promulgates, deliberately or unintentionally, its core beliefs. Power and organisational structures and the control systems reflect how the organisation officially works and can be defined and described in rational, objective terms. The other three – symbols, stories and myths, rituals and routines – are less rational and reflect what people, inside and outside the organisation, actually see and often remember most about the way the organisation conducts itself. These can have just as significant an effect in defining the basic beliefs or perceived beliefs of the organisation. To succeed an organisation must demonstrate consistency and compatibility between its beliefs and all aspects of its behaviour both in terms of

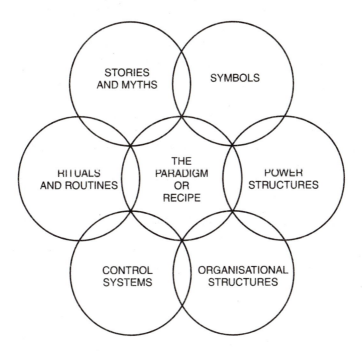

Figure 8.7 The cultural web

Source: After Johnson and Scholes (1993)

its internal management processes and its external relationships. When used to describe an organisation it is a powerful diagnostic tool which can enable better understanding of the areas in which change and improvement are needed. Later the effects of changes made can also be reflected in order to understand whether or not they have had the desired effect. An example of using the technique to describe the views a business had of its IT department, obtained from a 'customer survey' is given in Figure 8.8.

Clearly the business did not think highly of its IT department! In fact the management of the IT department had been working hard restructuring the IT organisation, improving the control of activities and getting line managers involved in decision-making about IT. However, the symbols, stories and rituals as perceived from the 'customers' had changed little over time – the IT management was largely unaware of these and the impact they had on its ability to work effectively in the business. This is partly to be expected given that IT managers are generally logical, rational thinkers and they therefore focus on the more rational elements of the 'web'. Even when these are actually made more effective, the other components will colour both internal and external perceptions of the function, based on past performance. Unless conscious efforts are made to change

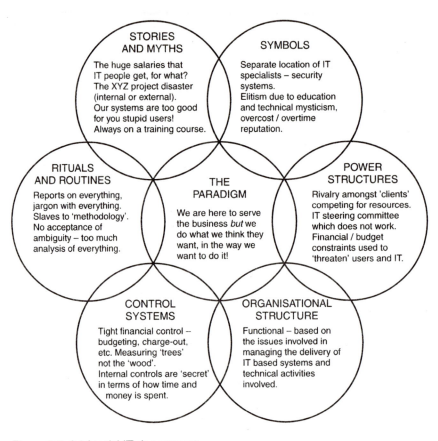

Figure 8.8 A 'classic' IT department

these elements of the web to make them consistent with the intended paradigm the organisation will not be more successful. This takes time and in the process it is necessary to 'unmake' history, eradicate old perceptions as well as create the required future. Traditionally IT management have not focused their attention on these softer aspects of their relationship with the business, resulting in the IT department's contribution being less valuable and less valued than it could and should have been.

Many organisations have recognised that there is a 'culture gap' between the IT function and many other parts of the organisation and are taking steps to reduce the gap. Much of the discussion in this chapter has been about ways of integrating the IT operational and management activities with the rest of the organisation, in order to eliminate the gap. These are summarised in Figure 8.9 which reflects the reality that many organisations are taking steps at various levels to enable the IT function to work effectively in partnership with the rest of the business and enable IS and IT strategies to be developed and implemented successfully over the long-term. It seems that concerted action is required at all levels, from the creation of an executive steering group to changing working relationships through new job roles at the 'coal face', if this is to be successful and sustainable.

ADMINISTRATIVE ISSUES

Most of this chapter has been devoted to considering the particular organisational and people management aspects associated with information systems. In doing so it has also addressed some of the administrative issues for which formal and informal policies and processes have to be established. Administrative issues fall into two categories:

(a) those which are general to the organisation where IS/IT should be treated no differently from any other business activity or function; and
(b) those that only affect the IS/IT activities of the business – such as data and information management issues as addressed in the last chapter. Some aspects of managing IT people also fall into this category and these were discussed earlier, as was the need for the governing mechanisms of the

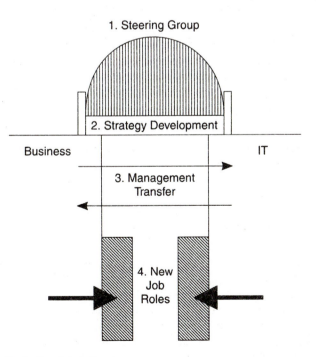

Figure 8.9 Reducing the culture gap

steering and planning groups. Aspects of managing technology procurement are also particular to IT and these were also considered in the previous chapter.

In principle IS/IT issues should be dealt with via the general administrative policies and procedures in force in the rest of the organisation. IS/IT should be seen to be an integral part of the business, and the more it has its own peculiar policies the less likely that integration will occur. Whilst, for instance, the acquisition of appropriate technology and the use of specialist IT services requires particular technical knowledge, the purchasing of IT products and services from both a financial and legal perspective, should be dealt with like any other procurement of any other business resources or services. No separate practices should exist which enable normal business policies to be ignored or bypassed by the excuse that IS/IT is in some way unique and should be dealt with separately.

Having said that, one or two aspects of the administration of IS/IT have often become different from normal management practice. One of these was dealt with earlier in terms of the way investments in IS/IT normally have to pass a multitude of tests, at least in principle, due to the lack of clarity about what the investment consists of: capital expense on 'machinery' and/or revenue expense on software, services and the use of internal people. At the other extreme too little thought has been given in most organisations to the process of managing and reviewing the attainment of the benefits used to justify the investment. This lack of a post-implementation evaluation of benefits gained tends to make a mockery of the stringency of the justification process. Many organisations realise this and the justification process becomes a 'game' that is played, often involving a 'conspiracy of lies', to ensure that what people want to do gets done. This is very disappointing and it is to be hoped that in the future the process of justifying and then evaluating the success (or otherwise) of the investments will become an integral part of the management processes discussed throughout this book.

Another aspect of administration of IS/IT that has often become a particular problem, and a problem which often compounds the difficulties of investment justification, is the way in which IT costs are allocated to the users of the technology and services. This is the subject of the rest of this chapter, because inept or inappropriate policies for 'charging out' or allocating IT costs can severely impact an organisation's ability to manage IS/IT coherently over time.

ALLOCATING AND/OR CHARGING OUT IT COSTS

Few aspects of IS/IT management have attracted as much academic attention or user dissatisfaction as so-called 'chargeback systems' – ways of either allocating IT costs to users or charging them for services used. Why is this rather irritating aspect of IS/IT management, which should perhaps be a minor accounting issue, be of any importance in strategic management? Because what may appear as charge-out to the accountant and IT department is seen as a **pricing mechanism** by the user. If the charge is a crude overall cost reallocation of a relatively arbitrary nature which the user can neither influence nor control, he or she will probably ignore it. Otherwise the charging system can significantly affect the implementation of strategy as decisions are made on the price of systems and services prevailing at the time of decision.

What must be remembered is that such charge-out systems are really **transfer-pricing** systems for the buying and selling of IT products and services, and must be constructed as such. If the IT group is set up as a profit centre or even a separate company then the charge to users is obviously a real price. The merits of such an acceptance of the pricing mechanism are strongly argued by Allen (1987) in terms of the benefits accruing when information service groups are made to 'pay their way'. He argues that when IT is managed as a profit centre it will provide a 'better service because it is rewarded for successfully responding to the users' and 'users determine their own budgets'. Many of the organisations who outsource IT argue that if the users have to pay 'real money' for services they will be more accountable and demand a good service. Though given no choice of suppliers this logic is a little weak. It must of course follow that:

(a) users can select the most appropriate supplier (internal or external);
(b) the IT supplying department can refuse 'unprofitable' work.

This arrangement is close to the definitions of **free market** as described earlier. Allen concedes that the profit-centre approach is not appropriate where the IT department is technologically backward or poorly managed because the users will choose outside suppliers in preference for most needs, and the IT department will not improve. If a free-market strategy is appropriate then so perhaps is a profit-centre approach, but it could be seen as the need for effective charging and user accountability determining the strategy, not the reverse.

Charging-out/pricing of development costs is relatively straightforward since the majority of IT costs are labour hours plus capital expenditure. Either a market or internal labour recovery rate can be used. The total project development cost can be identified relatively easily and performance against targets reviewed either against a fixed 'contract' cost or original estimate. Whether any over/under run is attributed to the IT 'supplier' or the user 'customer' is largely academic but may be a sensitive political issue!

Charging/pricing for other services is more problematic due to changing economic factors and usage of resources over an extended period.

The CIMA Management Accounting Guideline No. 4, *Charging for Computer Services*, recognises that:

> The problems of calculating a transfer price for computer services are complicated by the specialised nature of the services, their independence from the saleable end products of most businesses and the difficulty of matching the demand for computer services with their supply in the short and medium term.

Many charging systems for computer services are complex in design to address these problems, producing elegant accounting solutions but often ignoring the fact that transfer pricing is a matter of business policy, to enable overall business, not just IT and accounting, objectives to be met.

Most writers on this subject describe some or all of the objectives that Olson and Ives (1982) list for charge-out systems:

(a) to provide the basic accounting functions of cost recovery;
(b) to maximise IS benefits;
(c) to ensure equitable resource allocation amongst users;
(d) to regulate demand for scarce resources;
(e) to assist in planning;
(f) to motivate and evaluate IT management performance;
(g) to make users accountable for resources consumed.

A study carried out by Bergeron (1986) showed that if users are to be held accountable for meeting their IT budget they must be involved in its preparation and they must be charged in proportion to the services they use.

In order for this to happen the charges to users have to be understandable to the users. If they are difficult to understand they will not be used. These findings are similar to those of Olsen and Ives, and apply to both project development and systems operational charges.

Earl (1989) goes further and suggests that the charges should be based on things the user can see and influence, e.g. number of transactions, screens viewed, etc.

Returning to the objectives listed above, no charging mechanism will meet all of the objectives, so it is important that the objectives for charging for IT services are specifically stated and understood by everyone. The least contentious objective is the first – to provide basic accounting functions of cost recovery. In that case IT can be treated like any indirect function and its costs allocated on some sensible, if rather arbitrary, basis to 'direct' departments to satisfy management accounting requirements. Of the other objectives, three – (c), (d) and (e) – are essentially about 'planning' or regulating supply or demand and it would seem that using the charging system is no substitute for putting effective IS and IT planning mechanisms in place. Equally using charging as a way of maximising IS benefits is difficult to understand in that it can only affect how costs are dealt with. However, as has been said earlier, few organisations have processes for managing the benefits of IS/IT investments and hence the undue focus on the costs of IT. The remaining two objectives, – (f) and (g) –, are about accountability and performance measurement, both of which should be important in ensuring resources are used effectively. It is to satisfy these objectives that most charge-back systems are actually designed.

McKinnon and Kallman (1987) argue that the type of charge-back mechanism should relate to the stage of maturity of IS and its management in the organisation. They use the support – key operational – high potential – strategic rationale of an increasingly important application portfolio to demonstrate the need for increasing sophistication of charging/pricing mechanism. They argue that prices and the pricing mechanism should be clearly aligned with IS/IT policy, either encouraging use or trying to control it, and either encourage freedom of user choice or directly influence priorities. Irrespective of the detailed methods used, pricing is, and must be employed as, an instrument of strategy.

Taking this rationale further, Earl (1989) argues that the charge-out systems should reflect the role of IS/IT as a component of the business. He argues that normally IT is seen in one of three roles.

1 A **service centre**, whereby users are not charged in any way for IT resource consumption.
2 A **cost centre** whereby users are charged with costs representing the resources consumed such that IT costs are 'recovered' from the other functions.
3 A **profit centre** – whereby the IT function charges a price for everything to the users in order that they more than recover their total costs. As has been said earlier this implies a 'free market' strategy and hence the price will depend as much on what the customer will pay as the costs of the services – 'market pricing'.

Where IT is treated as a cost centre the charging method can either be based on average costs – i.e. charging the total cost of the resource (e.g. network) to the users in proportion to the use each makes of it; or standard costs – where resources are charged as they are used, the cost being calculated in advance based on estimated usage. The latter method, whilst administratively more cumbersome, at least means the users can relate activity to costs incurred. Also, efficiency and volume variances are not hidden and this encourages more careful use of the resource and better forecasting – avoiding wasted capacity, enabling more accurate sizing of resources and more timely procurement of extra capacity.

Earl considers the implications of the charging methods resulting from these three fundamentally different roles of IT as **service, cost** or **profit** centre, in the context of the application portfolio. These implications are summarised in Table 8.5 (sections 1–3).

Whilst none of the approaches is ideal in any situation, it can be seen that, if used sensibly, the methods of charging can address the issues associated with key operational, support and high potential applications – i.e. charging methods should not cause inappropriate behaviour. However, Earl recognises that none of the charging methods is suitable for strategic applications and he believes a fourth approach is needed – the hybrid (see Table 8.5 section 4). Here the way charges are made for a particular application will be determined by the nature of that application on the basis of ensuring the intended benefits are obtained. This can cause problems in accounting terms but the flexibility is essential if innovative, cross-functional, change-driven systems are to be developed. The focus is on benefit achievement not costs incurred, and in many organisations the charging system creates discussion about 'who pays', not 'who benefits', and hence strategic applications are rarely successful.

Table 8.6 is an attempt to bring together the application portfolio, the role of

Table 8.5 Alternative views of IT as a business component and implications of associated charging mechanism

Pros	Cons
1 Service centre	
• Stimulates experimentation • Avoids organisational conflict • Promotes use of services	• Allows uneconomic uses • No accountability • Creates excessive demands and no means of priority setting
(good for high potential) (tolerable for support)	(bad for key operational) (poor for strategic)
2 Cost centre (either average or standard costs)	
• Makes users justify requests • Controls on IT department • Makes users aware of cost of systems • Enables priority setting	• Can deter use of IT • Focus on cost not benefit • Often unsatisfactory in practice (difficult to define equitable charging systems)
(good for key operational and support)	(poor for high potential/strategic)
3 Profit centre	
• IT controls its costs • IT becomes pro-active (markets itself) • Encourages user decision-making on IT	• Users may go external on marginal cost basis (trading) • May create under-used IT resources • IT specialises in 'profitable' work
(good for support) (tolerable for high potential)	(bad for key operational/strategic)
4 Hybrid centre	
• Allows for different stages of IT development • Can accommodate innovation and new technology • 'Pricing' can be used as a policy weapon to achieve strategy	• Can be confusing to users, and accounting system is complex • Incomplete control of IT resource • Needs continuous review of charging practice • Can cause conflict in IT dept.
(good for high potential/strategic)	

the IT resource and the method of charging. It also includes the generic strategies that relate reasonably logically to the bases for charging, again meaning that behaviour required will be encouraged by the charging method. Like many things about IS/IT management there are clear cause-and-effect relationships. Charging policy becomes a pricing policy in the eyes of the user and inappropriate charging methods will lead to inappropriate use of resources to deliver the wrong set of applications. There are no simple answers and Table 8.6 suggests that a complex set of answers may be necessary – adopting different charging methods according

Table 8.6 Implications on the portfolio of view of IT resource and method of charging

Charging basis and related generic strategies	Service centre	Cost centre	Profit centre	Hybrid centre
No charge out (leading edge)	High potential			
Average cost (scarce resource)		Support		
Standard cost (monopoly)		Key operational		
Market price (free market)			Support and high potential	
Flexible (centrally planned)				Strategic and high potential

Notes: There is a cause-and-effect relationship between application mix/generic strategy/charging approach.

to the type of application. Given that there is a need to manage strategically to get an increased business contribution from IS/IT investments, it is probably obvious that one policy instrument that can be used to enable that strategy is the pricing of the IT resources. It is however a very unpredictable instrument if used carelessly and it may be best to not charge at all, treating IT costs as overhead, if the potential effect of the charging system is to nullify or even counteract the strategy.

KEY LEARNING POINTS

- In managing information systems resources the difference between achieving success and failure of delivered systems often lies in the calibre of specialist IT resources and how effectively they work with the other business managers and system users.
- Over time the technical knowledge needed to design and construct technology-based systems has decreased and this trend will continue, as more package software becomes available and languages become more 'natural' or 'user friendly'.
- This implies a changing role for IT specialists, but not as so many have predicted, the 'demise of the computer programmer'. New types of application will always need programming and users are unlikely to acquire the skills to develop large, complex systems without technical help.

- However, it may be that many of these skills will be bought in, as needed, from a supplier and the trend is towards outsourcing of the more technical skills required. But to get the best service from bought-in resources the organisation must be clear in knowing what it wants, and be able to determine whether the supplier has delivered the appropriate product or service.
- The role of the IT specialists has changed and hence the organisation and positioning of the resources is also evolving. An article by Venkatraman and Loh (1994) summarises this change neatly in its title – 'The Shifting Logic of the IS [in our terms 'IT'] Organisation: From technical portfolio to relationship portfolio'. They suggest that there are three key relationships to manage:

  (a) with the outside IT suppliers who will, they say, do more and more of the work through outsourcing arrangements;
  (b) with the business managers and system users to enable the business to gain the benefits available from IT; and
  (c) with other companies' IT specialists as more and more systems become inter-organisational through extended use of EDI (electronic data interchange) and even shared systems, as described earlier in the book.

- Even in smaller organisations using IT these relationships will need to be managed even if no dedicated IT resource exists in-house. In larger organisations the nature of the cultural relationship between IT specialists and the rest of the business people is often poor due to different, and potentially conflicting, interests and objectives. The fact that this 'culture gap' seems to be widening in many organisations was recognised in the Price Waterhouse Information Technology Reviews in 1992 and 1993.
- The softer issues as well as the harder, structural issues implied by the 'culture gap' have to be resolved if the IT resource is to contribute effectively. Historically many organisations have failed to address the core problems involved in having IT specialists in the organisation.
- The centralisation or decentralisation of the resource has often dominated a rational debate which should lead to a balance of both. Who 'controls' the resource seems to have been at issue, not how to maximise its contribution.
- 'Charging for IT' is rarely satisfactory from everyone's viewpoint but in many cases it can actually cause the organisation to do the wrong things, in the wrong way and may actually destroy any IS strategy that could have existed!
- There is no simple solution, but business managers, accountants and IT specialists all need to understand the implications, both good and bad, of any approach to charging.
- It is not good enough just to say 'It's OK we don't charge users for IT' –

that itself is a charging system with certain implications. The policy for charging will affect many others, including justification of investments and make-or-buy decisions, both of which are important judgements if the organisation is to do the right things, in the right way.

- It is too important an issue to be left to accountants and IT specialists! It is an important aspect of the management of IS – a matter of policy and principle, not a trivial accounting issue.

The final chapter is a summary of the key ideas, concepts and models in the book.

QUESTIONS FOR CONSIDERATION

1 For an organisation with which you are familiar:

   (a) Describe the way in which IT specialist resources are organised (including people in 'user' departments) and analyse the roles they are fulfilling in terms of the structure suggested in Table 8.1. Comment on any significant omissions or differences from the model and any implications for the effective use of IT.

   (b) Describe the processes in place for governing the use of IS and IT resources, especially to ensure appropriate matching of supply and demand. Assess the effectiveness of these processes (*** good, ** satisfactory, * poor) in terms of the activities described in Figure 8.5, and attempt to explain any aspects assessed as poor.

   (c) Use the cultural web (Figures 8.7 and 8.8) to describe the perception of the IT department from the business users' perspective. Ask someone in the IT department to do the same and compare the results. (A number of views could be taken.) Identify any significant differences in perception, the possible reasons for them and the consequences.

   Summarise the results from (a), (b) and (c) in terms of issues to be addressed to improve IS/IT management in the organisation.

2 The chief executive officer (CEO) of a newly privatised public utility has decided to establish profit centre-based business units to improve motivation and accountability. This includes the IT department. Currently all major business functions are heavy users of the central IT service, although a few, especially engineering, have developed a sizeable IT capability themselves. Advise the CEO on the pros and cons of his decision to make IT a profit centre and describe the potential long-term consequences. Suggest alternative ways that IT and the business units could be made more accountable for the effectiveness of IS/IT investments.

RECOMMENDED ADDITIONAL READING

Crescenzi, A.D. (1988) 'The Dark Side of Strategic IS Implementation', *Information Strategy: The Executive's Journal*, (Fall).

Earl, M.J. (1989) *Management Strategies for Information Technology*, Prentice-Hall, Chapter 8.

Earl, M.J. and Feeny, D., (1994) 'Is Your CIO Adding Value?', *Sloan Management Review* (Spring).

Price Waterhouse Information Technology Reviews (1992/3) and (1993/4).

Von Simson, E.M. (1990) 'The Centrally Decentralised IS Organisation', *Harvard Business Review* (July–August).

Zmud, R.W. (1984) 'Design Alternatives for Organising Systems Activities', *MIS Quarterly* (June).

OTHER REFERENCES

Allen, B. (1987) 'Make Information Services Pay Its Way', *Harvard Business Review* (January–Febrary).

Bergeron, F. (1986) 'Factors Influencing the Use of DP Charge-back Information', *MIS Quarterly* (September).

Johnson, G. and Scholes, K. (1993) *Exploring Corporate Strategy*, Prentice-Hall, Chapter 2.

La Belle, A and Nyce, H.E. (1987) 'Whither the IT Organisation?', *Sloan Management Review* (Summer).

McFarlan, F.W. and McKenney, J.L. (1983) 'The Information Archipelago – Governing the new world', *Harvard Business Review* (July–August).

McKinnon, W.P. and Kallman, E.A. (1987) 'Mapping Charge-back Systems to Organisational Environments', *MIS Quarterly* (March).

Olsen, M.H. and Ives, B. (1982) 'Charge-back Systems and User Involvement in Information Systems – An empirical investigation', *MIS Quarterly* (June).

Venkatraman, N. and Loh, L. (1994) 'The Shifting Logic of the IS Organisation: From technical portfolio to relationship portfolio', *Information Strategy: The Executives' Journal* (Winter).

Chapter 9

Summary and discussion of implications for the management of information systems

INTRODUCTION

This chapter attempts to bring together, in overview, the key ideas and approaches in the book and show how they form a sound and comprehensive set of principles by which information systems can be managed more successfully.

It is worth remembering that technology-based information systems have only become common in business in the last thirty years. During that time dramatic advances have been made in computer and communications technology and due to ever-improving economics and capabilities of the technology, the range of possible applications has exploded. Our ability to employ the technology often lags behind the capabilities of the technology. Hence many current technology developments, especially in the field of information storage and communications, have yet to manifest themselves in common use.

Over the same period of time the business environment has been changing equally dramatically, in terms of intensified competition on a global scale. Information technology is becoming a critical part of the business infrastructure that enables firms to compete in international markets. It is often said that in the 1980s western economies moved out of the 'industrial era', where the employment of capital to create economies of scale in production was critical, into the 'information era', where the acquisition and exploitation of knowledge will be critical to success. In this era, information will become a 'good' to be bought and sold and it will be available in abundance to all. The businesses that succeed will be those who can quickly extract and synthesise valuable knowledge from the information available. Without the use of technology this will be impossible. Many writers have compared the transition from the 'agricultural era' to the 'industrial era' with this new transition. Whilst from a western perspective that previous change brought enormous growth and created huge wealth, it should be remembered that many countries suffered enormous poverty as a result of western industrialisation. This new transition will undoubtedly create new wealth-producing opportunities, but it is not yet clear what the consequences will be for businesses in the different countries and economies in the world. Hindsight is a wonderful thing and it is easy to analyse the causes and effects of the previous transition – it is very difficult to predict the long-term implications of the 'information era' – it is not even certain that it has started!

In the meantime it is important for most organisations to address the management of information resources and the systems and technologies that enable their effective use.

OVERVIEW OF THE KEY IDEAS AND APPROACHES

This summary will reflect the overall structure of the book and is considered in four sections:

(a) strategy and planning for information systems;
(b) identifying the business information needs and opportunities;
(c) managing the applications;
(d) managing the resources.

In each case reference will be made to the specific parts of the book that provide the detailed discussion and relevant diagrams, checklists, etc.

Strategy and planning for information systems

As was described early in the book, for many years the issues associated with IS/IT were primarily internal and related mainly to the supply of technology-based systems to improve the efficiency or effectiveness of existing tasks (the DP and MIS eras). Planning was generally incremental and an organisation moved forward at a pace determined primarily by internal pressures to be more efficient along with its ability to design, develop and implement the IT-based systems. The main arguments for investment were due to the better economics of IT-based systems compared with manual methods. However, whether or not the full economic benefits were actually realised was rarely verified. Gradually businesses became dependent on these 'computer systems' and could not function without them. In essence, the initial purpose of investment in IS/IT was not to change the business, merely to improve the performance of existing activities.

It was really not essential at this stage to have an IS strategy – good planning of developments and resources was needed – but an 'IT strategy' (at least of sorts) to deal with the range of technologies and suppliers was normally developed in larger organisations. During the 1980s, however, it became clear that some organisations were using technology-based systems to change how they conducted business, to their advantage and the disadvantage of others. IS/IT had become a strategic weapon, whereby it was necessary, at least, to understand the business implications of IS/IT investments by competitors, customers and suppliers. At this point planning for IS/IT had three new dimensions – external focus, strategic impact and opportunities to change the conduct of business.

Also during the 1980s the 'PC revolution' occurred whereby the ability to deploy technology throughout the business became a reality. Previously technology and the development of systems had normally been centralised and hence planning and even strategy had been left very much to the IT (or DP! or MIS!) department, who responded to requests by business managers and delivered systems as required by the various functions of the business. This 'diffusion' of IT added a new dimension which produced the 'complex' environment described by Sullivan (see Figure 2.1). The ramifications of this environment are described in Figures 1.2 and 3.2 in terms of the degree to which benefits from IS/IT depend on the extent of change delivered and the relevance of an organisation's systems to its external business environment.

It was as if a juggler who had happily devised a system for keeping two balls in the air (DP and MIS) – one in each hand! – had suddenly been given five or six balls to keep in the air at the same time. The old, relatively simple, IT strategy was no longer enough. A new strategy was required to keep all these balls in the air at once. In fact two strategies were needed – IS and IT – but these two had to link into the business strategy, and the three were becoming increasingly inter-related and inter-dependent. Figure 9.1 (a copy of Figure 3.1) shows this, and Table 2.3 describes some of the problems resulting from a lack of IS strategy in this complex environment. One of the main reasons for these problems is that it is reasonably obvious that business managers are responsible for **business strategy** and that IT specialists should be responsible for **IT strategy**, although as IT became more diffuse in the organisation this strategy often became fragmented. The **IS strategy** is the problem, because it is a shared responsibility between business and IT management and, as often happens, shared responsibilities are not fulfilled by either party. Frequently, the IS strategy defaulted to the IT specialists who not only determined **how** things should be done but effectively decided **what** should be done, with at best only indirect reference to the business strategy.

New ways of thinking and new processes are required in most organisations if each of these strategies is to be optimal and the links between them are to be effectively established. This is a complex task, requiring continuing consensus to be achieved between the three key stakeholders in the IS strategy – senior management, line management/users and IT specialists. Figure 9.1 does not really reflect the complex reality of the situations in most organisations in terms of the strategic management processes. It depicts an ideal approach whereby a clearly defined business strategy can be converted into the appropriate IS investment strategy and thence into the best IT supply strategy. In most modern organisations strategy evolves or is crafted, as described by Mintzberg (1987) and others, in response to internal and external forces. Both the business and IT strategies are subject to ever-changing forces, such as the changing nature of IT suppliers and their products and services, and the strategies have to evolve and be adapted in the light of changing circumstances. These changes can occur at any time in both business and IT strategies and it needs a well-established and effective process if the IS strategy is to be kept optimal when factors affecting its viability are changing elsewhere. Figure 9.2, derived from work by Johnson and Scholes (1993) perhaps reflects the reality of the situation better.

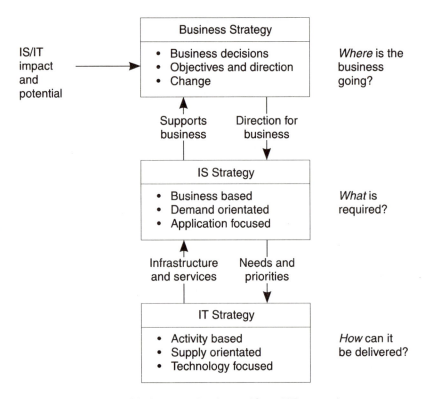

Figure 9.1 The relationship between business, IS and IT strategies

In such a complex, changing environment a range of approaches to IS and IT strategic planning are needed to cope with the mix of IS options and varying rates of change in aspects of the business and IT strategies. The five planning approaches described in Chapter 3, based on work by Michael Earl, appear to address many of the issues at the business/IS strategy interface. Figure 3.6 and Table 3.2 show how the business-led and organisational approaches are pre-requisites for success in devising truly strategic IS opportunities and investments, in harmony with business strategic initiatives.

A key component of the process of achieving the understanding and consensus of the three key stakeholders of the IS strategy is agreement on the nature and contribution of existing and future IS applications in the business. The application portfolio, used as a core model throughout the book, is designed to achieve this and has proved of value to many organisations in describing the IS strategy clearly and succinctly for all to understand. A version of the matrix is shown in Figure 9.3 to show the key questions that need to be answered in describing the contribution of the applications.

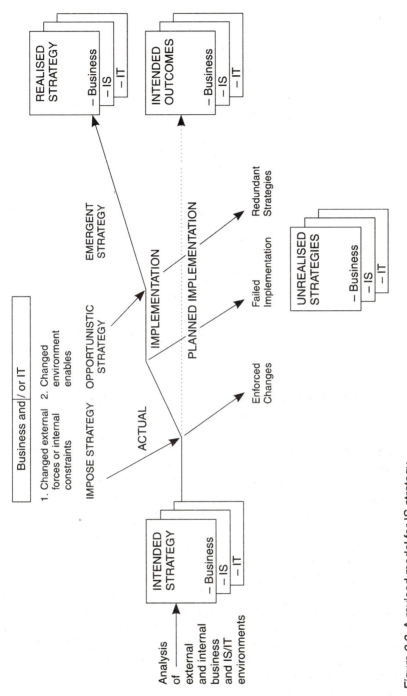

Figure 9.2 A revised model for IS strategy

Source: Adapted from Johnson and Scholes (1993)

STRATEGIC		HIGH POTENTIAL	
WHY	do we want to do it in strategic terms?	WHY?	– not clear
			and/or
WHAT	does the system need to do to gain the advantage?	WHAT?	– not certain
			and/or
HOW	best to do it?	HOW?	– not yet known
WHY	– to improve performance and avoid disadvantage	WHY	– to reduce costs by improving efficiency
WHAT	– actually has to improve and how much?	WHAT	– of existing necessary tasks?
HOW	– best to do it?	HOW	– best to do it?
KEY OPERATIONAL		SUPPORT	

Figure 9.3 Key questions on the application portfolio

The figure shows how the critical questions develop as we move round the matrix. In **support** the general objective is clear ('why' = efficiency) and 'what' is needed to be improved is determined by existing tasks and activities. The main question is **how** to do that most successfully, in terms of the use of IT. For **key operational** the 'how' question still has to be addressed, but in addition considerable thought may be needed to define specifically **what** has to be done, and to which systems, to avoid the potential disadvantage (why we need to do it). Again both 'what' and 'how' questions need to be resolved in **strategic** applications but in addition we need to clearly understand **why** we wish to do it in terms of the business strategy. Strategic applications require creative thinking and will cause change probably externally as well as internally, and the reasons for and potential benefits of such changes must be agreed on. By definition, the strategic systems cannot be copied from others (since we will already be potentially disadvantaged!) and hence their rationale has to flow coherently from the business strategy of the organisation. If one or more of the **why, what** or **how** questions is unanswered, it implies that the application is at best **high potential** and appropriate evaluation is needed to answer the outstanding questions before investing on a large scale.

In effect the applications portfolio should be the agreed product, at any time, of the IS strategy and it should evolve over time in alignment with the changing emphasis and priorities of the business strategy. It may well be constrained, in terms of when the applications can be delivered and at what cost by the IT strategy, but then the issue has become how best to satisfy the needs, not what those needs are.

Identifying the business information needs and opportunities

The key techniques for this are described in Chapter 4, and can be summarised in terms of three main components.

1. Techniques which enable the consideration of IS/IT opportunities and threats to be included in the situation appraisal from which the overall business strategy materialises. Figure 9.4 summarises this process, by which a 'good' strategy should match internal capability and ambition to the external environment in which the business operates. A number of techniques (e.g. five-forces analysis, see Table 4.1) can be used to appraise both business issues and IS/IT threats and opportunities, resulting from assessment of the external environment. These enable the 'market driven' component of the business strategy to be determined along with some IS strategic needs. A number of other techniques can be used to determine the 'internally driven' part of the strategy which attempts to maximise the use of resources and organisational competences in order to deliver success in terms of stakeholder demands.

At a simple level the consequences of this analysis can be expressed in Porter's generic business strategies of low cost, differentiation or focus, but this poses as many questions as it answers – e.g. by what means is effective differentiation to be achieved?

An article by Treacy and Wiersma (1993) argues that organisations can follow one of three paths to market leadership. These are:

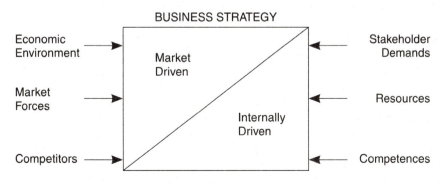

Figure 9.4 Forces which shape strategy

(a) **Operational excellence** Enabling products and services to be obtained reliably, easily and cost effectively by customers.

(b) **Customer intimacy** Targeting markets very precisely and tailoring products and services to the needs of particular customer groups.

(c) **Product leadership** Continuing product innovation meeting customer needs.

They argue that each of these requires a different set of competencies and use of resources. In the context of this book these 'leadership' strategies offer significant guidance as to the nature of the IS investments which should be made in support of the core strategy. In the terms of Michael Earl's planning approaches these strategies form the 'organisational themes' which should determine those IS investments which are 'strategic'.

2. The second set of techniques are those which enable the role of information in the industry, the business and the organisation to be understood and improved to advantage. Various levels of analysis can be carried out, but the ideal starting point is the external value chain, moving in through the customer resource life cycle view to the internal value chain, and on to more detailed process, activity and flow analysis. The result is a picture of the business in terms of information flow and usage, from which areas of potential opportunity and threat can be identified and improvements initiated. An article by O'Sullivan and Geringer (1993) explains how by understanding the value chain and in particular the role of information, major business performance improvements can be made by redesigning the way the chain works to the firm's advantage. The article also introduced the idea of 'natural' and 'contrived' value chains – the 'natural' value chain representing (the unattainable) optimum structure for the industry based on **what** needs to be done and the 'contrived' value chain which shows **how** (in often far from optimal ways) things are currently done. Table 9.1 summarises some of the differences between contrived and natural value chains, points which complement much of the more detailed discussion of value chain analysis in Chapter 4. In analysing the role of information in the value chain the purpose is essentially to enable the business to move closer to the natural value chain wherever possible.

3. The third set of techniques are those which enable the organisation to focus IS/IT investments on the achievement of its specific objectives. Those objectives are the statement of what is intended to be achieved in a certain time frame, usually the next year or two, within the context of the longer-term strategy. The most commonly used technique for translating these objectives to the requisite actions is the **critical success factor** (CSF) analysis (see example in Box 4.2). CSF analysis is a generalised technique which proves very useful in enabling management, with little real understanding of (or even interest in!) IS/IT, to ensure that the IS/IT investments are being driven directly by the business objectives. It is not usually a very creative technique – it tends to be problem driven and internally focused – but it is very valuable as a way of selecting and prioritising creative ideas derived from other techniques.

Table 9.1 Natural versus contrived value chains

Contrived value chain Represents *how* things are done by the resources in the industry/organisation:

- driven by organisation structures, historical evolution and compromise;
- is often very complex, confused and 'messy' and poorly understood;
- contains many reconciliation activities and reacts slowly;
- can take many forms, is continuously being modified to meet business changes.

Natural value chain Represents *what* has to be done to succeed in meeting market requirements:

- based on value-adding activities and the resources needed to carry them out;
- defines essential inter-relationships and dependencies and the ideal way to achieve business purposes;
- contains few reconciliation activities and responds quickly;
- usually only one ideal exists and it does not change significantly or frequently.

Figure 9.5 (a repeat of Figure 4.11) attempts to bring together the various tools and techniques described mainly in Chapter 4 into an overall structure which can define the required application portfolio for the business.

The discussion above has focused on the use of tools and techniques to formulate the future demand for IS in **one** business unit. Most large organisations consist of many business units and, if the same approaches are used in all of them, it enables opportunities and ideas to be compared and shared and also synergistic opportunities to be identified amongst the units, as explained in more detail in Chapters 4 and 5.

Managing the applications

As shown in Figure 5.2 the application portfolio that an organisation has or plans to have will result from a contribution of formal planning, based on some or all of the techniques and processes summarised above, **plus** informally driven opportunistic ideas for the use of IT. To succeed in the long-term an organisation must be able to manage the mix of application types in the portfolio, through their life cycles whether they result from formal planning or opportunism.

At the highest level the 'generic strategies', described in Table 5.3, offer essential guidance on how best to manage the delivery of applications in the different segments of the portfolio. That these can be shown to have relevant similarities to the planning approaches from which the applications usually derive (see Table 5.4), means that an appropriate delivery approach exists for the whole range of demands that will probably arise. Observation and research has

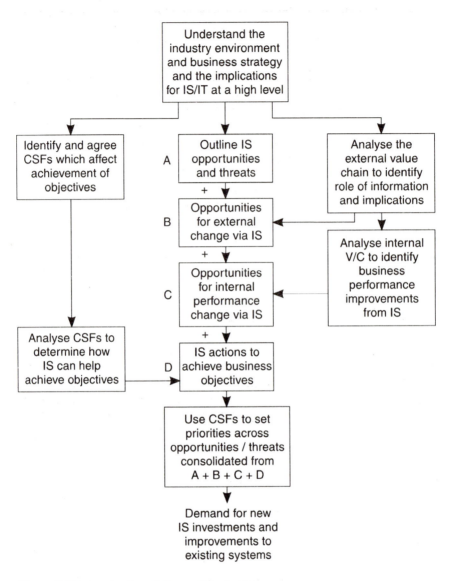

Figure 9.5 Determination of demand-summary

frequently shown that the combination of portfolio analysis, planning approaches and generic strategies is a powerful set of diagnostics for demonstrating why particular IS developments succeed or fail. A mismatch of approach and/or strategy to the contribution required almost always lead to failure.

Historically there has been an over-simplistic view of what is involved in the delivery of IT **applications**. The focus has been on IT development **projects** and although it is obviously important to manage the process that produces the technical solution well, it is not the whole story. In Chapter 6 the approach recommended recognises that a whole range of business- and IT-based activities (or 'projects') have to be carried out if the system is to work well and deliver the expected benefits. Clearly defined roles are recommended – in particular for the business-based 'application manager' whose prime responsibility is to ensure that the available benefits are obtained, through the undertaking of the appropriate mix of business and IT development and infrastructure projects. Whilst most organisations have ample policies, procedures, guidelines and standards to ensure that IS/IT developments can be managed well, very few organisations offer managers any guidance on what has to be done to manage the delivery of the benefits which justified the investment. Chapter 6 describes an outline **benefit management** process which begins to address this management responsibility. Chapter 6 also describes an overview of a **risk assessment** process which helps the business manager determine the probability of achieving the benefits, and enables him or her to take appropriate action to avoid unnecessary risks. Given that '70 per cent of all IS/IT investments fail to deliver the expected benefits', the process is obviously risky! and there is considerable scope for improvement by introducing a proactive approach to consciously managing for benefit.

The 'classic' systems development life cycle (SDLC) is described in Chapter 6 (see Figure 6.5) and the purpose and deliverables of each of the main phases are briefly outlined. This does not really do justice to the topic and any reader who is closely involved in systems development should read one of the many good texts that describe the framework in detail. However, what is often overlooked by those texts is that most systems development 'methodologies' were designed to improve the approach to large, complex systems which in general fulfilled a **key operational** role in the business. The ideal approach for these is often too rigid and too bureaucratic for strategic, high potential and support applications. The methodology has to be adapted for the requirements of these types of application and these variations on the basic theme are discussed in Chapter 6 – Figures 6.9 and 6.10 showing the changes needed to allow for either the prototyping required (high potential and strategic) or the use of packaged software (support and key operational).

In Chapter 5 it was argued that the range of potential benefits available from IT was increasing, but to achieve these benefits required increasing degrees of business change. Simple automation of existing tasks produces limited benefits but the potential business performance improvements which derive from value linking, acceleration and restructuring are enormous. These only arise, however, by a combination of well-designed and implemented IT plus well thought out and carefully implemented business changes. The more 'strategic' the applications become, the greater the degree of business change normally needed to deliver the improvement required (see Figure 5.6). Therefore the more work there is involved in the business development and infrastructure projects, the more success will rely on the quality of business management associated with the application. In this book the focus has been on the role of the business manager in the application development process. The increasing criticality of this role has long been recognised, but more often than not the 'business project manager', given the responsibility for an application's success, has received little specific guidance on how to succeed. Usually the role is seen as an 'add-on' to the IT development approach – a business person nominally responsible for what IT people are doing! The role can only add value to the process if it has clearly defined new, but complementary responsibilities beyond the scope of the current IT development approach. This role will vary according to the differing contributions expected by the various applications in the portfolio.

Managing the resources

Chapters 7 and 8 deal in detail with the management of the main resources involved. Chapter 7 considers information and technology and Chapter 8 the people and organisational resources, plus some key administrative issues. These in combination can be described as the 'infrastructure' required to enable the beneficial development and use of technology-based information systems. Traditionally the majority of these infrastructure elements were managed in-house in most organisations. Many can now be outsourced to other suppliers of services. Even many large organisations have outsourced some of their IT resources, and for smaller organisations it is not feasible or justified to have them all in-house. However, organisations must understand the role information, systems and the supporting technology and resources play in the business – i.e. have an IS strategy – before they can make the right decisions on the best sourcing options. More will be said on this towards the end of the chapter, but first a review of some of the main points in Chapters 7 and 8.

Information management

The latest buzz-phrase in IS/IT, at the time of writing, is 'legacy systems' – the 'heap' of previously built or acquired systems which often use old fashioned software to run on yesterday's technologies. They were rarely planned coherently, nor were they designed as an integrated whole – each was built in a particular way to satisfy a particular set of needs, at a particular time. Then, later and often with considerable extra effort, the systems were integrated with each other, in often far from ideal ways. Given the more dynamic business environment of today, new systems are needed to be put in place quickly to meet business changes and systems need to be 'flexible' (although people are rarely at all clear about what they mean by 'flexible'), to respond to changing business circumstances. At the same time lower cost, more user-orientated hardware and software options are becoming available and organisations want to take advantage of these, even if they do not wish to change the systems. The ability to deliver 'flexible' systems quickly or migrate systems from one 'platform' to another is often restricted by the way data or information is managed within the range of legacy systems. It is relatively easy to change a processing component of a system but it is much more difficult to change how data, used by many processes, is maintained and stored. This is exacerbated where systems are poorly documented and it may not even be known whether particular data items are used in particular systems!

The existing systems, the 'legacy', need to be assessed in terms of the information they contain or produce, rather than the processes they perform or the technology on which they sit. A strategy for change or migration should then be driven by the value and use of that information in the business. If the information resource is well structured and organised then migration issues from old to new environments often are easily resolved.

Every time organisations seem to be on the verge of addressing this key issue of information resource management (IRM), a new variable is introduced which either:

(a) suggests the IRM will resolve itself in some way at some point in the future! or
(b) that distracts everyone from dealing with the core problem while hardware or applications are changed! i.e. some convenient excuse arises for not tackling a difficult problem.

The information resources of many organisations are at best disorganised and at worst in chaos and yet more and more data is being collected, images, voices and documents can now be stored and accessed. Unless some overall approach is adopted in the organisation for the management of this information, then in a few years' time the 'legacy' problem will be much worse. The information resources trapped in the complex web of the legacy systems are the real items of value, but unless those items are rationalised and organised coherently then they will become difficult if not impossible to use in the future.

Considerable academic and business effort is now being expended on working out how the unsatisfactory legacy can be re-engineered to provide the required flexibility and speed of business response. It could be argued that adherence to well-documented 'best practice' in IRM in the past would have prevented much of the current problem. Whilst we consider how to re-engineer the past, 'worst practice' often continues in the present ensuring that the 'legacy' problem will be for ever with us, but on a larger scale. Chapter 7 attempts to show that information management is a business, not an IT, issue and that each organisation needs to establish a clear understanding of roles and responsibilities for what is a business asset or resource. This often involves some disciplines which are alien to the business users of the systems, even if they are familiar to IT specialists. This latter point often encourages the users to 'leave it to the IT people', an option which is more and more inappropriate as users have the capability to develop and run their own systems. In this book it is only possible to provide a framework or overview of information management – an overall set of principles or a philosophy for managing what in the 'information era' will be one of (if not *the*) most important resources in an organisation.

Technology management

Georges Pompidou once said, 'There are three ways to disaster. Gambling is the quickest. Sex is the most enjoyable. But technology is the most certain!'

This argument has perhaps also encouraged British managers, who are on average technology averse (and often proud of it!), to decide that technology should be managed by someone else. The analogy of cars is often used, to say the business manager only needs to know how to drive the car not how to build or service it. Agreed, provided that (a) the business manager is a good driver and (b) he or she knows what the capabilities and limitations of the technology are. To follow the analogy through, many business managers perhaps still need a man with a red flag walking in front of them, to protect the rest of the organisation!

It is not important, nor is it feasible, that business managers understand how the technology works. But IT is becoming an integral part of the business technology of every organisation and hence business managers need to be competent in making decisions about IT investment. It will always be necessary to take advice from technology specialists but that advice will never (a) be complete or (b) be totally objective, and will almost always be confusing, leaving areas of uncertainty, within which business managers can either try to exercise sound judgement or abdicate responsibility.

Chapter 7 attempts to do two things. First, it talks sufficiently about the technology (e.g. Box 7.1) to reduce the discomfort felt by some business managers, if only sufficiently to understand the issues which need to be addressed. Second, the key issue of how to justify investment in technology is considered – an issue which will become more difficult in the future. Why? The reason is that in the past the normal, if not always satisfactory, approach to justifying IS/IT investments was generally via 'IS' – i.e. the application benefits were weighed against the system development or purchase costs and costs of any associated 'IT'. In future many pure IT investments in capabilities (software mainly) and capacities (hardware mainly) will be to enable users to buy packages or build their own systems, and there may be no available application benefits to weigh against the costs. For instance, one major company invested nearly £2 million to standardise on one word processing software package. It replaced a wide variety of existing software, upgraded most PCs in the organisation and needed a huge retraining programme. No immediate benefits would occur. The long-term benefits of document preparation, sharing, storage and dissemination are largely 'intangible' but the organisation knew that one day they would have to standardise to avoid major inconvenience costs and hence made the decision in 1991. They could only make a decision based on software available at the time and they may have to change in the future – but then only **one** software set will need replacing by one more. This was a business decision based on advice from the IT specialists – if 'IT' had made the decision it is certain that everyone of the users would have protested to their management that it was not the best solution for them!

Chapter 7 also suggests how technologies can be classified in relation to the application portfolio – emerging, pacing, key and base (plus obsolete!) – as a basis for the IT strategy and management decision-making. If the organisation can accurately synchronise its application portfolio evolution with the appropriate technologies, at the right stage in their life cycles, then business benefits can be maximised from technology. If these three aspects are unsynchronised, benefits will be reduced and the costs of the technology will be the focus of attention. Many articles have been written about overall technology management strategies – whether it is best to be a technology leader, fast follower or conservative member of the majority. All agree that a 'trailing edge' approach is unlikely to succeed! If the approach to technology management can be closely aligned with the business requirements via the IS strategy then leader, follower, etc., are really irrelevant terms. It may be appropriate to take a risk with a new technology in one case **and** be very conservative in the choice of software in another. Whilst the main responsibility of business managers is to ensure the relevance of the IS strategy, it can only be of further benefit if they understand the technology management implications and issues of that strategy.

People and organisation management

From one perspective the thirty or so years of evolution of IS/IT in organisations can be viewed as one of continuous organisational conflict about the role, structure and reporting relationships of the IT specialists. It has never satisfactorily been resolved and some organisations, rather than understand the reasons for the troubled marriage, with a view to reconciliation, have opted for the convenience of divorce through outsourcing.

Chapter 8 tried to explain the issues by looking at four key aspects – IT organisation, the governance of IS/IT in organisations, the cultural relationships between IT specialists and the business functions, and the specific administration or policy issues that can affect the outcome. These all interact to affect the competence level of the organisation with regard to its use of IS/IT. Clearly the role of IT specialists is changing from one based on 'construction' to one based on 'services'. This changes the nature of the skills required by IT specialists and the way they need to be organised. In every aspect of business some things are best provided and managed centrally and others are best decentralised – the same is true of IS and IT. The 1993/4 Price Waterhouse IT survey recognised that centralisation/decentralisation was once more a major issue and then surveyed the factors that affected people's views as to whether greater centralisation or decentralisation was appropriate. The balance was almost exactly equal! as shown in Table 9.2.

The more IT resource is distributed, there is a need to govern its use to enable

Table 9.2 Issues affecting the role of the IT centre (from Price Waterhouse Information Technology Review 1993/4)

For centralisation		*For decentralisation*	
1 Need for IT expertise	(77)	1 Shift to autonomous business units	(70)
2 Integrating IT with corporate objectives	(76)	2 Culture gap	(54)
3 Cost containment	(46)	3 User friendliness	(51)
4 Client-server architectures	(44)	4 Commoditisation (of IT)	(45)

Note: (*n*) = percentage of times mentioned.

beneficial integration. The more it is centralised, there is a need to govern the allocation of resources. Organisational positioning and structure are not the only factors in success. Some additional set of management approaches – described in Chapter 8 (Table 8.3) in terms of the 'steering group' structure – is needed to ensure that the strategy for IS and IT and the actual implementation are consistent with the strategic and operational needs and priorities of the business. Most of management's energy in the past has been dissipated on controlling what the IT resource does and not on delivering the available business benefits. The steering group structure – or at least the activities – described redress that balance. Most organisations who say they are not getting 'value for money' from IT are getting it in proportion to the management time and effort they have put into achieving value.

Why there is often a poor relationship between the IT function and the rest of the business can be explained in a number of ways (Ward and Peppard 1994). Perhaps the most succinct is shown in Table 9.3 which describes the evolution of how organisations mature with technology in three eras.

This three-stage view summarises how organisations mature with new technology from the point of view of the technologist. Whilst the particulars are interesting in themselves the table perhaps explains in a simple way why organisations have found it exceedingly difficult to fully integrate the IT function. In phase 1, the technologist is exploring or pioneering, attempting to exploit the technology and the rest of the business is the normally unwilling subject of this haphazard and uncertain exploration. Not a satisfactory start to the relationship. Eventually the technologist (and the rest of the business!) realises the limitations of the technology and care has to be taken to avoid unacceptable effects on the rest of the organisation – the technologist becomes defensive – again not a very equal or mutually responsible relationship. Finally, in the third phase the technology can clearly deliver strategic change if managed well, but the technologist

Table 9.3 Maturing with technology

Phase	Mission	Purpose of application	Oganisational impact	The technologist	Nature of design
Phase 1	To design	To exploit new technology	By surprise	'Frontiersman'	Exploratory
Phase 2	To design carefully	To minimise social impact	By mistake	Tailor	Defensive
Phase 3	To design deliberately	To change organisation	On purpose	Agent of change	Strategic

After Hedberg.

is seen as the agent of that change – a source of potential revolution in the organisation. Once more this is a threatening role which is difficult to accommodate comfortably. Hence even if the technologist has the wit to recognise these changing roles and can acquire the skills needed, almost by definition he or she is an intruder or even a threat to the rest of the organisation. The natural reactions of any organism in such circumstances are to (a) pretend it's not there, and/or (b) reject it as soon as possible!

Approaches, such as the cultural web, described in Chapter 8, have been devised to help the different parties articulate, understand and then reconcile issues in the relationship. It is not a problem that will go away – it has to be managed positively by both IT specialists and business managers. It is not a question of who is right and who is wrong, but the end result of antagonism and blame is IS/IT investments which fail. Whilst it is unlikely that the business and IT people will ever have a completely common set of 'shared values' – it is important to achieve consensus wherever possible and recognise and respect the differences elsewhere. 'Cultural' problems in organisations are often relatively easy to identify and diagnose, but they are devilishly difficult to cure. Often due to a complete lack of shared values and no respect for the values of others, the IT function is 'culturally outsourced' from the rest of the organisation long before some event occurs that makes management seriously consider real outsourcing. In such circumstances, often as trivial as a call from an IT services supplier, the existence of a wide culture gap makes it easy to select what is effectively just another supplier, since the IT function is not considered integral to the organisation.

In fact the situation should be considered not as a choice **between** internal or external sourcing. There is a market place within which IT products and services can be purchased and to get benefit from those products/services the organisation may have to add further value internally. The suppliers offer products to satisfy the maximum number of customers, yet the main benefits from IS come from the excellence of fit with the organisation's unique business success factors and competences. Therefore there is a balance to be found between essentially 'commodity' products and services which can be purchased and value-added activities to exploit what can be purchased. The more a business wishes to exploit IS/IT within its business strategy the more it will have to have internal competence to add value. In many applications – such as basic accounting – value adding may be unnecessary but in others, especially those which visibly affect customers' buying habits, considerable value can be added to basic products. Therefore the selection of the source of product or service depends on the future contribution required. The achievement of that contribution will depend on the nature of the relationship of the business managers and the IT specialists involved – whether internal or external, as well as the competence of both parties.

Figure 9.6 describes a set of alternative views of that relationship which should assist sensible and consistent decision-making about sourcing options. The bottom one, where IT is a profit centre, is essentially an interim arrangement en route to one of the others. By 'outsourcing' is meant the nature of the relationship, even if the IT function is in-house. If the IT department is seen as adding 'unnecessary' cost then its costs can be tested against other suppliers – but it must be allowed to tender for existing work under the same conditions as the other parties. Often this approach has enabled the existing IT function to show greater cost savings than outsiders – which must prompt the simple question, why did they not do it before? And the answer is consistent and equally simple – users and management insisted on higher levels of service from and imposed internal constraints on the IT department, than they required of the new suppliers. At lower levels of service and without constraints (e.g. you must be based on existing company premises) the in-house IT function can usually reduce costs dramatically. **But** service levels also decrease, often to the dissatisfaction of users (if not management).

Every company has outsourced aspects of IS/IT over many years – buying a payroll package rather than writing a system is outsourcing – but outsourcing large parts of the IT capability is a relatively new phenomenon (since about 1988/9) and the long-term implications are not yet clear. But in every case, decisions should be taken for good business reasons and an inability of the IT function to work with the business is not a good business reason – it is a result of poor management.

CONCLUSIONS

This book is called the *Principles of Information Systems Management* and has attempted to describe the issues which have to be addressed, and, as far as possible, the means by which success can be achieved. The intention was that non-IT specialists could learn more about what they have to understand in order to ensure IS/IT investments and use are successful. To some extent that perpetuates

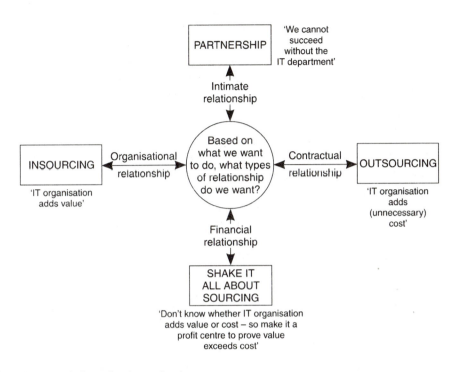

Figure 9.6 Sourcing in a mixed economy

the divide, described a few pages ago, between the IT specialists and others. Perhaps one day the activities associated with IS/IT will become a natural part of business life – just like managing people and accounting? Even in those disciplines there are experts and many business people struggle to deal successfully with human resource or financial issues. Even at the highest levels some executives are insensitive to good practice in managing people and others are ignorant of financial matters. However, proportionately more managers and executives either do not understand or are fearful or feel incompetent when faced with what they see as IT issues. Most IT issues should be left to specialists in IT, as with accounting, but the IS issues – which affect the quality and relevance of the information and systems to the business are the responsibility of the business managers.

This book has hopefully enabled business people to appreciate the role they play and the responsibilities they have in making IS/IT a successful component of their business. At the same time by presenting the issues and ideas in this way some IT specialists may be able to see a different, perhaps less introspective, view of how they can contribute to a business's success.

Whilst in the short-term the quality of an organisation's IT resources may determine what it is able to achieve through IS/IT, in the long-term an organisation will get the systems it deserves. Only through better management of **both** IS and IT will it achieve the benefits which can be delivered – this needs a partnership approach based on sound, agreed well understood **Principles of Information Systems Management**.

RECOMMENDED ADDITIONAL READING

Treacy, M. and Wiersma, F. (1993) 'Customer Intimacy and Other Value Disciplines', *Harvard Business Review* (January/February).

OTHER REFERENCES

Johnson, G. and Scoles, K. (1993) *Exploring Corporate Strategy*, Prentice-Hall, Chapter 2.
Mintzberg, H. (1987) 'Crafting Strategy', *Harvard Business Review* (July/August).
O'Sullivan, L. and Geringer, J.M. (1993) 'Harnessing the Power of Your Value Chain', *Long Range Planning*, Vol. 26.
Ward, J.M. and Peppard, J. (1994) 'Reconciling the IT/Business – A troubled marriage in need of guidance', Cranfield Working Papers.

Index